She Changes by Intrigue

GENUS:
Gender in Modern Culture

6

Russell West-Pavlov (Berlin)
Jennifer Yee (Oxford)
Frank Lay (Cologne)
Sabine Schülting (Berlin)

She Changes by Intrigue
Irony, Femininity and Feminism

Lydia Rainford

Rodopi

Amsterdam - New York, NY 2005

Cover design: Pier Post

The paper on which this book is printed meets the requirements of "ISO 9706:1994, Information and documentation - Paper for documents - Requirements for permanence".

ISBN: 90-420-1607-8

Printed in the Netherlands

Table of Contents

Acknowledgements

I would like to thank St. Hugh's College, Oxford, for appointing me to the Joanna Randall MacIver Fellowship, and giving me the time and space in which to finish this book. Many thanks are also due to Robert Smith for his enthusiasm, patience and keen sense of irony in supervising the original research; to Clare Connors, for sisterly solidarity; and to my parents for their unfailing love and support. Finally, by greatest debt is to Dominic, who has sustained me through this project from beginning to end.

Introduction

In spite of what the title of this book might imply, I do not intend to formulate a feminist theory of wily femininity; at least, not without introducing a number of disruptions and complications. I intend to examine the association of a certain sort of "ironic" intrigue with the figure of "femininity" in philosophy and theory, and investigate the connections between this association and contemporary feminist debates about gendered subjectivity and agency. But I also intend to problematize the figure of "femininity", questioning its hierarchical and historical position in philosophical discourses, and how feminism might relate to it. And I will be asking why irony should align itself with "femininity" and feminism, and analyzing the different forms it takes. In short, this is a book about writing, authorship, strategy and agency: how "woman" and "femininity" have been figured, and how feminists might re-write these figurations. It traces the mutual relations and implications of irony, femininity and feminism.

In recent years, one of the most sustained debates within feminist theory and philosophy has been over questions of subjectivity and agency. The basic premise of feminism – that it is a discourse whose aim is the freedom and autonomy of women – still holds, but the ways in which "women" and "autonomy" are defined have become ever more problematic. There has been an increasing anxiety about the political possibility and desirability of (referring to) an autonomous subjective category of "woman" because the ontological and epistemological foundations through which this category commonly gains significance are so embedded in patriarchal discourses. To found an identity politics on the basis of "woman's" sexual or biological difference seems to veer uncomfortably close to historical prescriptions of woman's natural "essential" nature, and inferiority, that feminism would seek to counter. Moreover, such a definition of "otherness" seems to be too general to allow for permutations of difference – such as sexual orientation, racial or cultural difference – other than those that sit within the confines of the "man" versus "woman" dialectic. If feminism is striving to release cultural forms and practices from phallocentric dominance, then maintaining a vigilance over other possible forms of oppression or exclusion is a political and ethical imperative.

The impact of these anxieties on opinions about the source and aims of feminist agency has been considerable. On the one hand, there are those that insist that some category of "essence", however nominal, is crucial in order for feminism to maintain the specificity of its political cause. Without a definition of sexual difference and sexually different subjectivity, there is no foundation on which to base feminism's critique of patriarchy and hope of liberation. On the other hand, some feminists believe that the interrogation of categories of essence, and a resistance to identity politics, should be the primary task of feminist interventions, because it is the sedimentation of such categories that leads directly to the marginalization and oppression of "otherness". At times it has seemed as if these opinions fall into irreconcilable "essentialist" and "constructivist" camps, but as theorists such as Diana Fuss and Elizabeth Grosz have pointed out, even if we accept the truth of this division, the two camps' positions on the relationship of feminism to prevailing patriarchal culture need not be mutually exclusive.[1] There may be points of incommensurability between Luce Irigaray's formulations of sexual difference and Judith Butler's interrogations of gender identities, but both thinkers begin from a position which acknowledges the peculiar double-bind of feminist critique: that it strives to challenge and break from the (unequal) sexual terms, relations and hierarchies of patriarchy, but that the cultural forms and discourses at its disposal are themselves enmeshed in patriarchy. Whether they refer to a "phallocratic order" (Irigaray, 1985b, 68) or "hegemonic masculinist cultures" (Butler 1999, 7), the question feminists constantly return to is how to engage with the cultural legacy of masculine influence.

The recognition of, and negotiation with, this legacy is not a choice. As Elizabeth Grosz asserts,

> The alternatives faced by feminist theorists are all in some sense 'impure' and 'implicated' in patriarchy. There can be no feminist position that is not in some

[1] See Fuss 1989 and Grosz 1994.

> way or other involved in patriarchal power relations; it is hard to see how this is either possible or desirable, for a purity from patriarchal 'contamination' entails feminism's incommensurability with patriarchy and thus the inability to criticize it. (Grosz 1994, 94)

The "binding of patriarchal terms" is both historically and politically necessary. Feminism is indebted to the structures it criticizes. It is a kind of parasite, sharing constitutive elements and practices with patriarchy without being at one with the whole "body" of these elements, or having a common goal. This means that any efforts to formulate a feminist agency will have to emerge, at least in part, from these structures, rather than from some "virgin" territory. However, to attempt this is a hazardous business, for it necessitates a balancing act between repeating, unpicking and reformulating prevailing sexual terms and figurations. Given the common ground of feminism and patriarchy, the question of how to make a "movement beyond" is highly vexed. How is it possible to intervene in these structures and discourses in such a way as to achieve a real refiguration of gender relations and hierarchies? From what position, and through what method, can a feminist provoke change and bring about (sexual) difference?

This book considers a particular response to these questions by analyzing irony as a form of agency for feminist discourse. Irony has long been thought of as a strategic means of questioning or countering established truths and ideas. Its philosophical roots in Socratic dialogue reveal it as a rhetorical mode which enables the emergence of knowledge – importantly, self-knowledge – without actively positing this knowledge, or claiming authority for it.[2] As such, irony operates from within the structure it interrogates, repeating the beliefs of the structure in such a way as to negate their value; thus implying that the *real* truth is another thing altogether.

Recent feminist writers have claimed or implied a special affinity between women and irony, and between feminism and irony on account of their "double" relation to the prevailing order of things: both speak from within this order – indeed, to a greater or lesser extent, are determined by this order – and yet both remain "other" to this order in some way. Interestingly, this affinity has been drawn both by feminists who are seeking more autonomous terms in which to

---

[2] There are countless books on the meaning and intention of irony. Some interesting historical perspectives on irony can be found in Dilwyn Knox, 1989; Norman Knox, 1961; Muecke, 1970; Wilde, 1981; and Stringfellow, 1994.

describe women and femininity, such as the philosopher Luce Irigaray, and by feminists such as Judith Butler, who are seeking to displace notions of gendered identity. Although these writers employ the figure of irony in different ways, and with different ends in mind, the ironic mode is considered as a form of internalized agency for the feminist: as well as reflecting her double relation to the patriarchal structure, it turns her alterity to her advantage, by using it to negate the terms of the prevailing hierarchy. In her book *Splitting Images*, Linda Hutcheon explains the basic idea:

> … the condition of marginality (with its attendant qualities of muteness and invisibility) has created in women a 'divided self, rooted in the authorized dualities' of culture. [This means that] the 'splitting images' they create through their double-talking ironies are a means of problematizing the humanist ideal (or illusion) of wholeness, as well as hierarchy and power. Contradiction, division, doubleness – these are the contesting elements that irony lets in by the front door. (1991, 97)

What Hutcheon says here suggests that women's "double-talking ironies" are both a reflection and criticism of the position in which they find themselves. In challenging a hierarchy where "woman" always comes second – habitually figured as an adjunct to the "ideal" of masculine subjectivity – the ironic woman does not simply seek a subjectivity of her own to replace the masculine ideal. Instead, she uses her secondariness as a form of "negative freedom", repeating it back to the patriarchal structure in order to undermine the authority of (sexed) subjectivity itself. Irony creates a way to unravel the prevailing "truth" of gender positions without being obliged to step outside these positions.

The exact process of this ironic "subversion" and its implications for different models of feminist theory are not as transparent as may seem from this initial description. I will outline some of the questions it provokes in a moment. First I would like to make a more careful definition of the nature of irony as it will be discussed in this book.

Described in the terms Hutcheon uses, irony sounds significantly more disruptive, more political, than one would assume a rhetorical method to be. Indeed, a common view of irony as a rhetorical trope is that it is always at one remove from any real "action": its Greek root "eironia" suggests a dissimulation or deception that is either too playful or defensive to be commensurable with serious political or ethical engagement (see Knox 1961, 38-42).[3] Most sustained considerations of irony focus on its aesthetic function, defining it as a device that "says one thing and means another", and analyzing the relative positions of its perpetrator, victim and audience.[4] Its action is thus regarded as being confined to discrete moments of narrative or argument, and having a specific devious or deflationary intention. When irony arises in the context of broader aesthetic and cultural discussions, it is often treated with suspicion. This is the case in current debates about so-called "postmodern irony", where its suspension or interruption of knowledge is regarded as at best a retreat into apolitical aestheticism and at worst a conservative or reactionary tendency. Richard Rorty clearly demarcates irony as the trope of what he calls "private perfection", associated with the "irrational" and aesthetic writing of authors such as Kierkegaard, Nietzsche, Proust and Derrida. Their work stands in opposition to the "human solidarity" of Marx, Mill, Dewey and Habermas, who are "engaged in a shared social effort … to make our institutions and practices more just and less cruel" (1989, xv-xvi and 125).[5] And Fredric Jameson's post-Marxist critique of postmodernism refers to postmodern irony as a kind of "monadic relativism" whose "philosophical ideology often takes the form of a vulgar appropriation of Einstein's theory of relativity" (1991, 412).[6]

However, the few analyses of irony which address it in more than purely aesthetic terms do not delimit its scope and import so easily. Paul de Man's essay, "The Concept of Irony", stakes out a radical negativity in irony's nature which refuses to be contained in discrete moments of speech or narrative. Indeed, he regards the limitations that are usually assigned to irony as defensive measures on the part of those who assign the limitations, rather than inherent qualities of irony: by bracketing off the function of irony they are attempting to

---

[3] Wayne Booth describes this aspect of irony as the "Snotty Sublime" in his half-serious list of the "genres" of irony (1974, 211). He describes its "special limiting delight" as, "what fun we can have if we realise that all values except our own superior ironic insight can be ridiculed".

[4] See Stringfellow, who quotes Quintillian's definition: by irony "we understand something which is the opposite of what is actually said" (1994, 11).

[5] Rorty aspires to a "liberal utopia" which gives up the (metaphysical) "attempt to hold all the sides of our life in a single vision" and admit to the incommensurability of public and private life and theory (xv-xvi). Irony is clearly ascribed to the "private" domain, and thus can serve no "public" or political cause.

[6] See also Jameson 1991, 217-59.

defuse its potential to damage the fundamental structures and categories of narrative and understanding.[7]

De Man defines irony as an ever-present danger of disruption and deviation in signifying systems. He follows Friedrich Schlegel's definition of irony as a "permanent parabasis" in narrative, which is rooted in the way narrative is posited through a dialectic of substitution, a system of tropes that builds through relations of resemblance and difference. If narrative takes place through the "tropological" movements of language – the "turning" between literal and figurative meanings – then irony epitomises the dark undercurrent of this movement: the propensity for words to "turn" at any moment, and mean something other than what their apparent context would indicate, or their narrator would intend. De Man describes how Schlegel's own work embodied this hazard, and scandalized dialectical philosophers such as Hegel because it seemed to endanger the respectability of the philosophical endeavour itself. One passage in his most famous work, *Lucinde*, pertained to be a highbrow philosophical argument, but on another (ironic) level, was a narrative describing a sexual act.[8]

De Man takes Schlegel's all-pervasive strain of Romantic irony and combines it with his own post-structuralist ideas of the arbitrary determination of language. The resulting characterization of irony is one which extends far beyond notions of rhetorical strategy into questions of knowledge and understanding. De Man calls irony the "trope of tropes" because it constantly underscores the fact that

> Words have a way of saying things which are not at all what you want them to say. You are writing a splendid and coherent philosophical argument but, lo and behold, you are describing sexual intercourse. […] There is a machine there, a text machine, an implacable determination and total arbitrariness […] which inhabits words on the level of the play of the signifier, which undoes any

---

[7] De Man posits three ways in which irony is typically "defused": by regarding it as an aesthetic practice ["*Kunstmittel*"], by reducing it to a dialectic of the self as a reflexive structure (which, he acknowledges ironically, is how he deals with it in his essay), and by absorbing it into a dialectics of history. This dialectical absorption, which De Man associates with the philosophies of Hegel and Kierkegaard, is a strategy that is of particular interest to me in this book. De Man comments that the curious relation of irony and history "can only be tackled when the complexities of what we could call performative rhetoric have been more thoroughly mastered" (1996, 184). I hope the latter chapters of this book will begin to do this.

[8] For an ironic reading of Hegel's scandalized reaction to *Lucinde*, see Krell 1996, 89-107. For a feminist, slant on Schlegel's "permanent parabasis", which roots its "obscenity" in its performative rendering of gender, see Redfield 2000, 103-30.

> narrative consistency of lines, and which undoes the reflexive and the dialectical model, both of which are [...] the basis of any narration. (181)

Irony's "turning", substitutive movement threatens to negate structures and systems of understanding as they are formed, because its movement is tied so intimately to the very construction and constitution of these structures. It strikes in the very moment that an idea is posited, an argument or narrative is performed. There is thus a persistent "riskiness", a peculiarly vertiginous quality to irony's action, which resists conceptualization. As De Man says,

> ... one could say that any theory of irony is the undoing, the necessary undoing, of any theory of narrative, and it is ironic, as we say, that irony always comes up in relation to theories of narrative, when irony is precisely what makes it impossible ever to achieve a theory of narrative that would be consistent. (179)

Once admitted, irony spawns other ironies, and their undercutting, unravelling movements become impossible to curtail.

It is this more invasive definition of irony which I will be analyzing in this book. Consequently, my treatment of irony will depart from most analyses of the "meaning" of irony which tend to consider it as a localized rhetorical trope. In fact, as I hope to show in my chapter on Kierkegaardian irony, once irony is treated "seriously", as a force which can affect the fundamental categories of meaning and interpretation (the "author", the "subject", "truth", "intention"), the power to limit the interpretation of irony to discrete events or fields – whether as particular, intended textual effects, or as the "realm" of private, aesthetic enjoyment – is radically problematized.[9] This is not to say that everything becomes relative, or that localized instances of irony signify nothing in themselves. Rather, it is to claim that irony introduces a peculiar "riskiness" into categorical and interpretative decisions which makes these decisions less self-assured, less certain, and imbues them with a sense of radical "otherness".

The "riskiness" of irony and its sense of radical "otherness" will be at the centre of my thinking in this book. The mutating characterization of irony that I will be employing seeks to preserve the vertiginous quality captured in De Man's essay, but does not necessarily have the dark finality of his definition. De Man's interest in irony is primarily epistemological and tropological, and is thus

[9] Wayne Booth reflects upon the fact that "everyone who writes on irony with any seriousness seems to face this [realization] sooner or later", (1974, 240-41), even though most of his book ignores this realization.

centred in quite a pure sense on the self-reflexive action of irony; its "undoing" and "disruption" of understanding and narrative. I want to draw out the political and ethical implications of this action: what irony's interruption might enable or allow, as much as what it interrupts. Of course, action and implications are not separable, which is why the stakes are so high – and irony is so much more than a trope – in De Man's essay. Nevertheless, I am hoping to explore the productive possibilities of irony's disruption in greater detail.

In the context of a discourse where the state and status of "otherness" is at stake, as it is in feminism, the disruption or disillusion associated with irony might be considered as exactly what makes it a potential force for subversion and, as Linda Hutcheon says, gives irony its "edge" (1994, 31-36). The structural and epistemological uncertainties provoked by the doubleness of irony means that its intervention is not simply a countering movement – a case of denying prevailing truths and asserting or implying new ones – but of (potentially) unravelling the whole structure in which the debate is being pursued. This is why Hutcheon's writing on feminist irony claims its doubleness as a form of agency that does not merely challenge women's marginalized identity in relation to men's, but problematizes the "humanist ideal [...] of wholeness" (1989, 97). In failing to engage with the "ruling" structure on this structure's terms, irony promises to shift the prevailing dialectic of power and open the terms of debate to more and different conceptions of "otherness" and "identity".

However, there are difficulties inherent in this promise, most obviously in the unpredictability of irony's "riskiness". Even as we might embrace the radical implications of an ironic agency, we are faced with the question of how irony can be co-opted for specific political ends when the direction and extent of its disruption is so unreliable? Surely the self-reflexive element of its structural unravelling will compromise the "intentional" capacity of the ironist? And if it constantly destabilizes the establishment of knowledge, then won't it prevent or destabilize the emergence of any new configurations of gender relations and identity? Compounding this uncertainty is irony's parasitical reliance on the structure it questions. Its "doubleness" may indeed work to unravel the constitution of terms from the inside, but there will inevitably be some repetition of these terms because the irony is constructed *through* them: it has no knowable life external to the prevailing structure. How, then, can irony's repetition resist compromising the structural disobedience that irony's "otherness" unleashes? Does the risk of complicity with the structure outweigh the potential for liberation?

Feminists who consider the subversive possibilities of irony are obliged to face these difficulties of intention and direction. Judith Butler, who orientates herself as a constructivist feminist, seeks to use the risks and disruptions of irony to interrogate prevailing notions of sexed identity and "essence." Emphasizing the strategic dimensions of irony, she describes and advocates a form of "gender parody" which displaces what she calls the "law of sexual coherence" by revealing that "the original identity after which gender fashions itself is an imitation without an origin" (1999, 175). In other words, the authorial and intentional complications put into play by a purposeful enactment of the ironic mode displaces the very notion of an original "source" of being which, employed in the context of gender, can disrupt inscribed "norms" of sex and sexuality:

> This perpetual displacement constitutes a fluidity of identities that suggests an openness to resignification and recontextualization; parodic proliferation deprives hegemonic culture and its critics of the claim to naturalized or essentialist gender identities. Although the gender meanings taken up in these parodic styles are clearly part of a hegemonic, misogynist culture, they are nevertheless denaturalized and mobilized through their parodic recontextualization (176).

Butler is seeking to open "gender meanings" to configurations beyond the biologically-ordained and heterosexist opposition of "male" and "female". Indeed, she calls for a plural definition of "gender", which acknowledges the social and cultural constitution of even its most apparently "physiological" aspects.[10] By emphasizing the discrepancies and uncertainties in this constitution of gender, its "identity" is reconfigured as a process – a "*stylized repetition of acts*" – which is susceptible to change (179). This is what she means by "recontextualization".

The question of where and how the agency for this reconfiguration might emerge is a difficult one. Butler resists questions about the parodist's individual agency because she asserts that "there need not be a 'doer behind the deed' […] that the 'doer' is variably constructed in and through the deed" (181). She is highly critical of the

---

[10] Butler dedicates much of her argument to de-bunking prevailing cultural assumptions that the reproductive functions and physiological attributes of "men" and "women" are absolute determinants of their "sex" and gendered identity. Her argument even extends to debates about chromosomal sexual determinants (1999, 135-41). Butler develops this analysis into her theory of gender "interpellation" in *Bodies That Matter* (1993, 7-8).

"epistemological model that offers us a pregiven subject or agent" because it "refuses to acknowledge that *agency is always and only a political prerogative*" (1992, 13). Rather than regarding subjective agency as an "a priori guarantee", Butler analyzes it as something that is constituted and reconstituted through the particular "matrix of power" – the structure of social, institutional and discursive forces – that surrounds it. Thus it ceases to be a matter of "instrumental actors who confront an external political field" and becomes "the permanent possibility of a certain resignifying process, one which gets detoured and stalled through other mechanisms of power, but which is power's own possibility of being reworked".

This shift to a contingent and contextual notion of agency is in keeping with the dissimulative, parasitical nature of irony: it operates within and through the prevailing discourse and thus any agency it might possess cannot be autonomous. Indeed, for Butler, the recognition of the embeddedness of the "agent" is a crucial part of gender parody's "denaturalizing" action: it admits that gender is constructed and mutable rather than pre-ordained and essential. However, precisely because the "agent" is embedded in and constructed through the discourse it undermines, it is difficult to determine the extent to which its parodic action *will* act to denaturalize and problematize prevailing gender identities, and the extent to which it will merely repeat them. If the "stylized repetition of acts" emerges from and repeats their "hegemonic, misogynist" context, then how can they knowingly or deliberately repeat themselves differently? The "possibility" of the "resignifying" and "reworking" of power will be just as much a possibility of the same power returning. Although Butler asks similar questions in much of her writing, her citing of drag acts as subversive practices of parody seems to brush over these difficulties and imply a fairly straightforward relation between mimesis and agency: it seems the more self-consciously performative and "artificial" the gender act, the more subversive it is. But given that these acts are re-enactments of existing gender acts, the mimetic element of the parody cannot be inherently subversive, or immune from complicity with the prevailing "matrix of power".

Questions concerning the agency and complicity of irony are further complicated when we consider the specific status of "woman" and "femininity" in the history of theory and philosophy. Many dominant structures of thought – including structures which have greatly influenced feminism – have not only figured "woman" as the negative version of the male positive, (passive to active, matter to form), but have aligned her with an ironic function in society and a mimetic pattern of thought.[11] The logic seems to be that as "woman" is secondary to "man" and "femininity" is characterized by qualities which oppose "masculinity", her position as subject can only ever be one of a copy or simulation; and her *modus operandi* will naturally be a negative, derivative one. So for a feminist to employ irony might be to risk complicity with the structure she counters twice: firstly through repeating the structure in general, and secondly, by repeating the specific ironic status which has already been deemed her "natural" position as a "woman".

An obvious case in point, and the example I will use throughout my book, is the gender hierarchy in Hegelian dialectics. The work of Hegel has been a key influence on many theories of liberation, whether Marxist, psychoanalytic, or feminist, primarily because its historical method of analysis challenges the immutable categories of transcendental philosophy and opens them up to change across time and in different material contexts. However, Hegel's model of self-recognition, which is at the core of the whole dialectical process, works through a logic of oppositions in which subjectivity is reached through the mastering and appropriation of an "other" object: the fulfilment of self-consciousness is determined through its negative relation to what is "immediate" or given in nature. From this emerges the common spirit of society's laws, customs and practices – what Hegel calls "objective Spirit" ["*objektiver Geist*"] – and self-consciousness in its infinite form, embodied in the self-reflection and knowledge of philosophy, art and religion – what Hegel calls "absolute Spirit" ["*absoluter Geist*"]. [12] In Hegel's analysis of the social and ethical order, which reflects the activity of *Geist*, subjective self-consciousness is only fully realized by men, and the journey towards its realization lies in opposition to the subjective and ethical determination of women. Man's life is characterized by "externality": "his actual substantive life [is] in the state, in learning, and so forth, as well as in labour and struggle with the external world and with himself" (1942, section 166, 114). Woman, on the other hand, "has her substantive destiny in the family and to be imbued with family piety is her ethical frame of mind". Not only is man's "powerful and

[11] See Hélène Cixous' famous polemic about the "universal battlefield" of sexual terms, in her essay "Sorties" (1986, 63-132).

[12] This is a very sketchy outline of Hegel's system and structure of consciousness, fitting only for the purposes of this introduction. I will return to the relevant passages of the *Philosophy of Right* and the *Phenomenology of Spirit* in later chapters

active" relation to "externality" opposed to woman's "passive and subjective" relation, but the struggle that defines man's determination manifests itself through his "diremption" from the unity of the family.[13] In other words, woman's inferiority serves the development of man's "self-consciousness". The principles she embodies – "particularity", "immediacy", "naturalness" and "substantiality" – must be negated in order to fulfil the masculine principles of "universality", "mediacy", "freedom" and "subjectivity".[14] In the *Phenomenology of Sprit*, Hegel calls woman the "internal enemy" of "universality", and defines her ambivalent function neatly in a phrase which will haunt this book, and which gives it its title:

> Womankind – the everlasting irony in (the life of) the community – changes by intrigue the universal end of the government into a private end, transforms its universal activity into a work of some particular individual, and perverts the universal property of the state into an ornament for the Family. (1977, 288)

The "irony" and "intrigue" of "woman" in Hegel's philosophical system are thus far from being subversive, because their dissidence is already inscribed as part of the logic of the dialectic, helping to serve its "universal" ends and perpetuate woman's "natural" marginality.

Given this double risk of irony's complicity – on both a local and historical level – the opportunities for a feminist to appropriate it as a form of agency seem negligible, the space for manoeuvre liminal. Luce Irigaray acknowledges this by qualifying the "strategic" possibilities of irony in relation to the writing (woman) subject. She suggests that women have no choice but to speak from their "eternally" negative position, precisely because they have no other history or language than the one which is indifferent to their (possible) sexual subjectivity. In conceiving of a feminist writing, she speaks of

---

[13] As he says in the same section of the *Philosophy of Right*, "it is only out of his diremption that he fights his way to self-subsistent unity with himself. In the family he has a tranquil intuition of this unity, and there he lives a subjective ethical life on the plane of feeling" (section 166, 114)

[14] Seyla Benhabib also describes Hegel's "rational ontology of gender" according to these opposing principles (1991, 129-45). Luce Irigaray's analysis of this ontology, and woman's corresponding "eternal irony", extends to Hegel's description of the physical differences between men and women. In *The Philosophy of Nature*, he figures women's sexual organs as the literal negative of the male organs, lacking the capacity to "emerge into opposition" to "become and independent and active cerebrality" (Hegel, 1970, 173). The female thus constitutes merely "the principle of conception". As Irigaray remarks, "What an amazing vicious circle in a single syllogistic system." (1985a, 223).

two "phases": one where the impossible masculinist legacy is repeated mimetically; and one where this mimesis is repeated deliberately, so that it ceases to be simply negative:

> There is, in an initial phase, perhaps only one "path", the one historically assigned to the feminine: that of *mimicry*. One must assume the feminine role deliberately. Which means already to convert a form of subordination into an affirmation, and thus to begin to thwart it. Whereas a direct feminine challenge to this condition means demanding to speak as a (masculine) "subject", that is, it means to postulate a relation to the intelligible that would maintain sexual indifference. (1985b, 76)

Although this strategic description acknowledges the problem of the specific status of "woman" in the history of thought, it is still difficult to see how the transition from negative, mimetic repetition to affirmative, deliberate repetition takes place. It seems unlikely that something as fully intended as this parodic strategy could arise from a position of *generalized* mimicry and irony. Irigaray maintains it is possible because women "are not simply resorbed in [the mimetic] function. *They also remain elsewhere*", beyond the "masculine logic". The question then becomes what is this "beyond" and how can it be employed to challenge masculine logic without being construed as a dangerously idealized "other" ontology, or by simply inverting the logic in a "feminine" version of the subjective / objective hierarchy?[15]

The particular questions provoked by Butler's, Irigaray's and other feminist conceptions of agency will be addressed throughout my book. However, for the most part my discussion will be seeking to go "behind the scenes" of these feminist interventions, to investigate why the connections between femininity and irony, and feminism and irony arise, and to disentangle the more radical and more reactionary strands of these relations. The continual motivation for this analysis will be the sense that more needs to be said about the particular nature of "woman's" designated negative or ironic status in prevailing

---

[15] Seyla Benhabib calls for a restoration of irony to the dialectic through a deflation of "the pompous march of historical necessity" which will give back "to the victims of the dialectic … their otherness, and this means, in true dialectical fashion, their selfhood." (1991, 143). Benhabib's article undertakes one such "deflation" by restoring to view the (unconventional) life of a "real", historical, female subject – Caroline Schlegel Schelling – which Hegel's generalizing prescription of "womankind" effaced. Although her strategy works to reveal the blundering determinism of Hegel's gender formulations, it is questionable whether retrieving a "selfhood" for the "others" of Hegel's system really challenges the logic that created the gender inequality. Her "selfhood" is still defined by her otherness to Hegel's historical necessity.

discursive structures before irony can be regarded as a form of feminist agency in narrative or theory. Similarly, the precise form irony takes in this context needs to be defined: a vague sense of it being a subversive force or a trope of "self-creation" is not sufficient.[16] By analyzing the figuration of "woman", the "feminine" and irony in the specific context of their relation to each other, I hope to clear up some of the difficulties and evasions associated with their troubling relation to "master" narratives.

I begin my book at the heart of these difficulties: with the question of how to conceive a specifically "feminist" agency within a male-dominated discourse. Chapter 1 analyzes the work of Julia Kristeva, which exemplifies the hazards and problems that characterize this quest. Kristeva combines many influences in her theoretical system – structuralist linguistics, revolutionary politics, psychoanalysis – but the overarching, dialectical structure of this system is inherited from Hegelian and Marxist philosophy and Lacanian psychoanalysis. Kristeva seeks a form of agency within this "signifying" dialectic which challenges the conventional view of subjectivity and sexuality as a fixed essence. Indeed, her suspicion of immutable categories of identity is such that in spite of her abiding concern with the masculinist hierarchy which governs these categories, she refuses to be called a "feminist": for her, feminism's focus on an independent female subjectivity perpetuates the notion of a natural, God-given identity. Kristeva focuses on the symbolic and psychic constitution of sexuality and identity, attempting to "position" the habitually excluded "feminine" term without subscribing "her" as a transcendent "essence" of "woman". However, as I hope to show, her dependence on dialectical logic forces her into a binary, oppositional mode of thought which forecloses her efforts to create a heterogeneous relation between sexual terms.

With this impasse in mind, Chapter 2 turns away from questions of the feminine and feminism in favour of more general questions concerning opposition and agency within the dialectical system. I focus on the possible advantages of adopting irony as a non-essential form of agency; for it preserves the possibility of a subjective truth without claiming knowledge of its absolute or eternal truth. I take as my example the work of Søren Kierkegaard: in particular his delineation of the concept of irony as an ethical force within the

[16] "Self-creation" refers to what Richard Rorty believes is the purpose of irony (1989, xv-xvi).

philosophical system which follows a dialectical structure and yet troubles the dialectical urge towards predetermination and absolutism. Kierkegaard uses the "infinite negativity" of irony to counter the objective, "world-historical" philosophy of Hegel, because, unlike Hegel, it never claims knowledge for itself, and thus does not exclude other possibilities. His treatment of irony as a serious concept and as something more pervasive than a "method" – a whole mode of being or "personality" – suggests a style of writing which does not sacrifice the perpetual return of alterity for the sake of a fully determinable agency. This chapter argues that it is only when he seeks to curtail this style for the sake of his "leap of faith" that his battle against the oppressive Hegelian structure fails.

The first two chapters set up a debate about feminism and irony which reflects the complications I have touched upon in this introduction. Chapter 3 carries this debate into a more detailed consideration of the negative status which femininity and irony share in dialectical philosophy. Both are figured as the "other" of philosophical self-consciousness which dialectical mediation seeks to "sublate". I explore the extent to which an ironic, feminist discourse which privileges alterity can disrupt the dialectical tendency to exclude or incorporate the other, given that alterity functions as a kind of "negative capability" within the dialectical process.

The second part of the book develops the questions and conclusions formed in Chapter 3. It responds in particular to the problem of the dialectic's subscription of the feminine and irony into a position of "essential" negativity. In treating this problem I examine deconstructive approaches to notions of written agency, as they seek to displace the rigid oppositional positions of dialectical logic.

Chapter 4 analyzes Jacques Derrida's reconception of the structure of dialectical time. By attending to the logic of its writing, Derrida reveals that not only does dialectical mediation fail to sublate what it regards as its "other", but that its whole possibility depends on what remains after this process. Its neat linear / circular temporality is thus a reflection of its own desire for completion, rather than a matter of "truth". Derrida reiterates this structure through the time of its writing so that it acknowledges the alterity of its own (legal) determination. This means that rather than treating alterity as something "beyond" the present structure – either as a transcendent "cause" or excluded, negative "other" – he regards it as a constitutive, although still unknowable, part of philosophical and authorial decisions. Derrida's style of writing liberates the feminine and irony from their idealized, perpetually negative state, giving them the capacity to be "affirmative" without simply repeating the prevailing structure. It also shifts the notion of gendered agency or subjectivity from being a "present" essence to being something highly contingent and radically contextualized.

While Derrida's work deconstructs the binary logic which so inhibits feminist irony, it shies away from engaging with a specifically feminist agency. For this reason, my final chapter turns to the work of Sarah Kofman. Kofman follows Derrida's displacement of the intending, "self-present" subject – redefining subjective and authorial decisions as contingent "propriation" – but engages in a more detailed analysis of the significance of gender to this "act" of propriation. She deconstructs the notion of essential femininity or masculinity, but also shows how the legacy of masculinist logic lives on in the "biographical trace" which returns as part of written propriation. This means that as a "woman" writer she bears a different relation to the "ironic feminine" than a "male" writer. In response to this difference, Kofman performs a highly "risky" double analysis of her main influences – Derrida, Nietzsche, and Freud – which plays out their transmutations and repetitions of masculine propriation and her own historically ironic relation to this, and their, influence.

My analysis of Kofman suggests that her genealogical mode of writing is unique in its ability to affirm an "other" sexual history without resorting to idealized notions of alterity and authority. The trajectory my book follows, from dialectical feminism, to dialectical irony, to deconstructive irony and deconstructive feminism, mirrors the long path of Kofman's negotiation. It seeks to unravel the complexities, repetitions and transmutations of the relation of irony and the feminine in philosophical and theoretical history; and it seeks to delineate the complications of agency and authorship that this relation provokes. And while, in my role as feminist academic, I largely maintain the tone of "straight" philosophical analysis, I also seek to make some claims on irony, by allowing my analyzes to form *through* the textual movements and styles of my chosen subjects of study. If, at times, I seem troublingly close to the texts I am analyzing, it is because I am trying to do justice to irony's parasitical otherness; or because irony's parasitical otherness is doing justice to itself.

Although it is impossible to predict the outcome of any negotiation with irony, I hope that what emerges from my attempt is a narrative of vigilance. It should be a narrative that reveals how the position and status of feminine "otherness" must not be allowed to remain unquestioned; and a narrative that shows how the feminist must maintain a radical interrogation of the returns of masculinist logic in the structure and style of her own writing, if she is to balance the marking of alterity with the pursuit of sexual agency.

Chapter 1

The "Impossible Dialectic": Julia Kristeva

"Womankind – the everlasting irony of the community."
G. W. F. Hegel (1977, 288).[1]

I. Feminist Dilemmas

Feminist or Feminine Agency?

If the perpetual problem for modern feminism is how to refigure categories and relations of gender and sex, then the theorist Julia Kristeva translates this problem into questions of essence, position and system.[2] According to Kristeva, to counter the binary structure of speculative, rational thought – which excludes "woman" or positions her as the "other" of the masculine norm – by establishing a stable position for a female "subject" (with the male as the female's "object" or "other") would be to adopt in reverse the sexual hierarchy which feminism ought to challenge. It would repeat the prevailing pattern of transcendence and unified subjectivity, and so risk repeating the pattern of woman's marginalized otherness. The starting point of Kristeva's work is the impossibility of an identity-based politics. As she says in her essay on feminism, "Women's Time", "the very logic

---

[1] Translation modified.

[2] I refer to 'system' here as a way of specifying the structure within which Kristeva addresses the problematic figuration of the feminine. The system to which Kristeva refers incorporates many different discourses and disciplines, including linguistic, psychoanalytic, biological and philosophical structures. According to Kristeva's project of "semanalysis", all of these fall under the category of "signifying systems" or "sign systems". For a brief explanation of this project, see Kristeva, 1986, 24-33.

of counter-power and of counter-society necessarily generates, by its very structure, its essence as a simulacrum of the combated society or of power" (1986b, 203). Any notion of a singular, fixed identity, like the unified transcendental ego of idealist philosophy, denies heterogeneity, and heterogeneity is the explicit aim of Kristeva's theoretical project.

Kristeva's theoretical tactic against what she considers as the stasis of classical thought structures is expressed as the "necessity" of elaborating "the dialectic of a process within plural and heterogeneous universes" (1984a, 14). Her emphasis on process and heterogeneity, on an excess or movement within and on the border of subjectivity and signification, relates to her conviction that the history of political, theoretical and artistic discourses during the twentieth century is not only inseparable from their interaction, but reveals, through their contradictory interplay, a potential space for change and revolution. This historical sense of a modern "culmination" reflects the largely Hegelian method of philosophical analysis that Kristeva adopts, where "self-consciousness", as knowledge, is reached through a path of negative moments; a structure built on the paradox that the subject requires mediation to know itself, and yet knows itself only as the very structure of mediation.[3] For Kristeva, this reading of subjective becoming resists the closure of Cartesian models. The subject and its discourse are always mid-stream, "in process", and thus permanently "on trial".[4] In analysing this turn towards process and production of experience, Kristeva identifies points of crisis or rupture in established methods and systems, and creates a space in which terms that these systems repress might be reintroduced. Yet this also leaves her with the problem of how this can actually happen when nothing exists "outside" the prevailing mediating process.

The intricacies of Kristeva's highly complex model of consciousness demand a close and careful analysis, which I will undertake later in this chapter. However, as far as specifically feminist debates are concerned, Kristeva's never-mastering process of becoming leaves her in a problematic position. Not only does it estrange her from liberal feminism's notions of the gendered subject, and this subject's possible agency in the political-philosophical

---

[3] As Hegel says, "Self-consciousness is born into this ocean, dripping with the water thereof, ie. never coming to absolute selfhood" (1946, 289).

[4] Kristeva's coinage, "sujet en procès", translates into English as both 'subject-in-process' and 'subject-on-trial'. For a commentary on the difficulties of translating Kristeva's subjective terminology, see Leon S. Roudiez's preface to *Revolution in Poetic Language* (1984a, ix-x).

system, (her "sujet-en-procès" never finally "becomes") but it means that feminism itself, as a movement, is only "a moment in the interminable process of coming to consciousness" (1984b, 203). This would appear to cut Kristeva out of the feminist picture altogether. Indeed, her accusations of the feminist movement's "anthropomorphism" (210), and her refusal to consider the problem of "woman" in any but symbolic terms, has led to great suspicion of her work being phallocentric among politically concerned (mostly Anglo-American) feminists (see Fraser 1992, 177-94). Yet she has also been condemned by feminists who, like her, are more concerned with difference and heterogeneity than with identity politics. Their problem stems from the form of agency that Kristeva employs in her attempt to "heterogenize" the discursive terms of rational thought.

Kristeva's theorizations of femininity emerge from established philosophical and psychoanalytic figurations of 'woman', which portray her as the 'other' of masculine subjectivity and the object of its desire. Following Freudian and Lacanian theories of language and the unconscious, Kristeva associates this feminine alterity with a force of potential disruption to symbolic and subjective unity. She posits the "semiotic" as a simultaneous and counter-dependent movement to the symbolic order of language and Law, which plays an equal role in the production of the "subject-in-process" (1984a 25, 40-41). Kristeva defines it as a movement, rhythm or "excess" of the producing system – present in language, and in particular in "poetic" language – which prevents the complete becoming or final identity of the speaking subject. The semiotic is the "revival of archaic pre-Oedipal modes of operation" within the symbolic (1977b, 58), and thus represents a threat to the (imagined) unity and coherence of the symbolic. The chronology of its function is highly complex. As an "archaic" drive, it harks back to a time before symbolization – indeed, Kristeva describes it as "originally a precondition of the symbolic" (1984a, 68) – but because it "exists in practice only within the symbolic", as a break in conventional linguistic functioning, the notion that it "precedes" symbolization is "only a theoretical supposition justified by the need for description". It is thus simultaneously a material drive and a fabrication or fantasy of the symbolic: it occupies an ambivalent space between the symbolic and its other.

Considered in structural terms, the movement of the semiotic raises the possibility that,

> … every speaker would be led to conceive of its Being in relation to some void, a nothingness asymmetrically opposed to this Being, a permanent threat against first, its mastery, and ultimately its stability. (1980b, 238)

Moreover, since its mode of operation is "pre-Oedipal", it suggests a psychoanalytic process of becoming which exceeds the constraints of the paternally-centred framework of psychoanalysis. The constant "threat" to the "stability" and "mastery" of subjective identity is inevitably a threat to the (Lacanian) paternal Law and its prohibition on desires for the maternal body. Kristeva has frequently asserted that her emphasis on the 'maternal space' is an attempt to put right the "massive *nothing*" which Freud offers (as) woman in his topography of the subject, and which Lacanian psychoanalysis has overlooked.[5] Thus the maternal function, coupled with the paternal, enables a "traversal" of phallic mastery, and the recognition of

> … a certain bisexuality which is precisely the possibility of exploring all the sources of signification, that which posits a meaning as well as that which multiplies, pulverizes, and finally revives it (1980, 165).

However, as far as feminism is concerned, here also lies the problem. Even if the semiotic *is* knowable only through the symbolic order, and represents, in metaphorical terms, a multiplicity of drives, the oppositional relation of "paternal" symbolic to "maternal" semiotic risks re-inscribing the feminine as *essentially* material, irrational and subversive, and thus still *essentially* "other". Kristeva's figurations of the symbolic significance of maternity do seem to teeter on the edge of biologism. In "Motherhood According to Giovanni Bellini", for example, Kristeva suggests that the mother, in her "growing" and "grafting" of an other (the child), acts as a radical questioning of rational and religious "unified" subjectivity, precisely because, as a "*filter*" and "place of a splitting", she "*is not there*" (1980b, 237-8). However, her depiction of this dislocation of singular identity quickly becomes something more prescriptive:

> Material compulsion, spasm of a memory belonging to the species that either binds together or splits apart to perpetuate itself, series of markers with no other significance than the eternal return of the life-death biological cycle. How can we verbalize this prelinguistic, unrepresentable memory? (239)

Rather than figuring the maternal as the "thoroughfare" or "threshold" ["*un seuil*"] of the nature / culture divide, this passage seems to place the maternal firmly on the side of nature. This worries feminist critics

---

[5] In an interview for the journal *L'Infini*, Kristeva stressed "the importance of the maternal space, to which I think certain recent psychoanalytic trends, notably the Lacanian trends, have not paid sufficient attention. I believe that the maternal function must be restored [réhabilitée'], just as it is also necessary to keep a distance from it" (1993b, 72).

such as Domna C. Stanton, who feel that some of Kristeva's figurations of the maternal represent not so much a challenge to prevailing notions of identity as a total negation of the feminine in discourse. Stanton comments:

> Although the maternal/semiotic is crucial to the Kristevan theory of art as the exemplary subversive practice, the mother remains, as the phallotext defines her, a passive instinctual force that does not speak, but is spoken by the male: 'the artist speaks from a place where she is not, where she knows not. He delineates what in her is a body rejoicing (*un corps jouissant)* (Stanton 1989, 164, citing Kristeva).

This does seem to be a slipping of the maternal metaphor or function into a dangerously phallocratic essence, which, as Stanton suggests, means that Kristeva "does not deviate fundamentally from the patriarchal oedipal script".

Symbolic or Hegemonic?

It is this seeming conflation of the mother with the material which "anti-essentialist" critiques pick up, although Kristeva's conceptual yo-yoing is harder to catch than most essentialist / constructivist debates tend to admit. Typical of this type of critique is Judith Butler's, which stems from what she regards as Kristeva's unquestioning attitude towards the "heterosexual matrix" of psychoanalysis, which leaves traditional sexual binarisms (male versus female), and hence essences, intact. In *Gender Trouble*, Butler challenges this framework in favour of a radically constructivist approach to systems of discourse, where notions of instinctual or material drives "prior-to" language and culture are reconceived as "reiterations" of the continual (re)production of language and culture. Thus Butler's section on "The Body Politics of Julia Kristeva" takes issue with what she regards as a strain of essentialism in Kristeva's potentially "subversive" concepts (1999, 101-119).

According to her reading, Kristeva's emphasis on the semiotic as the movement of instinctual, pre-Oedipal drives sets up a divided conceptual structure where the maternal function and body are attributed an "ontological status" prior to culture, and the paternal law which governs this culture is a purely repressive agent. Butler argues that this has two politically problematic consequences. Firstly, it raises doubts as to whether the maternal ontology is a "viable construct" or "even a knowable experience", because it lies beyond the symbolic realm of language and meaning. This means that any subversion provoked by the movement of the semiotic within the symbolic can only be temporary, because it "cannot be maintained within the terms of culture" (1999, 102). Secondly, Butler argues that in "restricting the paternal law to a prohibitive function" Kristeva is failing to realize that the semiotic / maternal space may itself be a product of the law:

> The law that is said to repress the semiotic may well be the governing principle of the semiotic itself, with the result that what passes as 'maternal instinct' may well be a culturally constructed desire which is interpreted through a naturalistic vocabulary (116).

Far from challenging the paternal law, this is as good as rendering it invisible, because it naturalizes its heterosexual laws of kinship. What for Kristeva is a "pre-paternal causality" should, according to Butler, be read as a "*paternal* causality under the guise of a natural or distinctively maternal causality" (Ibid.).

With such a hegemonic notion of the symbolic, and hence a permanently separate, repressed and pre-cultural essence of maternity, Butler claims that for Kristeva, a "full-scale refusal of the symbolic is impossible, and a discourse of 'emancipation' […] is out of the question"(109) Her politically-constrained "strategic task" is thus,

> … neither to replace the Symbolic with the semiotic, nor to establish the semiotic as a rival cultural possibility, but rather to validate those experiences within the Symbolic that permit a manifestation of the borders which divide the Symbolic from the semiotic (108-9).

Butler's critique of Kristeva is illuminating insofar as it raises the question of the sustainability of semiotic subversion in Kristeva's system. I would agree that this is a valid, and taxing, question, and will spend more time analysing it, from a slightly different perspective, in later sections of this chapter. However, I would also argue that Butler's assumption that Kristeva's semiotic is tied to the notion of a pre-discursive maternal ontology is not upheld by Kristeva's own descriptions of her topography. Even at her most apparently essentialist, when speaking of the semiotic, or theorizing the pre-symbolic maternal "space", Kristeva always stresses that the semiotic only exists within the terms of the symbolic. Her constant emphasis is on discourse, speech and representation, which is why her question to feminism in "Women's Time" is not "what is a woman?", or "what should a woman be?", but "what can be our role in the symbolic contract" (1986b, 99)? As Kelly Oliver notes, Butler fails to distinguish between the "symbolic" (function) and the "Symbolic" (order), a crucial difference which problematizes accusations of essentialism. As she says,

> The semiotic is part of the Symbolic. Which is not to say that it is confined within the Symbolic – although certainly we cannot talk about it except within the Symbolic order, because we cannot talk about anything outside of the Symbolic order. The semiotic moves both inside and beyond the Symbolic. The semiotic, however, does not move within the symbolic. Within signification, the symbolic is heterogeneous to the semiotic. The symbolic is the element within the Symbolic against which the semiotic works to produce the dialectical tension that keeps society going (1993, 10).

The logic of Kristeva's dialectic, is not, then, as simple as Butler suggests, nor is her notion of the Symbolic necessarily as hegemonic. Indeed, one could argue that Butler's conceptual structure relies on a far more hegemonic notion of symbolic power than Kristeva's. If libidinous, bodily forces are always already constructions of the prevailing discursive structure, then it is difficult to see how any subversive gestures are possible, let alone the "full-scale refusal of the symbolic" that she seems to demand from Kristeva. Butler's demand for a totally subversive, yet "culturally constructed body" (119), realized as a "knowable experience" (102), is not matched by the formulation of an agency that could bring it about. Her own suggested solution to heterosexual hegemony, a "subversive" gender parody, can only function within the confines of the culturally constructed body, as a *repetition* of the prevailing gender laws, so is far from being able to provoke a complete overhaul of these laws. This is not to say that gender parody is without its subversive possibilities, but they seem closer to being the smaller "tactical subversions and displacements of the law" (109) that Butler allows Kristeva's semiotic, rather than the "open future of cultural possibilities" that she promises through her own agency (119). While she accuses Kristeva of holding a too-repressive notion of symbolic law, Butler seems to put too much faith in its productive action. The instability and failures of the law may very well result in "unexpected permutations" (119), but these permutations won't *necessarily* amount to forms of liberation. They will also always possibly be embedded in the repressive patterns of the law.[6]

---

[6] Penelope Deutscher makes a similar point about the subversive potential of performative gender parody. As she says, "Butler is saying that heterosexuality is a constant parody of itself *and* it is a compulsory law", which must mean that "heterosexuality as a compulsory law is *sustained* by the fact that is a constant parody of itself" (Deutscher 1997, 31).

Moreover, Kristeva's apparent essentialism is not as easily attributable to her psychoanalytic influences (at least, not her *Freudian* psychoanalytic influences) as Butler would suggest. In fact, far from the "matrix" of psychoanalysis determining fixed positions for masculine and feminine, it is Kristeva's use of a psychoanalytic framework that disrupts the possibility of a certain sexual ontology. In her essay "Place Names" ["*Noms de lieu*"], Kristeva focuses on the disturbance that Freudian psychoanalysis provokes in the unity of the Christian Word and the closure of the Cartesian subject. She describes how the discovery of the unconscious provokes a confusion of the "cause" and "effect" of traditional logic, asserting that,

> … the notion of 'infantile sexuality' allows for the examination, not of he who does not speak (in-fans) but of what within the speaker is not yet spoken, or will always remain unsaid, unnameable within the gaps of speech (1977a, 468; 1980b, 272).

This emphasis on what Kristeva calls the "libidinal-signifying organization" or "semiotic disposition" in infancy could be interpreted as a teleological topography of the subject which places the (maternal) drive-filled semiotic in a separate, archaic domain; its "return" acting as a revolutionary "outside" to the identity of the speaking adult (1977a, 472; 1980b, 276). However, Kristeva is careful to show that the causality is not so straightforward:

> Instinctuality is simultaneously revealed as innate and hereditary, but, within the Freudian framework, it is already protected from substantialist interpretations. For although the child enters the world with polymorphous instinctual drives, these conflict with repression and the latter produces the several variants of libido fixation ('subjective structures'). It follows that neurosis – or the speaking subject – can never be dealt with at the level of the drive, or through a child at zero degree of symbolism, but rather always through a narrative 'texture', that is, a texture of language and phantasm: 'It was only after the introduction [within childhood's instinctual experience] of the hysterical fantasies [the parental seduction fantasy] that the texture of the neurosis and its relation to the patient's life became intelligible' (1977a, 472; 1980b, 275-6).[7]

This intrinsic "texture" of signification, and the belatedness of its phantasmatic structure, defeats the possibility of either a hegemonic Symbolic or a separate place or "space" of the maternal semiotic. The contamination of the boundary of each by the other precludes an absolute actuality of either. It is, instead, the translation of this perpetually contaminating topography into the terms of rational

[7] Kristeva is quoting Freud's "Sexuality and the Neuroses".

thought, with its "obsessional shackling to time", that forces them into the teleologized divisions – cause / effect, body / mind, semiotic / symbolic, maternal / paternal – hidden under the deceitful "unity" of "name" and "place" (1977a, 487; 1980b, 291). Kristeva's discourse highlights this name and place, and translates them through the narrative texture of psychoanalysis so as to undermine, not reinforce, their precision and identity. Her terms are never outside this texture: the originating place of naming "(the chora, space, 'topic', subject-predicate)" is a replacement not for what we "know" to be, but for what the speaker *perceives* as an "archaic mother". And by constantly repeating this texture she emphasizes the importance of this dynamic contingency in discourse:

> … how the units and minimal operations of any language […] revive, model, transform, and extend the pregnancy that still constitutes the ultimate limit of meaning where, if analysis is lacking, transcendence may take root.

"Place Names" ["*Noms de lieu*"] is thus a cunning title, for its contiguous terms demonstrate the very way the semiotic and symbolic interact in Kristeva's analysis, brushing against each other to reveal the insubstantiality of both terms. The Place of the proper Name is unfounded.

Ironically, this shows Kristeva's notions of the sex / gender division to be not so far from Butler's positing of sexual identity as "performativity". In *Bodies That Matter*, Butler expands this idea, asserting that the debate between constructivism and essentialism is futile, and the idea that "'everything is discursively constructed',

> … belongs to a kind of discursive monism or linguisticism that refuses the constitutive force of exclusion, erasure, violent foreclosure, abjection and its disruptive return within the very terms of discursive legitimacy (1993, 8).

Moreover, her performative notion of gender construction rests on the concept of "matter" as "not a site or surface, but as a process of materialization that stabilizes over time to produce the effect of boundary, fixity, and surface we call matter" (9). There is something beyond the determination of cultural discourse, but not an absolute "outside"; it can only be thought in relation to the discourse, at or as its most tenuous borders. Thus we are not "subjected to gender, but subjectivated by gender" and this emergence of the "I", or "naming" is "at once the setting of a boundary and also the repeated inculcation of a norm" (8). All this sounds quite similar to what Kristeva was doing in "Place Names", the main difference being that Kristeva's style of theorizing seems happier to accommodate the double time of the psychoanalytic model than Butler's.[8]

My point here is not simply to accuse Butler of being theoretically inconsistent, or to amalgamate the conceptual frameworks of the two theorists. Butler's Foucaultian model of "power" means that she is suspicious of the institutional power of psychoanalysis, and more concerned with "queering" what she considers as embedded heterosexist notions of material sexuality than Kristeva, who tends to consider these terms to be ambivalent. Yet their different gender relations, and Butler's confusion (like many others') as to the extent of Kristeva's collaboration with or subversion of the symbolic system, highlights the problem of the system in any consideration of the problem of gender: where or how to figure sexual alterity in the system; where or how to speak if you are a "woman" and hence other to the system; how to "be" outside when the other can not be known as separate from the system; how to even begin, when the beginning is already marked with the ontology of sexual difference?

The Anxiety of the System

When Kristeva tackles these questions in an explicitly feminist context, the difficulties and potential confusions surrounding her notions of gender and agency are compounded. In the early chapters of *About Chinese Women*, one of her few texts to confront the "woman problem" explicitly, Kristeva seems to express a paradoxical figuration of the feminine in order to highlight its problematic relation to the "sign and time" of her symbolic order (1977b, 35). The text oscillates between symbolic and semiotic, figuring women variously

---

[8] Butler is unwilling to accept the doubleness of Freud's attitude to the body and the ego's imaginary relation to it. In both *Gender Trouble* and *Bodies That Matter*, Butler argues that Freud posits a material body that precedes the conscious ego's imaginary perception of it, but that he also "confirms the indissolubility of a body part and the phanstasmatic partitioning that brings it into psychic experience" (Butler, 1993, 59). Following and developing Lacan's reinterpretation of Freud, Butler insists that the body and the ego's perception of it are simultaneously projected fantasies; indeed, that the body is itself a psychic "projection of a surface" (1999, 90, n. 43). (For a critique of this view, which asserts that Butler's formulation relies on a misreading of Freud, see Prosser, 1998, 40-42). Kristeva's reading of the body and ego-formation maintains a degree of Freudian ambivalence between materiality and fantasy. The bodily drives are still only knowable through the structures and fantasies of the symbolic but the semiotic represents a threshold where the (material) "other" of the symbolic breaks through. The "time" of the semiotic resists a straightforward sequentiality.

as mothers, *jouissant* bodies, witches and silent victims. The problem of Kristeva's project and her confusing position with regard to women and feminism is, I think, summarized in a brief paragraph which ostensibly suggests the ideal alternative to the repressions of "patrilinear society":

> A constant alternation between time and its "truth", identity and its loss, history and that which produces it: that which remains extra-phenomenal, outside the sign, beyond time. An impossible dialectic of two terms, a permanent alternation: never one without the other. It is not certain that anyone here and now is capable of this. An analyst conscious of history and politics? A politician tuned into the unconscious? Or, perhaps, a woman … (38).

The fact that Kristeva trails off here would suggest that her posited structure is indeed an *impossible* dialectic; something that cannot be realized, or perhaps even begun.

This sense of impossibility, and the anxiety it provokes are, I would argue, where Kristeva's work meets with feminism; or rather, like her contaminating terms, brushes against its boundaries. Her analyses of the way in which the material, the maternal, or the "feminine" are (or are not) figured within the prevailing structure of representation, relate to the wider anxieties about identity and agency in relation to this system. As she says in "Women's Time", the goal of the countering, questioning process she envisages should be seen as "an *interiorization of the founding separation of the socio-symbolic contract*, as an introduction of its cutting edge into the very interior of every identity whether subjective, sexual, ideological, or so forth" (1986b, 210). It is this 'contract' between gender, identity and system that makes her work so interesting to my analysis of the problems of contemporary feminism. The fact that Kristeva frequently refers to the specific relation of femininity to the system as a "pregnancy" embodies both her relation to the anxiety of the system and the confusions which arise from this relation. If pregnancy represents an "escape from temporality", or a "*jouissance* which breaks the symbolic chain, the taboo, the mastery" (1977b, 35), it can also be a "fundamental fetish, phallus-substitute" and hence "just another myth designed to restore time (even if different) at the very moment when time breaks up"(36). Is pregnancy an ethical encounter with the other, without mastery, or a product of kinship structures and thus a repetition of the same old patriarchal strictures?[9] Kristeva's

[9] For another description of pregnancy as an "embodiment" of ethical relations, see Kristeva, 1986b, 206: "Pregnancy seems to be experienced as the radical ordeal of the splitting of the subject: redoubling up of the body, separation and coexistence of the

"impossible dialectic" seems to be poised between a radical refiguration of sexual terms and a repetition of traditional sexual hierarchies. How, and whether, the dialectic could reach fulfilment in a way which would bring about the new ethical, theoretical and socio-symbolic "space" that Kristeva calls for, are taxing questions (1986b, 209). In order to explore these questions, and their implications for feminism, I intend to step back from the explicit feminist debate and explore the topography of Kristeva's system, and her anxiety about the system's anxieties. I hope that a close analysis of her encounter with the system – and the alternations of its terms and hierarchies – will ease some of the confusion about Kristeva's position in relation to the "problem of women", and determine to what extent she manages to reconcile "difference" and "heterogeneity" with the logic of a dialectical approach.

II. Sexual Revolution

The drive for change

So, to begin with the "impossible": how to trigger or provoke change within prevailing, and inherently speculative, structures of subjectivity and signification. While Kristeva uses the Hegelian notion of the historical "moment" to open up the closed consciousness of Being, her "revolutionized" dialectic must necessarily resist the Hegelian movement towards containment in an absolute "knowledge" or "consciousness"[10]. Following on from the Marxist inversion ["*renversement*"] of the Hegelian dialectic – the radical shift from "abstract ideology" to "material reality" – Kristeva stresses the irresolvable contradiction in the terms of the logical dialectic, refusing the transcendent, internalizing movement of the "Aufhebung", and positing instead the scissions inherent in the supposedly "neutral", "natural" terms of "*signifiance*" (1974, 14; 1984a, 17).[11] However, the problem in following a "necessity of change" within the confines

---

self and of an other, of nature and consciousness, of physiology and speech. [...] The arrival of the child, [...] leads the mother into the labyrinths of an experience that, without the child, she would only rarely encounter: love for an other."

[10] In this section of the chapter I am referring to Kristeva's *Revolution in Poetic Language* (1984a), and entering into the minutiae of its analytical movements.

[11] This radical shift is what Louis Althusser describes as "over-determination": the "decontamination" of the "kernel" of the dialectic from its "mystical shell" (1979, 91).

of a dialectical approach is immediately apparent when Kristeva describes this desirable "excess":

> one must still posit an "outside" that is in fact internal to each closed set, since otherwise the set would remain enclosed, even if internal differentiation could be extended indefinitely. One must, then, decenter ["*excentrer*"] the closed text and elaborate the dialectic of a process within plural and heterogeneous universes (1984a, 14).

To "decenter" "an outside" which is yet internal to the closed terms of discourse: Kristeva's language recognizes the inherent problem in seeking a new signifying practice, "on the outer boundaries of the subject and society". For, unlike Marxist theory, which posits a material reality in opposition to the Hegelian "consciousness", Kristeva theorizes the inseparability of any knowledge or experience from the discursive system, and removes the possibility of positing "change" in any purely phenomenological way: the project must be deconstructive before it can be reconstructive. Kristeva identifies a "movement" which, she says, "surpasses the stases of desiring structuration", yet rejects what she calls the "grammatological deluge of meaning" which arises out of the "*ingathering*" ["*recueillement*"] of the Derridean form of deconstruction (142, 141). According to her logic, if there are "only everywhere, differences and traces of traces" (Derrida, 1987a, 26), then there can be no revolution or "*jouissance*", no break in the perpetual process of "becoming", and no "renewal" of symbolic and social structures (142). Thus while it is impossible within the analytical discourse to affirm a wholly new space, position or "free energy", there is for Kristeva a "necessity" to posit the potential movement of the "ex-centric", if the *reconstructive*, as well as deconstructive potential of the "negativity" of the dialectic is to be kept "in process" (141-145). Kristeva's posited rupture is thus both material and symbolic; between the "becoming" of dialectical logic and the "différance" of the engrammatized system of language:

> … we must designate an event that occurs before and within the trajectory of Hegelian negativity, an event that lies between and beneath the psychoanalytic distinction between "desire" and "need", one that moves through and is inherent in biological and signifying development but links them together (146).

This event on the threshold of divisions seems to be a way of opposing "sign and time" without falling back into binarisms. Its "*scission*, *separation*, or *rejection*", ruptures both the "grammar" of a movement towards being, and the perpetual *jouissance* of the semiotic (146). Most importantly for Kristeva's social project, it enables the analysis of a "subject" while still denying any pre-constructed notions of language. The "subject-in-process" ["*sujet en procès*"] defies the teleological "law" of the symbolic – its potential for (self-)destruction is apparent with every semiotic pulsion – and is forever caught in a negative movement, rather than the essence of becoming:

> We view the subject in language as decentering the transcendental ego, cutting through it, and opening it up to a dialectic in which its syntactic and categorical understanding is merely the liminary moment of the process, which is itself always acted upon by the relation to the other dominated by the death drive and its productive reiteration of the 'signifier' (30).

Positing for the sake of necessity is one thing, but how can the ruptured subject and discourse of "revolutionary" texts be situated, without inscribing them into an ontology that leads inevitably to a metaphysical notion of presence (an *an-und-fur-sich*)?[12] This is where Kristeva adopts the simultaneously symbolic and material value of Freudian negation (rejection) by theorizing the "thetic moment" of symbolic rupture – the "break" in the subjective process which produces the signifying dialectic – as occurring in the space of the "chora". The position of this space arises from the term: a borrowed Platonic word which indicates "an essentially mobile and extremely provisional articulation constituted by movements and their ephemeral stases" (25). Plato used the term in *Timaeus* to indicate the space, "receptacle" or "situation" that is needed for "all living things to come into being", but he also asserts that it can only be posited or apprehended through a sort of "bastard reasoning" or "dream" (Plato cited in 1984a, 26, n. 13). It is not in itself a "certain something" ["*une telle*"]. Kristeva adopts this term because it encapsulates the ontological and temporal indeterminacy she attributes to this stage of (semiotic) functioning.[13] The chora carries the articulation of the libidinal drives "in a motility that is as full of movement as it is regulated" (25). In other words, it represents the rhythmical pulsions of the drives, and their "disposition" towards being structured and regulated, but is still too amorphous and mobile to accept definitive positioning in the symbolic order.[14] Kristeva's description of the

---

[12] I am thinking here of Derrida's comment: "breaks are always and fatally reinscribed in an old cloth (of epistemology) that must continually, interminably be undone" (1987a, 24).

[13] As Kristeva asks of Plato's term, "Is the receptacle a 'thing' or a mode of language?" (26, n. 12).

[14] Kristeva writes of the "insurmountable problem for discourse: once it has been named, that functioning, even if it is pre-symbolic, is brought back into a symbolic

chora's liminal space mimics the bastardized logic of the primary processes of psychic organization, as described by Freud: it is a modality of significance prior to the symbolic, a negativity prior to negation, and an ordering before inscription into the law. Always ambivalent, it is inscribed in a fictive "afterwards" as a moment "prior to" inscription. The thetic phase is thence located in the movement of the chora, so negates its own "moment"-ousness on any temporal or logical scale. This means that Kristeva's tracing of the "subject" moves from the phenomenological concern with the "operating and producing consciousness" – the "I" as origin – to a concern with the "producible consciousness" (36, n. 36):

> … only since Freud have we been able to raise the question not of the origin of this thesis but rather of its production. […] The Freudian theory of the unconscious and its Lacanian development show, precisely, that thetic signification […] constitutes the subject without being reduced to his process precisely because it is the threshold of language. Such a standpoint constitutes neither a reduction of the subject to the transcendental ego, nor a denial [*dénégation*] of the thetic phase that establishes signification (44-5).

This reliance on drive theory means that Kristeva's conception of semiotic agency ("free energy" and new "positionality") is prior to any subjective / symbolic presence or taking place. In Freudian terms, it coincides with the death drive: the desire to return to an archaic state before consciousness, the "urge [...] to restore an earlier state of things" (Freud 1991a, 308). If this "prior" force is to refuse entry into the internalized contradiction of the dialectic, it must constantly repeat its movement of rejection, for the moment its potential is realized it will be contained by the "grammar" of symbolic logic. However, if this movement remains as a perpetual repetition, it cannot meet the demands of what we might call the other side of Kristeva's threshold theory: the "need" of the dialectical method to perpetuate the "logic of scission" and thus fulfil its "revolutionary" potential (Kristeva 1984a, 172). This leads Kristeva to inscribe the semiotic as a "regulating process" through the psychoanalytic principle of negation, so as to push the repetitive rejection to a point where it will be "more than a mere mark"["*enfin plus qu'une marque*"] (173, 172).

---

position" (26, n. 13). Kristeva's terminology here is clearly attempting to deal with this problem. In later texts, Kristeva draws more explicit associations between the chora and maternity, For example, in *In the Beginning Was Love*, she describes the chora as "an ancient, mobile, unstable receptacle, prior to the One, to the father, even to the syllable, metaphorically suggesting something nourishing and maternal" (1987c, 5).

> … rejection must become positive: rejection engrammatizes, it marks One in order to reject it again and divide it in two again. As a step toward the development of the signifier, the engram is rejection's self-defense, its relative immobilization, which, in turn, allows the reactivation of drives: re-jection. Without this stasis (on which the symbolizing thesis will be established) – presented by Freud both in *Beyond the Pleasure Principle* and in his article on *Verneinung* – rejection could not produce something new and displace boundaries; it would be a merely mechanical repetition of an undifferentiated 'identity' (171).

In other words, only through the "re-" and not in the "-jection" can the death instinct be admitted into the path of "becoming" without it ending as a repetition of pure loss:

> The prefix 're' indicates not the repetition of a constant identity, but rather a renewal of division through a new unifying stoppage where something more than a mere mark – a representamen and an ego – will finally crystallize, and then be re-jected once again (172).

Dialectical Freud

However, the exact relation between the logic of drive and the logic of dialectic in Kristeva's system is somewhat confusing, and the consequences of this relation for her conception of systematic agency should give us pause for thought. The "stasis" that Kristeva points to as being presented by Freud is clearly related to the debate in "Beyond the Pleasure Principle", triggered by the death drive's perpetual movement towards inertia.[15] Kristeva is careful to stress the "two opposing tendencies" of "the objective laws of living matter", which are the "indispensable precondition" for rejection: "its division and stoppage and […] the principles of multiplication and constancy, the latter ensuring the preservation of the organic cell" (Kristeva 1984a, 173-4). Following Freud's change of thought from "Beyond the Pleasure Principle" onwards, Kristeva moves from positing this repetition as being solely an ego-instinct – thus "including the so-called self-preservative instincts of the ego among the death instincts" – to an equation between its move towards stasis and the libidinal

---

[15] Freud traces the origin of the death drive's apparent impulse towards inertia through its action in the ego-instincts and sexual instincts, in an attempt to work out whether the compulsion to repeat is inherently conservative or oriented towards progression and change. His problem is that the logical connection between repetition and progression would mean that the death instinct would be connected with the sexual instincts rather than the ego-instincts, as would be expected (1991a, chapter vi).

instincts (Freud 1991a, 326).[16] Thus rejection's impulse is towards the other (the "constructive" coalescence with other cells) and a logic of renewal: "the Eros of the poets and philosophers which holds all living things together" (323). This is also, importantly, a narcissistic movement.[17] For Kristeva, the stasis of the representamen is a displacement of the negative excess of rejection from the body onto the process of signification. It is a *thetic* heterogeneity, and thus establishes the preconditions for identification and "positionality" which bring about the ego and the sign:

> Its [rejection's] tendency toward death is deferred by this symbolic heterogeneity: the body, as if to prevent its own destruction, *re-inscribes [re-marque]* rejection and, through a leap, *represents* it *in absentia* as a sign (Kristeva, 1984a, 171).

The difficulty and problem with Kristeva's mingling of psychoanalytic and dialectical logic lies in the "*in absentia*". In Freudian terms, the agency of this stasis – the "leap" of Kristeva's quotation – remains in darkness.[18] It is only visible in the libidinal movement towards the other. It is the "fiction" of the ego ideal and leads towards the normative laws of the social code, yet is also its own constitution, coming ultimately from the narcissistic action *prior to* object relations and the positionality of the sign (1991b, 367-79). And according to Freud, narcissistic agency can never be known as a "discovery", only recognized through its effects (1991c, 89). Thus rejection, as both the logic of repetition and the logic of renewal, is has an indeterminate status: it is a potentiality, even a contamination

---

[16] Freud explains, this is a change in the dualism of his topography of instincts, from a division between the ego-instincts and sexual instincts to being between life instincts and death instincts. Thus impulses towards death and life act through both the ego and sexual instincts, rather than death being confined to the ego, and life to the sexual instincts.

[17] As early as his essay "On Narcissism", Freud suggests that the setting up of the ego ideal which leads to object choice was rooted in the "self-love…enjoyed in childhood" and suggests that there could be "a special psychical agency which performs the task of seeing that narcissistic satisfaction from the ego ideal is ensured" (1991c, 88-9). Freud went on to define this narcissistic agency in terms of the (oral) satisfaction of the primary identification with the "father of individual prehistory"–a prior-to-object which enables identification with objects, and the development of the super-ego: see 1991b, 370; and 1991e, 134-140. I will return to the concept of identification later in the chapter.

[18] Freud likens the problem of his originary debate to "a darkness into which not so much as a ray of a hypothesis has penetrated". He breaks off from the scientific approach into an explanation of inertia through Platonic myth (1991a, 331).

of order and positions. It constitutes the "breaking off" of the logic of the drives.[19]

Kristeva's "leap" turns out to be a very different one. She feeds the drive logic and the narcissistic agency of Freud back through the logic of the dialectic. What was neither certain presence or absence (the "return to an earlier state" which is also the "new psychical action" of narcissism) becomes a certain absence, and yet an absence which must be both visible and "knowable". For Kristeva, the rejecting stases in the signifying process prevent the "pure 'nothingness'" of repeating the "motility of the chora" – and thus the fantasy of identification with the mother's body – which results from the foreclosure of the thetic phase. Yet the "purity" of this nothingness results from the failure of the rejecting process to *know* its own agency:

> In immediate representation it appears as pure 'nothingness', although such a representation does not see that 'referent' in its true economy, namely as that from which representation itself results (Kristeva 1984a, 182).

Following the dialectical drive to knowledge, the narcissistic agency in Kristeva's structure takes the form of the Hegelian agency of consciousness, where its negation must move beyond the immediate, the movement of its own mediation, in order to reach a "true" consciousness. It must realize,

> ... the fact that this nothingness is specifically the nothingness of that *from which it results*. For it is only when it is taken as the result of that from which it emerges, that it is, in fact, the true result; in that case it is itself a *determinate* nothingness, one which has a *content* (183, citing Hegel 1977, 50-1).

To an extent, this shares the double mediating / constituting movement of the psychoanalytic agency. Yet the way in which the Hegelian agency is already determined, and *knows* its determination, removes the particular impulse towards "otherness" indicated by Freud's libidinal aspect of rejection. Being determined as well as being always in process means that Hegel's "true" consciousness finds the negative agency with which to propel itself forwards (beyond the immediate and into "truth") in the knowledge of this negation as its own mediation. "True" consciousness – the knowledge of itself – is its

[19] See Freud's "breaking off" of his drive-theory argument, in "Beyond the Pleasure Principle" (1991a, 332), which relates to what he says in "Negation": "the performance of the function of judgment is not made possible until the creation of the symbol of negation has endowed thinking with a first measure of freedom from the consequences of repression and, with it, from the compulsion of the pleasure principle" (1991d, 441).

own source. In effect, consciousness creates and controls its own mediation by positing its "origin" as beyond its immediate self and its process, and then denying it as being anything other than its own process: "a *determinate* nothingness, one which has a *content*".

Kristeva translates this nothingness from Hegel's language of identity into the language of affect: from the "presence *of consciousness*" into the "very movement of negativity" (184, 183). Yet even so, the logic is shifted towards a dialectical pattern of agency and mediation. In Kristeva's psychoanalytic "leap", the "in absentia" of the symbolic representation of rejection is a "determinate nothingness". The stasis of rejection *contains* the libidinal aspect of its narcissistic agency in the knowing "beyond" of its own self-propelling process. As a result, the potential heterogeneity of the movement of rejection in the Freudian structure – towards the other and as narcissism, towards identification and "prior to" positionality – is curtailed. The logic of renewal becomes a sequence of self-determining and uprooting ["*Hinausgerissenwerden*"], and the logic of repetition is re-inscribed as the "before" of the process, which must be denied if it is not to be the death of the logic. Once translated into Hegelian terms, the action of the chora – originally Kristeva's agency of change, and part of the simultaneity of terms in Freud's libidinal narcissistic agency – becomes the "other" term posited and denied by the (auto-)ontology of the dialectical process: the "nothingness of that *from which it results*". The potentially transgressive movement is reconceived as "a jolt, a necessary violence, consciousness' 'internal cause'" (184).

Threshold Speculation

This hybrid of Freudian agency and Hegelian logic has a subtle, but significant, impact on Kristeva's theories of revolutionary signifying practices. She argues that modern avant-garde literature resists the process of "unifying conceptual thought" (185) by organizing the symbolic around the libidinous "jolts of recognition", and these jolts resound as "unthoughts" on the level of the signifier. These are the rhythms and glossolalia she identifies in texts by, amongst others, Lautréamont, Mallarmé and Artaud, which endanger the subject's unity by admitting the negativity which symbolic laws in the prevailing capitalist society repress. However, because this negativity is, according to dialectical logic, already determined as part of the historical path towards knowledge, it undergoes a "reversal" which "introduces discourse" and sublates it into a "signifying thesis". This means that borderline texts which act as Kristeva's "subjects" begin to resemble historical "ego-texts", which contain (and determine) their own agency and thus "know" themselves:

> The text moves toward scientific knowledge of the process that perturbs and exceeds it only to the extent that this latter precondition (signifying thesis) is met (187).

> The modern text combines rejection, its signifying reversal and its "knowledge": it constitutes a process, but one that analyses itself endlessly (188).[20]

Thus the libidinal possibility of the semiotic agency becomes a narcissistic version of a Hegelian "pure universality" of knowledge.[21] Projected into the now necessarily temporalized, materialist process of subject production, Kristeva then posits the possibility of textual "practice" as well as "experience", a dialectical, materialist analysis, which preserves the self-determination and objective knowledge of the Hegelian process without, she claims, repressing the "moment of 'sensuous' and 'immediate activity' that Freudian rejection opens up (206). This analysis-in-practice will, Kristeva claims, finally allow her aim of "social" – rather than simply "subjective" – change or revolution.

Yet by translating rejection into dialectical terms, she has altered its determination. In place of the thetic phase, practice offers "not an identifying addressee [...] but rather processes and objective laws to discover" (206). And because these "objective laws" are part of the "course of historical processes", the direction and purpose of its revolutionary agency is already inscribed as part of the laws' internal logic: "the process of rejection finds its place in them all the more logically since its own logic is none other than that of renewed contradiction". The analysis Kristeva describes now is, in effect, a kind of *historical* reality testing, where the movement backwards is a speculative viewing and "knowing" of the refound object.[22] The

---

[20] Kristeva makes a distinction between the avant-garde texts of the nineteenth-century, such as those by Lautréamont and Mallarmé, which do not proceed towards the knowledge of their "practice", and those of the twentieth-century, which coincide with the "recasting" of Freudian negation through the analysis of historical materialism.

[21] Hegel defines the "pure universality of knowing" as being "self-consciousness as self-consciousness, which is the simple unity of knowing" (1977, 485).

[22] I adopt Freud's term here, used in 1991c, 440: Kristeva's analysis parallels Hegel's description of scientific method, whose nature "is to be in its being its own Notion ... This alone is the rational element and rhythm of the organic whole; it is as much

psychoanalytic "cure" thus becomes a movement forwards, set on the path towards sublation: the negation of the negation (a positive move) which denies the "subject" while preserving it on a "higher" level.

III. Sexual Ethics

Liminal Repetitions

If we are to relate Kristeva's theorization of semiotic agency to the difficulties surrounding her figurations of femininity and maternity, we can see that the problem is more "borderline" than a failure to introduce heterogeneity into philosophical discourse, or a too easy acceptance of the "heterosexual matrix" of psychoanalysis. Kristeva *does* succeed in forming a topography of a subject-in-process that lies "before and within" Hegel and "between and beneath" psychoanalysis. Indeed, contrary to the standard feminist critique of Kristeva's agency, the "position" of the chora *itself* – as a repetition prior to signification which disrupts the very notion of "self" – means that the association between the forces of the semiotic and a pre-Oedipal, feminized negativity never quite collapses into an essentializing embodiment of "the maternal / nurse figure" (Butler 1993, 41). As I have shown above, the bastardization of drive logic contaminates any separate terms or certain ontology. However, having harnessed this heterogeneous logic, Kristeva translates the agency into a structure of "becoming" which is too quick to accept the Hegelian comfort of dialectical intention. The consequence of this is to cut short the potential radicality of Freudian negation, which lies in its capacity to disrupt the singular progression of subjective consciousness.[23] The "excess" movement of the chora that was the contaminating agency of the subject-in-process is displaced onto the stasis of the thetic phase, which no longer identifies with the other, but with the structures of a "universal" process – which turns out to be its own self-process. Thus even though the action of the semiotic serves to disrupt the unity of the subject, and the authority of the (paternal) law, its negativity is sublated, and becomes a necessary part of the determination of the symbolic. The alterity of the libidinal movement is (re)incorporated; its "excess" is reconceived as an impossible reality which, rather than

knowledge of the content, as the content is the Notion and essence – in other words, it alone is *speculative philosophy*" (1977, p. 34).

[23] As Jacqueline Rose asserts, the "ambiguity of the concept" of the death drive "is the concept itself", because its return to stasis is also "the oscillation of position, the displacement of psychic levels and energies" (1993, 95).

dislocating the binary structure of the symbolic, will always serve some collaborative function as other *on the boundary* of the two terms.

Kristeva has produced an "impossible dialectic", but it is not her idealized alternation of "never one without the other"(1977b, 38). The "truth" she writes of summoning in *About Chinese Women* is a "truth" that is "neither true nor false, that cannot be fitted into the order of speech and social symbolization, that is an echo of our *jouissance*". What she summons through her revolutionary semiotic agency might potentially be all these things, but its potential disturbance is reincorporated into the signifying system as part of the internal determination of the dialectic. Its negation is negated (made positive) and it thus becomes impossible to think of its alterity as being truly "other". Instead, it assumes a fetishized, phallic status that remains stuck in the same paternally-centred symbolic organization.[24]

At this point in my analysis, the temptation is to raise the ghost of Lacan, a permanent, veiled, presence in Kristeva's writing. Translated into his terms, Kristeva's logic of the stasis could be regarded as a repetition of his structure's erection of the phallus as "the signifier of [an] Aufhebung" (Lacan 1982a, 82).[25] Lacan's subject is identified by the division of the signifier, the substitution for the mother /primary object positioned "in the place of the Other". It follows a dialectical movement, which negates the unknowable and claims it as its self-determining "truth". As Lacan says,

> If the phallus is a signifier then it is in the place of the Other that the subject gains access to it. But in that the signifier is only there veiled and as the ratio of the Other's desire, so it is this desire of the Other as such which the subject has to recognize, meaning, the Other as itself a subject divided by the signifying *Spaltung* [*splitting*] (83).

However, even if Kristeva's semiotic agency does refer back to a veiled, phallic mother, the pre-objectal aspect of its narcissism does leave a mark, a difference, on the repetition of the dialectic (we might, perhaps, call it the mark of impossibility), which would seem to

---

[24] One might go so far as to describe Kristeva's notion of "practice" in the same terms she uses to diagnose poetry's convergence with fetishism. It, too, seems to be a "stasis that acts as a thesis" or a "displacement of the thesis onto the realm of the drives" (1984a, 85).

[25] Lacan insists "the phallus can only play its role as veiled, that is, as in itself the sign of the latency with which everything signifiable is struck as soon as it is raised ["*aufgehoben*"] to the function of signifier". This seems to parallel Kristeva's "leap".

enable an analytical "occupation" of the borderline site of the system's own anxiety.[26] Kristeva develops this occupation in her analysis of two psychic "extremes" in *Powers of Horror* and *Tales of Love*. These texts can be viewed as an exploration of the mark of impossibility and a narrative history of the (fetishized) semiotic "space" from two different analytical perspectives: in *Powers of Horror* in terms of the "loss" on the maternal borderline of signification; and in *Tales of Love* in terms of a metaphorical "recovery" through paternal identification. Together, they mark a movement from an imagined "revolution" of terms (the "rejection-become-positive" of "Revolution in Poetic Language") to a provisional transformation: an analytical position where the "cure" of the symbolic structure, like the analysed subject of Kristeva's psychoanalytic method, can be "anticipated in an always anterior future" (1984a, 215).

Abjection

Kristeva's description of abjection as "the want" of the "object of want" is a similar movement towards the borderline of theoretical distinctions as her description of the logic of scission in *Revolution in Poetic Language* as the "re" of "rejection". However, *Powers of Horror* makes a further movement into the boundary of the dialectical terms in speaking from and as the "mark" of her agency's impossibility. Abjection is acknowledged as the collaborative movement in the system, which inscribes what is to be denied within primary narcissism, and hence what creates the "in absentia" of the thetic phase. As Kristeva says,

> … all abjection is in fact recognition of want on which any being, meaning, language, or desire is founded. One always passes too quickly over this word, 'want', and today psychoanalysts are taking into account only its more or less fetishized product, the 'object of want'. But if one imagines (and imagine one must, for it is the working of imagination whose foundations are being laid here) the experience of want itself as logically preliminary to being and object – to the being of the object – then one understands that abjection, and even more so abjection of self, is its only signified (1982, 5).

[26] Some feminist critics defend Kristeva from accusations of Lacanian phallocentrism by pointing to her "occupation" of the maternal space as a way of "unveiling" the phallic mother. In her analysis of "Stabat Mater", Jane Gallop interprets Kristeva's speaking from the "double space" of the maternal as being a mimesis of the phallic mother, and, hence a *dephallicizing* of her (1982). I will return to this view of "Stabat Mater" later in this chapter.

Abjection treads the ground between the rule and the ruled out. It is the sense of revulsion felt as encountering a loathed piece of food, "a piece of filth, waste or dung", certain bodily fluids, decay, or a corpse (2). Yet, as Kristeva asserts, this revulsion is provoked not by a perceived "lack of cleanliness or health", but by "what disturbs identity, system, order. What does not respect borders, positions, rules. The in-between, the ambiguous, the composite" (4). What is abject is that which breaks socio-symbolic taboos – "the primers of my culture" (2) – but, more specifically, is "something rejected from which one does not part, from which one does not protect oneself as from an object" (4). Anthropologically and psychically speaking, it is exemplified by the fantasy and prohibition of the maternal body.

The movement of abjection thus represents a threshold: it is a "composite of judgment and affect, or condemnation and yearning, of signs and drives" (10). And precisely because it is in the most liminal of spaces (a "hyphen" or "comma"), it reveals *as absent* the other (the "unknown") that was so crucially covered over by the incorporated negativity of the phallic Mother:

> The archaic economy is brought into full light of day, signified, verbalized. Its strategies (rejecting, separating, repeating, abjecting) hence find a symbolic existence, and the very logic of the symbolic – arguments, demonstrations, proofs etc – must conform to it. It is then that the object ceases to be circumscribed, reasoned with, thrust aside: it appears as abject (15).

Kristeva's exploration of abjection alters the balance of her "impossible dialectic", and comes close to deconstructing the agency, and hence the anxiety, of her system. She calls it a "narcissistic crisis", because it points to the libidinal drive whose negation by the thetic phase makes narcissism appear as "a regression to a position set back from the other, a return to a self-contemplative, conservative, self-sufficient haven". (14) The abject crisis reveals that "such narcissism never is the wrinkleless image of the Greek youth in a quiet fountain". Instead, the "conflict of the drives muddle its bed, cloud its water, and bring forth everything that, by not becoming integrated with a given system of signs, is abjection for it". This is a telling image, because it marks the obfuscation of the speculative view, a halting of the self-reflective "knowledge" that propels the rejecting process of Kristeva's dialectical "subject". It occupies an ambivalent position rather than a prescribed identity. The abject asks "Where am I?" rather than "Who am I?", and the question itself problematizes the notion of "position" (8). It 'shatters the wall of repression and its judgments", so that delineations are perforated, and classifications are demoted to mere "seeming" (15). This breaking of logic, and Kristeva's descriptions of it, can be seen as marking a return to Freud. The drives, the unaccountable excess, "muddle" sequentiality again, so that only the material "frame" of symbolization – the affect – remains as the mediation. The "archaic economy" thus empties out its own figuration without losing access to the symbolic altogether. Its action admits the provisionality of the law.

Put in these terms, the figuration of the abject can be viewed as providing an outlet for the (feminized) negativity of the semiotic in Kristeva's dialectic, because it interferes with the structure and sequence of narcissism; and thus with the inevitability of the movement of sublation which incorporates the maternal and turns it into a fetishized historical "moment". There is "nothing either objective or objectal to the abject". It "upholds 'I' within the Other", rather than containing the Other within the repeating, rejecting ego (15). Abjection's constant exposure of the threshold of the law reinscribes alterity into the narcissistic agency. The "pure" loss of the mother can become a retrieving loss, an "undeath". Its possible discourse, Kristeva suggests, is an unravelling, parodic one:

> The "narcissistic crisis" on the outskirts of the feminine, shows up with a comic gleam the religious and political pretensions that attempt to give meaning to the human adventure. For, facing abjection, meaning has only a scored, rejected, ab-jected meaning – a comical one (209).

This "comic gleam", which shows up difference, provisionality, an *in*difference to the law, as an agency within the prevailing agency of the system, suggests a position that the "feminine" can inhabit, for the "feminine" is always elsewhere to its symbolic figuration – "mother", "chora", "jouissant body", "Woman" – and must be if it is to resist (re-)incorporation. To follow the path of this ironic art, where (echoing Mallarmé's phrase) "nothing will have taken place but the place", is surely to create a threshold which may unsettle and displace the binary positioning of the sexes and of gendered identification in the subject. It may, perhaps, answer Kristeva's call for "never one without the other". Yet as Kristeva reaches this threshold, she trails off from the possibility. "Whom", she asks, "would agree to call herself abject, subject of or subject to abjection?" The ironic-abject could only be possible if an analyst could "manage to stay in […] the void […] the unthinkable of metaphysics" (209). It seems that for Kristeva this possibility must always remain in the conditional ("who could …" "who would …"). Her chosen descriptions, the "void", the "unthinkable" and later, the "labyrinthian muddy canals", prove that she is cannot tolerate the liminal identity of this abject subject (247). For within Kristeva's logic, a threshold seems to mutate rapidly into a void, "profound absence" or "truth": the loss or *jouissance* that identity brings to the other.[27] Kristeva's need for known "meaning", an object to discover and interpret through a transferential analysis, leads her to reinscribe the undead forces in her system as a "determinate nothingness", leaving the abject literally "ob-scene" (1982, 157-73).

"Hainadoration"

It is of little surprise, then, that *Tales of Love*, like the "necessity" in *Revolution in Poetic Language*, almost takes us back to the impossibility with which we began: how to allow heterogeneity in the system without negating its (dialectical) structure altogether. Kristeva seeks a recovery from the "narcissistic crisis" through the other side of her impossible agency, the identification or "new psychical action" posited by Freud in several of his essays (Freud, 1991c, 69).[28] The book moves from being a historical-psychical study of abjection, to a study of metaphor and identification through "love" which seeks to "cure" or at least "cover" the void of abjection.

Kristeva is concerned with re-establishing what she calls the "amatory states" of the Western psyche: the capacity of the subject-in-process to maintain a provisional identity and the structures of the ego ideal, in the face of the continual threat from the "narcissistic crisis".[29]

---

[27] I am thinking here of Lacan's inscription of feminine sexuality into a relation with the symbolic order where it is both the 'lost' (castrated phallus, mourned object) and the 'truth' (the foundation of symbolic identity, the desired other.) Hence his suggestion: "Might not this *jouissance* which one experiences and knows nothing of, be that which puts us on the path of ex-istence? And why not interpret one face of the Other, the God face, as supported by feminine *jouissance*?" (Lacan, 1982b, 147).

[28] Freud developed his theory of this agency in his chapter on "Identification" in *Group Psychology* (1991e, 134-140). Here he suggests that identification with a prior-to object establishes the ego ideal and object choice. He call this prior-to object the "father of individual prehistory" [father of "personal prehistory"] in "The Ego and the Id" (1991b, 370), where his analysis of the "special psychical agency's" relation to the ego ideal evolves into the theory of the super-ego (1991b, 367-79).

[29] As she says in "Evénement et revelation": "We [...] know the mechanisms of this transfer which makes the human psyche an *open system* capable of self-organization on condition of maintaining a kind of link with an other: these are the *identification* of primary narcissism "revealing" the subject, and the *idealization of the word* of the other. I have called this the amorous state" (1984b, 5).

The thetic side of narcissism is reasserted in what is depicted as a battle with chaos:

> Narcissism protects emptiness, causes it to exist, and thus, as lining of that emptiness, insures an elementary separation. Without that solidarity between emptiness and narcissism, chaos would sweep away any possibility of distinction, trace and symbolization, which would in turn confuse the limits of the body, words, the real, and the symbolic (1987a, 24).

Once again Kristeva forges a dialectic on the threshold of terms: another inscription of stasis that "screens" over the "void" of the abject and seems to return to the symbolic "leap" of a knowing self-process. And yet, once again, this dialectic has been slightly displaced. The corollary absence (the veiled, phallic absence in opposition) has asserted itself within the agency as impure, threshold, non-present, so that the return to a determining structure of "objective laws" can no longer be comfortably "objective". Consequently, Kristeva's descriptions of the subjective process in *Tales of Love* return to Freud's notion of identification, because it is an action which, crucially, takes place "before any choice of object" (Freud 1991e, 135). Kristeva takes up the archaic focus of Freud's primary identification, the "father of individual pre-history", whose ambiguous, bisexual status follows the pattern of the future inscription into socio-symbolic laws *without* yet being part of that inscription as an object:

> That enigmatic apprehending of a *pattern* to be imitated, one that is not yet an object to be libidinally cathected, leads us to wonder whether the loving state is a state without object and reminds us of an archaic *reduplication* (rather than imitation), 'possible before any choice of object' (1984b, 25).[30]

It is interesting to note the change in Kristeva's emphasis from mimesis (the narcissistic reflection of the self-determined subject) to reduplication (a doubling, or repetition, which disregards the notion of matching to an originary model). As with the "cloudy waters" of abjection, the specular structure of Kristeva's dialectical agency in *Revolution in Poetic Language* has lost a degree of its integrity. It carries with it the recognition of the non-objectal abject, its marking of the *provisional* law, and the "un-dead" threshold that this law denies. Moreover, the "bisexuality" of the father of individual pre-

---

[30] The "bisexuality" of the father of individual prehistory is due to "him" being identified with prior to any recognition of sexual difference. Freud says identification is, more accurately, "with the parents", but he refers to the father in his discussion in order to "simplify" his "presentation" (1991b, 370).

history admits the possibility of a movement towards an other which is not inhibited by the placement of sexual oppositions.

Kristeva turns again to the double impulse of Freud's narcissistic libido, towards self-preservation and towards death. Only this time the libido is not cut short by self-determination and self-knowledge. Both hatred and love *towards the other* are maintained in the "amatory space" – the "lovehate" [*hainadoration*] – which Kristeva posits as the transference of identification:

> Freudian dualism finds its strongest expression in this impossible harmonization of amorous space, in this fractured space of lovehate. Love is a necessary seeming, which is to be restored, aroused, promoted endlessly. This, in order to analyse it, in other words to dissolve it down to its framework, its carrier wave – which is hatred (125).

This means that the identification necessary to the thetic stage is no longer perceived as a foreclosing "leap", but as a permanently alternating space, "only for the time being and forever". Identification is *with* the symbolic, and creates a unified "identity", yet it is an identification with an other's language (the "father of individual prehistory") and an other which is not subscribed as a desired object:

> When the object that I incorporate is the speech of the other – precisely a non-object, a pattern, a model – I bind myself to him in a primary fusion, communion, unification. [...] In being able to receive the other's words, to assimilate, repeat, reproduce them, I become like him: One. A subject of enunciation. Through psychic osmosis / identification. Through love (26).

Transference becomes the metaphorical space where the pattern of the symbolic, of "objective laws", is maintained – thus creating provisional borders and a provisional self – but not "known" or categorically positioned. The permanent suspension of the "lovehate" incorporates both what would be transcendent or speculative in the system and the anarchic, heterogeneous action of the drives. Transferential identification with the father of individual prehistory thus absorbs objective and narcissistic forces into a subjective / aesthetic process which carries the mark of the abject. This means, in turn, that the transference of psychoanalytic practice, which resurrects the transference of archaic identification, can begin to "cure" the modern crisis of identity that Kristeva diagnoses in many of her writings.[31] Psychoanalytic transference creates a "screen" over emptiness without excluding otherness; it works

> … by preserving a *typology of discourses* (for instance, the 'poetical' is not the 'philosophical' discourse, which is not the 'analytical'), and setting for itself the regular task of being, on the one hand, a scene of metaphor production (as in the amatory state or in poetry) and, on the other, a scene of *provisional* interpretation. It is the *provisional* (this means such-and-such, for the *moment*) that inserts *duration* instead of the *absolute* in psychoanalytic interpretation. *Psychoanalysis is the most internalized moment of Western historicality* (277).[32]

Herethics or His law?

Could this, then, be the point of successful reconstruction of Kristeva's system, following the deconstructive action of the "impossible" abject? The agency of identification in *Tales of Love would* seem to be bordering on being an "interiorization of the founding separation of the socio-symbolic contract" (1986b, 210). Indeed, her definition of transference as an *internalized* historical culmination suggests that she considers it to be as close as her topography of the subject can get to becoming the "impossible dialectic": the impossibility of a separate, external agency acting on the system has certainly been incorporated by her threshold dialectic. Nevertheless, the result is not really the radical "heterogenizing" of the dialectical structure that she suggested in her earlier work. Incorporation may be a suspension which refuses transcendent knowledge, and thus admits difference, but the necessary *alternation* of terms within the space of Kristeva's transference – the residue of her dialectical frame – means that a hierarchy remains. There is still a more defined separation of archaic and symbolic domains, between the "not I" and the provisional "I", than Freud's agency of identification suggested.[33] This means that even though there is not a

---

[31] This crisis is described in *Revolution in Poetic Language* and *Powers of Horror*, but is explored in most detail in *Black Sun* (1989) and *New Maladies of the Soul* (1995b).

[32] Although it was written before *Black Sun*, *Tales of Love* stands in a therapeutic relation to it, describing in cultural rather than specifically clinical terms the transferential "cure" for the melancholy that *Black Sun* describes.

[33] Kristeva quotes Freud's definition of the father of individual prehistory as being "the most primitive aspect of affective binding to an object", but in the same paragraph slides this *affective* description into the capitalized terms of *identity*: "Freud has described the One with whom I fulfil the identification…as a Father" (1987a, 26). This cuts short "his" bisexual possibilities.

"leap" from pure loss to self-determining identity, Kristeva must still posit a "leap" between "having" and "being": the having of incorporation and the being of provisional identity (1987a, 26). To contain the division between the Phallic Father and abject mother neither inscribes nor erases it. As Kristeva notes, the father of individual prehistory is "endowed with the sexual attributes of both parents, and by that very token [is] a totalizing, phallic figure" (33).[34] The "path" of narcissism that Kristeva chooses sublimates both the "muddy canals" of the abject and the definition of the speculative into a "lay religiosity" which "has God descending within Narcissus and impos[ing] the Self as the pedestal of a new religion": the leap of "generalized symbolism" (136). The result is a provisional unity of contradictory terms; a religious Self which has no hope of an afterlife.

Ironically, this leaves difference little more room than Kristeva's self-determining topography. Heterogeneity and materiality are no longer the "pure" loss or Other of the specular structure, but they are still covered up, "screened" over as an un-dead presence which threatens the provisional process of "becoming". The abject, the maternal, the "feminine" are effectively buried alive. It is therefore not surprising that the woman's "domain", and indeed, Kristeva's own writing, comes to be figured as melancholic: the undead mother is walled up inside Kristeva's subject, and mourning is doomed to incompletion.[35]

Thus when Kristeva comes to call for a new feminine ethics – a "herethics" – in "Stabat Mater", it appears less as a castration of the Virgin Mary, the ideal Phallic Mother, than an incorporation of her *jouissance*.[36] The text of "Stabat Mater" performs a threshold dialectic which incorporates a history of the religious, symbolic significance of maternity and a less legalistic, more material meditation on the

[34] Kristeva continues, "its very existence and my being able to take myself for it – that is what already moves us away from the primal maternal satisfaction and situates us within the hysterical universe of loving idealization" (33-34).

[35] Kristeva refers to herself as a "melancholy theoretician" in 1989, 66. Nicolas Abraham and Maria Torok refer to this incomplete mourning of a (lost) object in their essay, "Mourning or Melancholia: Introjection *versus* Incorporation". Their analysis compares it to a walling up ("encrypting") of a loss that cannot be acknowledged (and is thus buried alive), and is connected to an incorporation of an "object word" (1994, 125-38).

[36] Kristeva even claims that "herethics" will "swallow up the goddesses" and "remove" their "necessity" (1987a, 263). Thus I disagree with Jane Gallop's view that Kristeva is dephallicizing the phallic mother. She merely incorporates her abject possibility within the phallic framework.

experience of pregnancy and motherhood. The way the double, split text proceeds *is* heretical insofar as it disrupts symbolization; mimicking the "rational" and "irrational" oppositions of the dialectic, and thus marking the "undeath [*a-mort*]" of abjection (263). Its sense or meaning emerges from neither the right-hand nor the left-hand column, but from the interaction and cross-contamination of the two "sides". As Grace M. Jantzen comments,

> The movement between the two columns [...] enacts the movement within the split self, the pleasure and challenge of doing justice simultaneously to the rational, linguistic self of the symbolic and the less articulate, but more creative and imaginative "semiotic" self. And the text as a whole enacts a deeper metaphor: the embodiment of the word, the articulation of the flesh: incarnation, becoming human / divine in a context and process of natality (1998, 201-2).[37]

Yet even as a new space seems to emerge, and it seems possible that otherness will be admitted rather than sublated and objectified, it is re-incorporated. For the "herethical" figuration works through paternal identification, in order that "bonds, thoughts, and therefore the thought of death [are] bearable" (1987a, 263). The terms of the Christian Phallic pregnancy – a "fundamental fetish phallus-substitute" (1980b, 272) – are repeated, and although they are marked with what they exclude (the other, the mother, the abject, *jouissance*) their authority is not finally displaced. Semiotic agency is suspended and separation remains, so that the only "comfort" for the maternal seems to be that she is an internalized rather than an absolute otherness; one which figures its own collaboration and its own impossibility or undeath:

> The love of God and for
> God resides in a gap: the bro-
> ken space made explicit by
> sin on the one side, the
> beyond on the other. Dis-
> continuity, lack, and arbi-
> trariness: topography of the
> sign, of the symbolic relation
> that posits my otherness as
> impossible. Love, here, is

[37] While Jantzen is critical of Kristeva's structural association between women and motherhood, and of the abject figuration of separation as "death", she regards "Stabat Mater" as a text in which a "new imaginary is suggested, a gap between the dying Christ whose image is the symbol of the West and the emerging natal, full of new life and potential" (Jantzen 2003, 130). I would argue that Kristeva's reassertion of the dialectical structure curtails this new imaginary.

> only for the impossible.
> For a mother, on the other
> hand, strangely so, the other
> as arbitrary (the child) is
> taken for granted. As far as
> she is concerned – impossible,
> that is just the way it is:
> it is reduced to the implacable.
> The other is inevitable,
> she seems to say, turn it into
> a God if you wish, it is never-
> the less natural, for such an
> other has come out of myself … (261-2).

Paternal identification within a dialectical framework incorporates the "excess" of the system (the *jouissance*, the baby, the absolute) so all that remains is the suspension of alternating terms within a provisional identity. The "herethical" is thus suggestible, or imaginable, but not possible; the other / child of its theoretical "space" is never quite realized / born. It thus seems appropriate that Kristeva should have described this text, and her position in relation it, as representing the "scar" of Freud's mourning (1984c).[38] For her dialectic marks, yet masks, the "open wound" of the impossible, undead feminine.

Although Kristeva's more recent work has only occasionally returned to an explicit consideration of femininity and female sexual identity, her figuration of femininity seems to remain in this "undead" space, so that it becomes a kind of shorthand for whatever remains exiled or unspoken within the symbolic system.[39] It thus becomes translatable into other forms of estrangement and marginality: an "irony of the community".[40] In spite of its different repetition – as semiotic, as abject, as undead "herethical" mother – and of her

---

[38] In her interview with Rosalind Coward, Kristeva says that in transference the theoretician is "positioned precisely on the place of this scar" (1984c, 24). Freud describes mourning as an "open wound" throughout his works.

[39] See Kristeva 1991 and 1995a, where she figures exile and estrangement as a form of incomplete mourning for the lost "maternal" origins and mother tongue. In "an New Type of Intellectual: The Dissident", she describes exile as the means of reaching beyond the "romantic melodrama" and "complacency" of modern feminism: "You will have understood that I am speaking the language of exile. […] How can one avoid sinking into the mire of common sense, if not by becoming a stranger to one's own country, language, sex and identity?" (1986c, 298).

[40] Kristeva makes an explicit reference to Hegel's declaration in an interview for *L'Infini*: "If it is true that femininity is a strangeness, an 'irony of the community' (Hegel), the woman should be able to make manifest her solidarity with other forms of strangeness and marginality in the modern world" (1996a, 46).

increasingly borderline analyses, Kristeva's engagement with the problem of changing the symbolic system has circled back to where it began: a demonstration of its anxiety, its impossibility.[41] Yet in the process, *through the repetitions*, Kristeva has marked the desires and identifications of her own structure. These marks do not resolve the problem of femininity in the system, nor feminism's relation to it, but they do suggest how the problem may be approached; which, as I indicated at the beginning of this chapter, constitutes half the problem. The marks reveal that as far as the feminine is concerned, the problem of Kristeva's dialectic is that it is dialectical. The problem of the system *is* the system; the system's desire for a pre-determined structure. Only if this circular irony were realized, and the systematic desire resisted, could the excluding hierarchy of terms perhaps begin to be altered.

[41] In more recent works, such as *Sens et non-sens de la révolte*, and *La Révolte intime*, Kristeva has modified her purely dialectical notion of "revolt", refiguring it as a movement of "re-volt", an anamnesis that returns to the past and re-elaborates the most archaic phases of psychic development (the narcissistic relation with the mother, identification with the father of individual prehistory and with the Oedipal father). Kristeva portrays this "re-volt" as the means of achieving "a reformulation of our 'carte psychique'" (1996b, 111): the subject renews itself, accepting and affirming the law, without closing itself off and becoming fixed. Although this model continues to emphasize the importance of the unconscious and the sense of alterity in psychic and social identity, one could argue that it represents a movement towards conservatism and individualism, which makes a change in the sexual bias of the system less possible. One could cite, as an example, her essay "Le sens de parité", which takes the biblical inscription of the difference between the sexes as the only starting point from which to claim "the singularity of each individual" (1999, 50). For a broad discussion of the political difficulties of Kristeva's recent work see Brandt 2001, 85-96.

Chapter 2

The Anxiety of Irony: Søren Kierkegaard

"One moment, then, appears as the essence that has stepped to one side as a universal medium, or as the subsistence of independent 'matters'. But the independence of these 'matters' is nothing else than this medium, [...] 'matters' posited as independent directly pass over into their unity, and their unity directly unfolds its diversity, and this once again reduces itself to unity. But this movement is what is called Force. One of its moments, the dispersal of the independent 'matters' in their [immediate] being, is the expression of Force; but Force, taken as that in which they have disappeared, is Force proper, Force which has been driven back into itself from its expression. First, however, the Force which is driven back into itself must express itself; and secondly, it is still Force remaining within itself in the expression, just as much as it is expression in this self-containedness."
G.W.F. Hegel (1977, 81).

"But the fact is that whether one tumbles into a little diving pool or plump into the great sea he swims all the same. By all means. Then we, too, must swim and try to escape out of the sea of argument in the hope of either some dolphin taking us on its back or some other desperate rescue."
Plato, *The Republic,* I, 5 § 453 d.[1]

If the problem of the system is its seemingly infinite capacity to subsume or incorporate attempts at opposition, then any alternative agency must first resist this urge towards mastery. Kristeva's repetition of Hegel's self-determining impulse means that her subjective agency is based in a leap (between "having" and "being") which precludes the possibility of a different form of negative mediation. The resulting compromise – a merging of psychoanalytic sublimation and dialectical impotence – incorporates the feminine "other" that she tried to acknowledge, and curtails the possibility of an

[1] Quoted on the original title page of Søren Kierkegaard's *The Concept of Irony*, (1841). See Kierkegaard, 1989, 418-9 (translation modified).

alternative subjective and ethical structure. Nevertheless, in her struggles to make a "space" for the other within the dialectic, and to create a truly heterogeneous notion of (sexed) identity, Kristeva's work serves as an important delineation of the complex relation which any feminist writer has to the legacy of "masculine" thought.

The question now is perhaps a more general one: how to begin to figure otherness without consuming one's own attempt? As Kristeva's semiotic suggests, there *is* the potential for a force which questions the (sexual) determinations of the analytical structure. However, if its interrogative power is to be sustained it is essential that, unlike Kristeva's incorporated, "revolutionary" abject, this force does not succumb to the determinations it criticizes. It must remain (at least in dialectical terms) truly ambivalent, risky, even "mad", in a way which Kristeva's dialectic could not tolerate.

It is at this point that the figure of irony suggests itself for analysis, for irony can be considered as exactly this kind of force. Even its basic dictionary definition supposes an ambivalence or doubleness which may resist the subscribing force of the philosophical absolute. As a form of "dissimulation" or "pretence" which feigns "ignorance [...] as a means of confuting an adversary", it argues from within the structure or concept it interrogates, without ever fully revealing its own position or "truth" (Oxford English Dictionary, 1989). Thus it might function as a form of "negative freedom" for one who, like the figure of "femininity", is both contained by and excluded from the prevailing philosophical structure.

This definition needs to be developed if irony is to be considered seriously as a form of agency for feminism, so I intend to turn away from explicit considerations of the question of "woman" and "femininity" to an exploration of the concept of irony in the work of Søren Kierkegaard. This is not as arbitrary a movement as it may first seem. While Kierkegaard's work has usually been classified as "theological" and "existential" rather than "feminist", "psychoanalytic", or "post-structuralist", he shares common ground with Kristeva in negotiating with a Hegelian structure of thought. However, where Kristeva is largely loyal to Hegel's dialectical operation, Kierkegaard criticizes it and tries to find possible ways of disrupting its incorporative logic. Kierkegaard's elaboration of irony is central to this search, for he considers it as an "ethical" force acting within and against the dialectic. His irony preserves the possibility of a subjective truth while questioning the assumption that this truth can be totally present and known. It censures the dialectical positing of an "absolute truth" for failing to account for what is unknown or "other" to this abstract category. An extended analysis of the nature of Kierkegaardian irony thus promises to provide further illumination of the inherent problems in dialectical accounts of "otherness"; as well as extending some of the possibilities that Kristeva foreclosed for fear of losing "positive" agency.

Throughout this chapter I will argue that it is Kierkegaard's "performance" as much as his analysis of the "concept" of irony which is particularly remarkable, and which distinguishes him from other dialecticians. I try to capture the style of this performance in my own writing; both because it has been neglected by many philosophers and theorists, and because it underlines my efforts to find a new way of figuring "otherness". As will become apparent, it is impossible to know where Kierkegaard's ironic path will end, but having followed it some distance, I will step back to the question of its possible relevance to feminism and feminist agency.

I. Either

The Chivalrous Battle

The work of Søren Kierkegaard deals with the notion of the subject and agency within the philosophical system: indeed, with the subject *as* a form of agency, counteracting what he deemed to be the too-easy movement of assimilation in the Hegelian philosophy of his time.[2] His earliest works trace the exclusion of all that is contingent, particular, individual or phenomenal in the realm of the world-historical, and show the illusory nature of dialectical "progression" and "mediation", since these movements are dependent on that very exclusion. As he says wryly of Hegel,

> … when the phenomena are paraded, he is in too much of a hurry and is too aware of the great importance of his own role as commander-in-chief of world history to take time for more than the royal glimpse he allows to glide over them (1989, 222).

Depictions of Hegel as an arrogant conqueror and despot are not infrequent in Kierkegaard's doctoral thesis and first published work, *The Concept of Irony*. In fact, the whole premise of his exposition of

---

[2] The majority of Kierkegaard's tutors at the university of Copenhagen were confirmed (and sometimes excessive) Hegelians, which is what *The Concept of Irony*, his doctoral thesis, is mainly aiming at, and treating ironically. See Howard V. Hong's and Edna H. Hong's Historical Introduction in Kierkegaard 1989, pp. vii - xxv.

the concept seems to be the indifference of the Hegelian system of philosophy towards anything but its own generalized conceptual aim. Within the first paragraph Kierkegaard's introduction demands

> ... of the philosophical knight a deferential propriety and a profound enthusiasm, in place of which one sometimes hears too much the jingling of spurs and the voice of the master (9).

The language is already that of power and combat, and Hegel apparently follows a very different code to Kierkegaard's preferred chivalric one. Instead of undertaking a quest, following humbly a path of discovery, Hegel gallops towards a place he has somehow already conquered. The whole movement of the Hegelian dialectic is projected towards its all-mediating goal. Through the Notion's "recognized moments" towards the ultimate freedom and knowledge – "self-consciousness", the "world-historical", "Spirit" – its direction could only be possible if the structure already knew the ending; in a sense, if it was already there. Kierkegaard objects to Hegel's recurring leap towards the known, the self-determining structure of his system, because it means that his imperious blindness concerns not only the incidents on the way but the beginning of the whole philosophical journey. Countering this insensibility, Kierkegaard insists on the particular, on the system's constituents: the determinants rather than the determined. What must be remembered as being "of great importance" is "that the phenomenon remain inviolate and that the concept be seen as coming into existence [*tilblivende*] through the phenomenon" (9). Interestingly, given his apparent respect for the inviolability of the phenomenon, Hegel's implied recklessness towards it (and given my interest in the negation of "feminine" alterity in the dialectic), Kierkegaard specifies that the phenomenon is "always *foeminini generis* [of the feminine gender]". The philosopher knight must treat "her" with care, must be an "amorist" rather than a conqueror, and while "he ought to have a sense of his own predominance" he "should use it only to help the phenomenon obtain its full disclosure".

Kierkegaard is clearly rebelling against Hegelian mastery: the Force of the dialectic whose "self-containedness" consumes even the independent elements that mediate it – as the epigraph to this chapter shows. Only by admitting these independent elements into the dialectic as *independent* elements, by allowing and facilitiating their "full disclosure", can we avoid such structural tyranny and perhaps begin to see a "cause" or "truth" beyond this abstraction. And yet, apart from assigning its gender, what Kierkegaard means by the phenomenon is not immediately obvious. It is not phenomenal in the Hegelian sense of the proximate "truth" internal to the movement of appearances.[3] Kierkegaard is evidently trying to specify some kind of essence or point of arrest in the mediating progression of philosophy which is not merely the base for sublation, nor a stasis in the sense of a known, self-enabling moment. He sets his example by his chosen concept, irony, which is conceived not as an abstract philosophical idea, but only through its manifestation in the "historical-actual, phenomenological existence" of a particular human individual: Socrates. For, as Kierkegaard explains, "the concept of irony makes its entry into the world through Socrates" (9). Noting philosophy's failure to value the history of concepts, as opposed to their eternal value, Kierkegaard explains that this is because while "concepts, just like individuals, have their history, [...] they nevertheless harbor a kind of homesickness for the place of their birth". Kierkegaard is thus radically at odds with Hegel's history of philosophy as well as his phenomenology, because Hegel's only admission of a beginning to philosophy – the beginning of a principle – is as an objective beginning:

> What philosophy begins with must be either mediated or immediate, and it is easy to show that it can be neither the one nor the other; thus either way of beginning is refuted. [...] The principle of philosophy does, of course, also express a beginning, but not so much a subjective as an objective one, the beginning of everything (Hegel, 1976, 67).

Kierkegaard's beginning, on the other hand, is clearly a subjective one. He introduces his revelation of Socrates the phenomenal-concept in "The View Made Possible" by distancing his structure and its premises from the Hegelian system. While adhering to the negative movement of the dialectical form, the "view's" "point of departure" is specifically *external*, unlike the system where "every element is essentially determined *ad intra* [internally], held and carried by the system's own conscience" (Kierkegaard 1989, 28). Kierkegaard exposes the circular logic of Hegel's beginning, which is hidden by his insistence on objectivity. If the whole system hinges on a self-determination, a coming to consciousness through the mastery of a self-posited "other", then it survives solely by perpetuating this

[3] This proximate truth will, according to Hegel, be sublated in the process of mediation: "In pressing forward to its true form of existence, consciousness will come to a point at which it lays aside its semblance of being hampered with what is foreign to it, with what is only for it and exists as an other; it will reach a position where appearance becomes identified with essence ..." (Hegel, 1977, 316).

autonomy, which means denying anything beyond its own mediating structure. It is thus (ironically) inevitable that Hegel should only claim the beginning as objective ("the beginning of *everything*") because as far as his system is concerned, the system *is* everything. Kierkegaard suggests that this beginning is actually subjective rather than objective, as its self-identical nature admits no other and perpetuates the illusion of system / consciousness equivalence. Thus it "appears to have the possibility of making every element a point of departure, but this possibility never becomes an actuality …".

Kierkegaard's external alternative to the dialectic's point of departure is precisely an admission that the beginning is not an objective totality. Philosophy's pursuit of abstract or universal "truth" can take place only through what is really other to itself: the actual, the phenomenal, the unknown. Thus if there is a premise it must be one of difference – the "higher actuality" or unknown "something positive" – and its beginning as a "view" or an abstract, generalized, written form of the pursuit of "truth", cannot presume to be anything other than subjective (28). Kierkegaard describes this in terms of resembling an incarnation. The absolute determination is infinite and other, but is manifested through an *actual* individual, which is the finite, partial form of the infinite.[4]

The way Kierkegaard maps the system's phenomenality and origin through the historically present individual may bring to mind a Fichtean idea of the phenomenal, where it is traced back to consciousness, which is the original fact (Fichte, 1970). And yet this is not right either because *The Concept of Irony* remarks on the particular "presuppositionlessness" of Fichte's idealism and its resulting incapacity to "let itself be born" (Kierkegaard 19891 274). Where the Hegelian movement has at once too much and too little subjectivity (too much in consciousness' positive, self-determination, too little in its failure to conceive of consciousness as an existence as well as a philosophical Notion/category) the Fichtean movement is too negative. "I=I" makes subjectivity an infinite, metaphysical category and abstract identity alone, and so excludes its possibility as finite historical actuality. The premise of its structure is, again, self-identical and its subjectivity has "no content" (273). It seems that actual existence (of concepts, phenomena and categories) in the philosophical "view" can only be born of a structure – that is, become

[4] Hence the biblical reference in Kierkegaard's description of the beginning, which quotes John 4:14: "We may say either that it is the word that creates or the silence that begets the individual" (29).

a present individual without the categorical individual being its whole transcendent purpose – that neither hides its origin/constituents within its teleology, nor sacrifices the general or universal to the particular. Philosophical positivity must be undermined continually if the balance is not to tip towards and repeat the self-created "truth" of a merely abstract structure. And this is what Kierkegaard is aiming at when he insists on drawing the concept of irony through its "life" in Socrates:

> As a rule, irony is understood ideally, is assigned its place as a vanishing element in the system, and is therefore treated very briefly. For this reason it is not easy to comprehend how a whole life can be taken up with it, since, after all, the content of this life must be regarded as nothing. But we forget hat a position is never as ideal in life as it is in the system; we forget that irony, just as any other position in life, has its spiritual trials, its battles, its retreats, its victories. [...] This is the purely personal life with which science and scholarship admittedly are not involved, even though a somewhat more intimate acquaintance with it would free them from the tautological *idem per idem* [the same with the same] from which such views often suffer (166).

Kierkegaard's "view", admits the phenomenal / individual on condition of a different balance of positivity and negativity. He calls it the "Mellemvœrende", which means the "something between", history and philosophy:

> Both of them ought to have their rights so that, on the one hand, the phenomenon has its rights and is not to be intimidated and discouraged by philosophy's superiority, and philosophy, on the other hand, is not to let itself be infatuated by the charms of the particular, is not to be distracted by the superabundance of the particular. The same holds for the concept of irony: philosophy is not to look too long at one particular side of its phenomenological existence and above all at its appearance but is to see the truth of the concept in and with the phenomenological (11).

The "incarnated" individual is thus a fitting representative of this precarious balancing act, for it does indeed act as a bridge between the abstract and actual, and is the total essence of neither one.[5] In fact it is at this point that Kierkegaard's chosen subjects – irony as "topic" and "concept", and its subjective manifestation as Socrates – begin to seem more pertinent and self-reflexive choices in relation to his philosophical system than they at first appear. For while he barely

[5] Kierkegaard compares Socrates to Christ insofar as they both form this bridge and both have the capacity to communicate "life and spirit" and release "the individual's locked-up powers" (29). However Kierkegaard is careful to point out that the two personalities are as dissimilar as they are similar See the extended footnote, 14-15. I will return to the significance of the Christ / Socrates analogy to irony's structure later in the chapter.

describes it in explicit terms, the "Mellemvœrende" is clearly equatable with an ironic movement: a balance reliant on an infinitely negative "something between". This means that in order to maintain the balance to which Kierkegaard aspires, the "existence" (Socrates) that is countering Hegel's abstract, universal force must be ironic about the concept (irony) for which it stands, and by extension, about its own particular essence. Socrates, the human phenomenon on which the ironic concept of irony converges (philosophically) and from which it came (historically) must also be "in between". Henceforth, "concept" and "existence" are described only in terms of each other, through the "between" of the other, and neither description is ever final. Irony is Socrates' method and life, yet Socrates is only ever present as the infinite negativity of irony: as a silence (11); as a vacant gaze (52); as a phantom (94); as a vampire, who sucks the blood of his lover without revealing himself (49); as a floating presence (48, 152); as a midwife, who is without the power of thought, but helps thoughts to be born in others[6]; even as a nisse who is made invisible by his hat (12).[7] But among all these ambiguous descriptions, the most significant is, perhaps, when he is described as being "like a dash in world history" (198). This, it seems, is the summary of his (and irony's) figuration as the "in between", for it combines Kierkegaard's definition of him as "magnificent pause" or "cryptic source" and as a "turning point", in history (198-200). And, given Socrates' ironic status as barren facilitator of other's wisdom, it is a pleasing (ironic) coincidence that "dash" in Danish, ["Tankestreg"] translates literally as "thought-line".[8]

---

[6] Kierkegaard refers repeatedly to Socrates' inheritance of his mother's skills as a midwife. In *Thaetetus*, Socrates attributes his mode of philosophizing to this inheritance. He compares himself to the midwife who, too old to bear children herself, attends other women in childbirth (1987b, 149b): "My midwifery has all the standard features, except that I practise it on men instead of women, and supervise the labour of their minds, not their bodies [...] I have *this* feature in common with midwives – I m yself am barren of wisdom. The criticism that is often made of me – that it is lack of wisdom that makes me ask others questions, but say nothing positive myself – is perfectly true" (150c). This analogy is, of course, well known in philosophy, but it accrues an interesting significance in the context of Kierkegaard's attempt to balance the (feminine) phenomenon / particular with the (masculine) concept / universal. In this sense, the ironist's employment is regarded by Kierkegaard as being more feminized than that of the world-historical conquering philosopher.

[7] According to Scandinavian folklore, a nisse is an elflike creature, benevolent if treated properly by the households in which it appears, which may be invisible when wearing its pointed red cap.

[8] See 198, footnote 461 for explanation of this translation.

Light and Shadow

However, this play of ironies does not necessarily take us further away from the "self-containedness" of Hegel's dialectic. After all, irony is itself a dialectic, an epistemological structure which according to most definitions dissimulates ignorance in order to ascertain the truth. This would comply with rather than defy Hegel's conception of mediation, which allows differential elements as the "being-for-another" which is the expression of the Being of Force in its "self-containedness".[9] Kierkegaard's Socratic "thought-line" could then be defined as a brief ethical "moment" on the way to universal knowledge. In fact, Kierkegaard came to disregard *The Concept of Irony* for being too Hegelian, and redrew "existence" as a dialectic of "faith". Irony is referred to in his later works as only a "stage" on the way to achieving the religious state of "inwardness", the emptiness and ignorance that waits for the singular absurdity of divine revelation. I will discuss this "downsizing" of irony later in this chapter. However, as far as Kierkegaard's ironic existence is concerned, it seems far less determinable and sublatable, and far more absurd, than one would expect of a negative dialectical moment. This can be seen not only in the play between existential phenomenon and concept but in Kierkegaard's own references to Socrates.

Kierkegaard continually emphasizes the impossibility of defining or positing within the negative balance of Socrates' method. Thus, he argues, although Socrates' dialectical form is in essence truth-seeking, the Essence of this Truth cannot be proven or "known" in its finite form. Throughout the Socratic dialogues values or essences are developed in line with the Greek philosophical ideas of immortality. Truth, Beauty, Virtue, or any other abstract form exist as immortal Ideas, before and beyond mortal existence. So while mortals may glimpse some likeness or reflection of the pure form in recollection – enough, at least, to use the abstract Idea as guide or measure in their pursuit of the ideal – it is utterly inaccessible, even to philosophers (Plato 1993c, 100b-107a; 1973, 50-57).[10] Socrates never "look[s] at

---

[9] Hegel himself described the Socratic dialectic as "the universal irony of the world" (Hegel 1974, 400)).

[10] It is a paradox of Socrates' thought that philosophers, who are supposedly engaged in a life which reaches most closely to the truth, must find that their philosophical truth is the realization of their inability to find that truth. As Harold Tarrant says in his general introduction, "The most depressing aspect of Socrates' disavowal of knowledge is the fact that his best-known doctrine […] is that virtue is knowledge. The result would be that neither Socrates nor anybody else with whom he is familiar

things […] with [his] eye" for fear of suffering the fate of those "who study the sun during an eclipse. For some of them ruin their eyesight unless they look at its image" (Plato, 1993c, 99 d-e). A copy or image is no guarantee of the original, of course, which is why when he speaks of the Idea, Socrates does not posit anything: he speaks with his face covered, claims the responsibility for what he says lies with nymphs or the divine (Plato, 1973, 37-8 & 76; 1993b, 40b). Thus when he follows the dialectical method in conversation – pursuing truth by testing the truths of others' statements – his speech is effectively a form of ventriloquizing: the arguments that test others' ideas are themselves the testing of Other's Ideas.[11] Positive value or conclusion are always held off by the negative movement of Socrates' questioning. All that is certain is that he cannot "know" for certain, and yet this also means that the possibility of the Idea continues to lie within this certainty; although still as a further uncertainty. So, as Kierkegaard points out, although Socrates uses actuality to unfound the Sophists' "excess of ideas", he

> … has no qualitative determinants with respect to the phenomenon's relation to the idea; to him one thing was just as good as another because everything was always metaphor and only metaphor – just as one must also regard it as having the idea only in abstraction when one finds that God is just as perceptibly present in a straw as in world history, since it all boils down to his really being present nowhere … (Kierkegaard 1989,17).

As far as the Socratic method is concerned, then, this rules out the stark Hegelian choice between "immediate" and "mediated", without the alternative to these choices being a similarly stark objectivity. Moreover, its doubling of "truth" means that the subject spoken of and the subject who speaks of it are also caught in the same state of being negatively "in-between". Conscious of this double-layered non-essence, Kierkegaard does not simply refer to Socrates' ironic "personality" as it is mediated by Plato or Xenophon or Aristophanes. Thus in the chapter where Socrates is supposedly drawn, "The View Made Possible", the "truth" of his personality emerges through the

---

can be virtuous – unless of course the knowledge of one's own ignorance can suffice to yield virtue" (Plato 1993a, xx).

[11] Which is not to say that the Idea definitely belongs to the immortal or the gods. The argument in *Euthyphro* makes it clear that the failed aspiration to reach knowledge of the Idea is a failure on *human* terms and not just an inability to match Zeus. In addition to this, the truth about the existence of an immortal state (in relation to the soul and the Idea) is also left up in the air. See Plato 1993c, 99d-e for Socrates' discussion of what he calls his "secondary approach to the problem of causation", and 1993b, 41c-e, for his discussion of death as either annihilation or change.

various ways in which those that have "recorded" Socrates voice have failed to capture his essence. Xenophon fills up the "cryptic nothing" of Socrates' irony with "the useful" (153); Aristophanes with an "implicit" emptiness; Plato treats irony as "a negative power in the service of a positive idea" (122). Indeed, Plato is the most guilty of obscuring the view of Socrates precisely because he explains him too much. He "lets the negative be seen", so forces a choice between "light" and "dark": a choice which implies a speculative self-projection "behind" the mediation. This means that unlike Socrates he fails to

> … take delight in the alternation of light and shadow found in a syllogistic aut / aut [either / or] when it almost simultaneously manifests broad daylight and pitch darkness, manifests the infinitely real and the infinitely nothing (81).

As the term "aut / aut" suggests, the ironic movement is not a matter of choice or decision, of one or the other, but a simultaneity, which is also a repetition, which nevertheless avoids being the *same* because it is caught between and takes account of the other. Kierkegaard argues that it is Aristophanes who comes closest to the truth of Socrates, precisely because he leaves him hanging, suspended in a basket just above the ground, "like Mohammed's coffin" floating between two poles (48 & 152). The image is one of formlessness and absurdity, the singular defying the general, but unable to be determined. Kierkegaard's own "account" of the existence of irony can thus be no more than an account of the difficulty of expression:

> I could try to chase together a host from every corner, but, to say nothing of the fact that the lengthy argumentation necessary […] would bore the reader, I also believe that the whole section, instead of coming like a soft whisper, as is the nature of irony, would come whistling. To have to demonstrate irony through additional research […] would […] rob it of the surprise, the striking – in short, would enervate it. Irony requires strong contrast and would utterly vanish in such boring company as argumentation (90).

Not intending

Perplexing as it is, then, Kierkegaard's thesis as a whole lies in ironic relation to its subject, in the sense of both topic and individual: if it fulfilled its claimed intention to explain the concept of irony, it would fail to express the very essence of that concept. Positive explanation would inevitably fall into the loud blustering of which Hegel's dialectic stands accused, which is no doubt why Kierkegaard says "Irony met its master in Hegel" (242). To master irony is to appropriate and conceptualize it, and thus to finish it off. Kierkegaard claims that Hegel uses "one single dialogue from Plato as an example of the Socratic method without explaining why he chose this particular one" (221-22). He calls Socrates the "founder" of morality, but skims over the negative and arbitrary method by which Socrates "founds" it, by portraying him as having already arrived at the good (235)[12]. Then, having neglected the defining method of Socrates' irony, he conflates it with his critiques of Romantic irony (265-71), whose defining feature was a "self-created actuality", an exaggerated, essentialist subjectivity and the resulting conviction that through the ironic artist one could "obtain a world" (275).[13] Hegel cuts off the *possibility* in irony – which to Kierkegaard is as close as one can get to its defining characteristic – by making it known, (pre-)determined, mastered by its philosopher-creator and all its subsequent commentators.[14] For Kierkegaard, irony must always remain unknown, a possibility, the other element in the balance between temporal and eternal, actual and conceptual, historical and

---

[12] Kierkegaard stresses that "the movement in Socrates is toward arriving at the good. His significance in the world development is to arrive there (not to have arrived there at some time). […] Now, this does not mean that he arrived there almost toward the end of his life, but that his life was a continual arriving at the good and having others arrive at it" (235). Kierkegaard is drawing back from the Hegelian movement which regards the good as the inevitable (and thus already determined) culmination of Socrates' philosophy. Rather than considering morality as if it is already "ordered in a totality" (230), Kierkegaard seeks to portray the fluctuations between positive and negative movements in Socrates' method, and maintains that morality can also come into being ironically and negatively. Indeed, the Socratic resistance to (positively) "actualiz[ing] the good" allows "the being-in-and-for-itself become visible in the qualifications of the manifold" (235, 236).

[13] Kierkegaard says this of Friedrich Schlegel and Ludwig Tieck, both of whom were central in Romantic theory and art. Kierkegaard objects to their treatment of art as a form which may aspire to the infinite, through the (self-) detachment and reflection of the artist. As he says prior to this comment: " In this there [is] a twofold difficulty. In the first place, the empirical and finite *I* was confused with the eternal *I*; in the second place, metaphysical actuality was confused with historical actuality." Romantic metaphysics thus have the same end as Fichte's according to Kierkegaard. He extends his critique of Romantic irony, and in particular of Schlegel's *Lucinde*, into parody in the first part of *Either / Or*, which I will examine later in this chapter.

[14] Hegel (as Kierkegaard acknowledges) distinguishes between Socratic and Romantic irony on the basis that Socratic irony is directed at people, in the service of "defending the Idea of truth and justice", whereas Romantic irony is directed at "the Idea itself" (Hegel, 1942, 101). Kierkegaard agrees with many of Hegel's criticisms of Romantic irony, but is claiming that Hegel's furious concern to counter the Romantic's infinite scepticism leads him to go too far the other way, in vociferously emphasizing the "positive content" of Socratic irony (269), and in providing a very sketchy and confused picture of Socrates. For Hegel's critiques of Romantic irony see Hegel 1993.

philosophical. Always silent, it is "the abstract equal sign between two unknown quantities" (71).

Yet this ironic relation is very difficult to grasp hold of, especially when the form of a thesis is one predetermined in the knowledge that is to be posited, proven and publicly defended.[15] If the writer/philosopher is always in ironic relation to his subject, if the chosen subject / concept is the one which undermines the concept's authority, if this concept /force can then only be figured as a singular historical phenomenon/personality, if the singularity of this phenomenon /personality cannot be predetermined or known without destroying its singularity, and if it stands, like the author, in ironic relation to its own manifestation as the concept – a "turning point" or "dash" as much as its pure source or essence – then the fact that the thesis remains standing at all begins to be incredible.

Many critical readings of Kierkegaard fail to get to grips with (or, rather, ease their hold over) the vertiginous relations of different "subjects" and different ironies in *The Concept of Irony*, and more peculiarly, do not engage with Kierkegaard's playful expression of the sheer difficulty and complexity of writing this irony. Implicitly or explicitly, they try to confine discussions of Kierkegaard's irony to its purpose or intent, characterizing it as a strategy against Hegel's system. Roger Poole, who interprets Kierkegaard's works in the light of his later claims that his writings represented an "indirect communication", reads Kierkegaard's irony as a deliberate part of his "writing practice" (Poole 1993, 45). He argues that the negative content of the thesis (irony-as-Socrates) stands in opposition to its form, which is seemingly busy making the view of Socrates "possible", "actual" and "necessary" in dialectical terms. Thus, while on a literal level Kierkegaard seems to be pursuing a philosophical definition of irony which is not wholly alien to Hegelian conceptuality (52), on the other (ironic) level, the sheer negativity of irony remains "unassimilable to any objective system" and the "Hegelian machinery" of the system is shown to be redundant (45).

This is certainly one of the effects of Kierkegaard's exploration of irony, and to a large extent, Poole's view accords with the way I have described Kierkegaard's (non-)characterization of irony-as-Socrates. However, Poole brings to his descriptions of Kierkegaard's irony a

---

[15] One only needs to compare the inordinately complex and numerous theses at the beginning of *The Concept of Irony* with Socrates' ambiguous position in his hypothesizing, to realize this.

level of intention which, I would argue, Kierkegaard is constantly at pains to problematize. For all the time that the silent, floating, phenomenal-existential figure of irony exceeds and negates Hegelian determinations, it also undermines its own authority and independence, its own power to step beyond the system it inhabits. In fact, it is thoroughly lacking in intentionality: working from the inside, claim to "know" of a separate, better system. It coexists with and feeds off this system, so always returns to it in some way. We must remember that Kierkegaard finds that the only way in which he can form an "account" of irony's "soft whisper" is to "draw a line over" others' texts "over which at times irony's roguish face will be allowed to peek" (90). This is as true of the thesis' relation of Hegel as it is true of Socrates' relation to the classical texts that describe him. Thus Hegel and Socrates, form and content do not quite stand in purposeful opposition to each other, but constantly invade and return to each other. Their perplexing relations cannot be explained as a singular strategy or practice.

Jean-Paul Sartre acknowledges that Kierkegaard's structure depends on as much as it differs from Hegel's structure, but his essay 'L'universal singulier' recuperates intention in a different way. Sartre focuses on what he calls the "anti-dialectic" formed between Kierkegaard and Hegel's relation, or misrelation (1972, 162). The temporal paradox of Kierkegaard's transhistorical subject is that it cannot be "known" and always exceeds "determinations", and yet, it is precisely through such known determinations – through Kierkegaard's words, through his interpretation of the dialectical system which "lives" beyond his death – that he announces this existence. For Sartre, this is the point of irony, precisely because "failure" – the extreme of negativity – cannot be incorporated by Hegel's "positive", "objective" system. However, Sartre too seems to undermine the negative balance of ironic existence in pushing it too far the other way. Kierkegaard's failure has "the absolute character of negation – in fact historical negation is, at the heart of a relativism, an absolute" (168). Kierkegaard may call the Socratic existence "infinitely negative" but it is never an absolute, and neither can the "point" of his irony be something as certain as "failure". Sartre makes Kierkegaard's anti-dialectic more of a "project" or "intention" than can be possible given the anxious complications of intention in Kierkegaard's own writing. This is inevitable, given Sartre's insistence on the "non-knowledge" remaining a *rational* non-knowledge, but it results in an insensitivity to the style of

Kierkegaard's irony – its peculiarly risky, irrational aesthetic – which unfounds notions of intention the moment they are approached.

Kierkegaard's thesis appears to be the attempt to take this aesthetic, and its ethic, into account. It thus refuses to settle into a definition of irony as either uncontainable negation or sublatable moment. As Sylviane Agacinski says,

> That irony could name *both* a negatively subjective moment in the history of self-consciousness (Socrates or Kierkegaard, for instance) *and* the grammatical category that puts into question the articulation of a subject ("irony") and its predicates (meaning conceived of as the possibility of a *serious* "thesis") is truly ironic. For the two mutually exclusive meanings of irony thus conceived enter into a self-obliterating relationship between the self *as* consciousness and the self *as* grammar [so that it is] impossible to decide whether irony is what allows consciousness to come into being or what prevents it from ever taking place (1988, 17).

This "self-obliterating" balance creates an anxious textual predicament, but anxiety seems to be the only way to remain true to irony's essential "riskiness". *The Concept of Irony* acts as a complication of subjects: as the unthought specificity in the universal-philosophical, in the concept, in the figuration of the concept and in the "writer" and writing of this figuration. All these steps or complications work to separate the overwhelming conflation in the speculative dialectic of the means and the end, or mediation and truth. Irony unhinges the certain knowledge and empties out the security of self-positing and intention. As Poole's and Sartre's readings show, an expectation of radical change or new beginnings upsets the balance, the liminal "Mellemvœrende" that keeps irony afloat between abstraction and essence. To define irony as a radical asymmetry – an excessive "essence" of the particular which upsets the universalizing speculative – or as an absolute of negative indifference, amounts to the same thing: a loss of risk and possibility, and a pandering to sameness. To put it in more phenomenal terms, irony could be compared to a flirt. Its desire may be implied as a radical freedom or licentiousness and yet it always holds itself back, "pulls back with a skeptical reserve".[16] If it crossed over into the positive, fulfilled its

[16] This is perhaps also why Socrates, the plentiful source of irony, was such a skilled seducer, and why the true, observing ironist, according to Kierkegaard, must be an "amorist" (Kierkegaard 1989, 9). This is not to be confused with the seducer-ironist portrayed by the likes of Schlegel (criticized and pastiched by Kierkegaard in *Either /Or* in particular) other than in the extent to which the Socratic-ironic seducer shares in the speculative. The Romantic seducers are the extreme of speculation, trapped in a

promise, and slept with its target; or if it turned its back, became abrupt or rude, then it would cease to *be* flirting, for there would be conclusiveness instead. The constant taking into account, the anxiety about the staging or positing of irony is thus a means of taking responsibility rather than an intention or self-consciousness. It cannot be dismissed as "bad faith". It is a preparation for the "truth", "conclusion" or "subject" that is always possible, but whose arrival will always be one of chance as far as the ironic text or subject is concerned, because its knowledge (of the Idea, the infinite, the abstract) is other; belongs to the other. Irony, or the responsibility of irony, could thus be said to act as an ethical vigilance working from within the epistemological.

So to push irony along the lines of intention and fulfilment is to let the risk and responsibility fall out of its structure. At this point irony slides into Hegel's definition; where the unknown must be known, where the "conceptions" of its "concrete" truth "must … be explicated and presupposed to be unknown in terms of what they really are" (Hegel quoted in Kierkegaard 1989, 267). This compulsory injection of "earnestness" and "positive content" destroys the risk and destroys irony's possibility:

> For irony, nothing is an established order; it plays helter-skelter ad libitum [at will] with everything; but when it wants to declare […] something positive […] its sovereignty is thereby at an end (269).

Thus Poole, Sartre (and even I, in my striving for elucidation) are, like Hegel, guilty of only "referring to" irony (244). Kierkegaard's guilt, within the logic of irony, is not his "failure" to posit a complete thesis, a work which separates itself finally from speculation, nor even to claim failure as the essence of its existence, but the extent to which he *does* all these things. Indeed, he acknowledges this in the same breath as the one in which he accuses Hegel.[17]

---

positive-abstract which forecloses any interaction with the object of seduction. There is nothing to flirt with. I will come back to this later.

[17] In effect, Kierkegaard disclaims his own thesis, just after his complaint against Hegel's "earnest" irony: "The difficulty here is that, strictly speaking, irony actually is never able to advance a thesis, because irony is a qualification of the being-for-itself subject, who in incessant agility allows nothing to remain established and on account of this agility cannot focus on the total point of view that it allows nothing to remain established" (269). See also Kierkegaard's admission, following the comments on Hegel "referring" to irony, that he cannot "lament justifiably over Hegel in the same sense as Hegel laments over his predecessors" (244).

II. Or

And yet, if Kierkegaard's irony is so radically undetermined and non-essential, so far from the Force of Hegel's dialectic, why is he not happier with its play of "light and dark"? Why is the anxiety of his style so exaggerated? Why does he suddenly "curtail" irony at the end of *The Concept of Irony* and leave it behind as the main way to an ethical truth in his philosophical structure?

I will admit to a degree of dissimulation at this point, in not having answered this question before. However, it was necessary to follow the logic of risk in Kierkegaard's irony, to delay its return to truth, in order to allow its possibilities – of negation, disruption and ethical vigilance – to proliferate.

The answer to these questions is, inevitably, ironic. It is precisely because Kierkegaard does not, or cannot leave irony behind that he attempts to do so; and it is in this attempt that he fails to leave dialectical "mastery". For if the shift that Kierkegaard makes from "knowledge" to a kind of uneasy "faith" in the truth is the answer to the need to undermine the deterministic Force of the dialectic, it is and must also be a repetition of the problem. Having charted irony's, risk, therefore, I will now briefly chart its return.

The "One Event"

Kierkegaard's "personality" avoids the sameness of dialectical reason by making Socrates the temporal embodiment of the unknown. As a historical-phenomenon he is an admission of the individual into the universal and the actual into the abstract. Yet because he is neither a fully grounded individual (in the sense of an attained "self-consciousness"), nor concretely actual (he floats, he disappears, he drinks hemlock in a nonchalant manner), he is also a prevention of historical phenomenology. As well as denying essence and postponing determination, this "incarnation" is the condition of the ironic risk happening at all. Without a premise, without Socrates' first assertion or question, the "risk" would be no risk because it would be an irreducible negativity: there would be no promise of its possibility. In receiving that first truth from some "other" source (whether divine, or from the speaker he is questioning) rather than making it, and in acknowledging that this reception is wholly arbitrary, the personality remains open (responsible) to other possibilities while being able to speak and begin. So far so good. However, in radicalizing the divide between (eternal) Idea and (mortal / historical) idea Kierkegaard's premise undermines the whole mimetic relation between the two that Platonic and Hegelian dialectics rely upon. This leaves the personality with an almost impossible choice: either it must speak only and entirely in another's words – indeed in the words of another which may not ever arrive, and cannot be willed into existence – or it must give up on the idea of the pursuit of truth altogether and admit that the whole temporal structure is simply the desire of a fictional and unnecessary "force." These two options are not necessarily mutually exclusive, nor are they impossible to assume while everything remains suspended between ironic poles (as in, for example the playful space between Kierkegaard's descriptions of the personality and his contradictory footnotes). The problem comes when these indeterminable "options" must be translated into the temporal structure of the dialectic, which it must if Kierkegaard's philosophical "actuality" is to exist at all. Unlike the ironic risk, the dialectic in which it is working can only move in one direction – linearly, towards fulfilment of itself – so the radical otherness of the personality can only be admitted if the risk is in some way curtailed.

In fact, we see this in Kierkegaard's structure from the very beginning, in the fact that his personality is an *incarnation*: an "analogy" between finite and infinite. Kierkegaard is quick to point out that his "personality", "such a *status absolutus*" could happen, "could be given only once"; in other words, as Christ. However, in order that this "once" can be admissible in a structure that does not entirely deny its own temporal possibility, its singularity has to be negotiable:

> … we must not disregard the fact that the analogy to this, history's repeated attempt at this infinite leap, also has its truth. *What Plato saw in Socrates* was such a personality, *an immediate conveyor of the divine* such as this (28-29).

The movement that initially undermines the essence of Socrates on a temporal level reinstates his essence at an infinite level. In its apparent need for some (even unreachable) connection to a point of stability or certainty, Kierkegaard's philosophical structure puts its "faith" in a unique event which, if it could be repeated, would lend the ironist's manoeuvrings the authority of the absolute.

This faith in the return of the absolute, the repetition of the "one event", marks the return of the dialectical force in irony, and the curtailment of irony's license of risk. However, we are not back to where we started, and Kierkegaard's chivalrous battle is not lost, because Hegel's apparently certain knowledge of the truth is constantly marked by the unknown of its expression; the non-coincidence of promise and premise that keeps it going in the temporal. Even as Kierkegaard draws the analogy between Socrates and Christ he expresses a "little asthmatic doubt" that the analogy may lie as much in dissimilarity as in similarity, and that it is possible "only because there is a contrast". As long as irony is anxious, therefore, and continues to mark the non-coincidence of truth and its mediation, there can be no complete return to "self-containedness". The linear purpose, the "law" of the "force" will continue, but since it relies on an "other's" truth and an undecidable essence, the "actualization" of the "force", "force *proper*" as Hegel calls it, will never quite take place.

If Kierkegaard tried no harder than this to alter the force of the dialectic, as is the case throughout most of *The Concept of Irony*, then he would at least remain true to the uncertainty of irony's aesthetic. However, even this uncertainty seems to be unsustainable. For having reached the point where curtailment is seen as an "always already", as the necessity of the risk existing within the dialectical structure, Kierkegaard tries to reclaim a larger territory for risk. He "decides" to "curtail" irony and aspire instead to the absolute risk that lies in the "infinite leap" beyond. Thus he concludes *The Concept of Irony* with a strange compromise between the arbitrary premise of the "unknowing" ethical irony and the aspirational promise of a *religiously* ethical irony: a "controlled element", which has lost its uncanny, amorous analogies, and is regarded as a "guide" (327). Irony as "guide" disciplines the human desire to attain "the perfect prematurely" (329) and teaches "how to actualize actuality":

> … life's content must become a genuine and meaningful element in the higher actuality whose fullness the soul craves. Actuality hereby acquires its validity, not as a purgatory – for the soul is not to be purified in such a way that stark naked, so to speak, it runs bland and bare out of life – but as history in which consciousness successively matures, yet in such a way that salvation consists not in forgetting all this but becoming present in it (328).

This uneasy mixture of dialectical self-consciousness and religious aspiration – the (Hegelian) precursor to the continual "leaps of faith" throughout the rest of his works – represents Kierkegaard's attempt to end the proliferation of anxieties that his portrait of irony has engendered. Just as Sartre tried to reclaim the "returning-to-self" of irony as the point, the purpose, the "truth" of irony, in an attempt to leave behind the anxiety of irony, so Kierkegaard cannot ultimately resist claiming the incarnated personality as "irony in its total endeavour" (122). Kierkegaard, like Sartre, thus simulates an end and dissimulates in pretending that this movement is the logical conclusion of irony. Yet it seems that because he has followed the logic of risk to a further degree, allowed the possibility of the irrational aesthetic to permeate his whole structure, this conclusion must be altogether more radical and more impossible. The "movement" of controlled irony recognizes the contingency of its "successively" historical maturation in the face of the infinite; but nevertheless resides in the historical to control its longing for "higher actuality". The "personality" is still an insistence on the ethical in the epistemological; its determination *is* other and thus what it is or when it will arrive is accidental in the terms of its inner economy (325). And yet the *event* of this accident has on some level become a matter of will or choice, so that responsibility for and openness to the other's words or truth slips from being an unintentional self-effacement to a purpose, an action, that seems to assume the possibility of a return-to-self (as truth):

> Actuality [...] will not be rejected, and longing will be a sound and healthy love, not a weak and sentimental sneaking out of the world. [...] Therefore actuality acquires its validity through action. But action must not degenerate into a kind of fatuous indefatigableness; it ought to have an apriority in itself so as not to lose itself in a vapid infinity (329).

Contingency may have been admitted into the structure, but this final stroke can only be interpreted as a repetition of the predetermination that Kierkegaard's structure set out to avoid. In attempting to leave behind the dialectical anxiety that his ironic performance continually marked, Kierkegaard curtails the risk and the openness to alterity that are so important to his delineation of a more chivalrous, ethical force in philosophy. Ultimately, the risks of this ethical force have been overcome and forcibly concluded by the religious desire for absolute truth. However, given the complications of time and determination that have been elaborated before this final "leap" we may perhaps ask whether the "controlled" religious irony *can* herald a permanent escape from the temporal anxiety of the dialectic, whether it *can* act as a genuine conclusion to Kierkegaard's concept of irony. This is a question that I hope to answer in the afterword that follows.

III. Afterword

Any further attempt will be a repetition. I mean this in the double sense of the word that the double bind of Kierkegaard's irony creates. As the "aut / aut" of Socratic irony, repetition is the almost simultaneous alternation of differentiated terms; the negative movement through time of the questions which empty grand assumptions of their claims to truth and leave room for another possibility. As the "recollection forwards", which Kierkegaard ascribes to Plato but which Kierkegaard's "personality" adopts in *The Concept of Irony*, repetition is a form of immanence whose possible realization lies in a patient acceptance of the finite and a translation of the ethical relation to the infinite into finite terms.[18] Both of these repetitions repeat themselves in Kierkegaard's irony, and in his attempts to cope with their non-coincidence, they repeat throughout his works. This is why repetition is to be expected in Kierkegaard's writing beyond *The Concept of Irony*, and why, in turn, any further analysis of these works is also susceptible to repetition. Mine is no different. The final part of this chapter stands as an afterword, then, instead of an extended analysis of the rest of his authorship, in order to control this risk.[19]

Kierkegaard ostensibly "gives up" irony as an explicit presence in the rest of his works, but it lives on as both the challenge to Hegel's system and as the dissimulating, anxious rehearsal of irony's ethics and aesthetic within the Christian framework.[20] The change of "subject" does not necessarily mean an escape from irony's double-bind, especially since in relation to the "System" this bind is also a degree of freedom. The compromised irony-as-personality in *The Concept of Irony* continues its existence through Kierkegaard's consideration of "inwardness": the ideal state of mortal existence which, combining the two sides of *The Concept of Irony's* personality, holds itself back in ironic reserve while at the same time revealing

---

[18] Kierkegaard ascribes the "recollection forwards" to Plato in *The Concept of Irony* (1989, 125). The definition of "repetition" as a "recollection forwards" comes in *Repetition*, (1983, 131). Its description as a form of "immanence" comes in the retrospective of Kierkegaard's works, by the pseudonym Johannes Climacus, in *Concluding Unscientific Postscript to Philosophical Fragments* (1992c, 263).

[19] In writing an expository chapter, I too must necessarily curtail irony.

[20] Kierkegaard's most virulent ironic attack on Hegel is throughout *Concluding Unscientific Postscript*. For an analysis of this attack as one which "transcends" the Hegelian tendencies of *Irony*, see Cross 1998.

itself in an emulation of divine revelation in the finite.[21] "Inwardness" is thus the difficult balance of the ethical in philosophical and phenomenal existence, expressed as the relation or non-relation between infinite and finite, and the extent to which it can be (temporally) posited. As if to bolster this balance, Kierkegaard's authorial responsibility reflects the simultaneous demand to reveal and conceal: while his texts clearly exposit views, concepts, poetry and philosophy, these texts are narrated by pseudonyms: a sequence of "editors" and "writers" who enable Kierkegaard to maintain his ironic dissimulation.[22]

"A" or "B"?

None of the pseudonymous authorships play out these concerns as obviously or elaborately as *Either / Or*: a whole book devoted to the "alternation of light and shadow" that was Socrates' ironic delight (1989, 81). Neither philosophy nor poetry, it builds on *The Concept of Irony* as a critique of Hegel, a parody of Romantic irony, and a serious and playful debate about which "view" of life is the most worthy of pursuit.

The debate is between different individuals' "aesthetic" and "ethical" views; but this could just as easily be seen as a debate about whether to choose hiddenness or revelation. Papers "B", dominated by the expositor Judge Wilhelm, are contrasted (by the accidental editorship of Victor Eremita) with the enigmatic fragments of Papers "A", whose most identifiable author is Johannes, recorder and protagonist of "The Seducer's Diary". From even a cursory glance one can see the complex levels – the "Chinese box puzzle" – of observation and comment (1992a, 32).[23] Kierkegaard is hidden behind the "editor", Victor Eremita, who, as his name indicates, is himself

[21] "Inwardness" is an ambiguous term much like "personality" and is never entirely defined. For discussions of it see Kierkegaard 1989, 177 & 451; and Kierkegaard 1992c, 189-251.

[22] Victor Eremita, Johannes de Silentio, Constantin Constantius, Vigilius Haufniensis, Nicolaus Notabene, Johannes Climacus, Anti-Climacus, Hilarius Bookbinder and Frater Taciturnus – whose names reveal their subjects, and all of whom are admitted as pseudonyms in "A First and Last Declaration" (1992c, 625).

[23] I have chosen to quote from Alistair Hannay's translation of *Either / Or*, although it is slightly abridged, rather than from the full 2 volume translation by Howard V. Hong and Edna H. Hong (1987). Hannay's translation seems to capture the playful tone of the book more precisely. However, good scholarly practice would obviously recommend the Hong edition as well.

well hidden from the world.[24] The fragments of Papers "A" are tracts on different aspects of poetic and speculative observation, which in turn form a commentary on roles and elements in "The Seducer's Diary."[25] Then Johannes, the arch-seducer, creates the scene of his conquest and narrative – what he terms love's dialectic – through his powers of ironic and invisible speculation. Half romantic poet and half dialectician, he creates himself and his object through a kind of poetic mediation, never dropping his ironic distance, so that he "leaves no footprints" and "everything finite and temporal is forgotten, only the eternal remains" (251, 375). Finally, the Judge brings his evasiveness into the focus of ethical revelation: the "open-heartedness, uprightness, publicity" of conjugal love (408), and the ethically-binding act of "choosing oneself absolutely" (524). This commentary / correspondence, Wilhelm insists, "remains a secret", and yet it is revealed, via the hidden editor(s), to all the readers (590).

The Seducer

From the explicit bias of the book, there would seem to be an easy choice to make with regard to the two views. Author A (I will call him Johannes for the sake of convenience) combines the worst features of Romantic and Hegelian speculation, being such a master of the form that he speculates himself out of existence. His actions and seductions mediate the temporal into his desired poetic unity, steering him away from any *actual* relation or contact with the finite.[26] Even in the act of seduction he has only a "parastatic" body, so that Cordelia, his lover and prey, feels at times that she "embraced a cloud" (251). Johannes

---

[24] Kierkegaard comments in his *Point of View* that Victor Eremita is writing from "the safety of the monastery" (1939, 12).

[25] To mention a few: the myth of the seducer (Johannes calls himself a "myth"); the fragmented characteristics of the contemporary figure of the Romantic poet (melancholy, a tragic striving, the contemplation of "modernity", the subjective creation of the poetic object, aspirations of (infinite) perfectability) which are united in the figure of Johannes; and the parallel references to speculation – often parodic in the fragments – which Johannes claims as his method to unitary perfection.

[26] The depiction of Johannes is an extension of the critique of certain Romantic writing in *The Concept of Irony* – specifically of Schlegel's *Lucinde*, which Kierkegaard described as the "attempt to suspend all ethics" (1989, 289; see also Schlegel, 1971). His distaste for Schlegelian irony lies in what he regards as its disregard of finite, historical actuality for the sake of its efforts to maintain a position of infinite detachment – and thus a God-like perspective on the world's contradictory totality. In this regard, Kierkegaard is in accord with Hegel's critiques of Romantic irony, but Kierkegaard's constant parodying of Hegel's systematization of irony makes it clear that Hegel is also guilty of bypassing irony's finite ethical possibilities.

has conspired to make Cordelia the instigator of their broken engagement, so she is not sure after the event that the seduction and desertion have taken place at all (253). Moreover, whereas the fragments in the rest of "Papers A" form in part a critique of the "Romantic" elements in the aesthetic view, they counter the solipsistic presumption of the infinite with a dialectical mediation. The rule of poetic unity simply becomes the rule of abstract principle and concept, so simply repeats the pattern of presumed totality and self-determination. Thus the observing, creating, Romantically ironic individual described in "The Seducer's Diary" is reflected as Don Giovanni, the "principle" of desire, in "The Immediate Erotic Stages": for only if an individual and his individual act are *representative* of the concept of seduction, can dialectical mediation be achieved. The seducer "exists only in the moment, but the moment, in terms of its concept, is the sum of moments, and so we have the seducer" (100). (There is a sharp parody of this self-propulsion in the section entitled "Crop Rotation").

So whether the relation of "love" is mediated through the striving poet or through the principle of desire, the result is the same. Actuality is never achieved, everything remains in the abstract and universal and, despite the aesthetic preoccupation with love and seduction, there is neither the *experience* of seduction nor any form of ethical relationship. The woman "zu Grunde geh[t]" (292),[27] the "finite and temporal [are] forgotten," and all that remains are image, myth and melancholy (375-6)[28]

The Judge

In terms of the failings of mediation and speculation – attacked in *The Concept of Irony* and so clearly on display here – Author "B", Wilhelm the Judge, must win the debate. As Kierkegaard's pseudonym Johannes Climacus writes in *Concluding Unscientific Postscript*, "part I is an existence-possibility that cannot attain existence, a depression that must be worked upon ethically" (1992c, 253). If there is ethical work to be done, then Judge Wilhelm is surely

---

[27] "Zu Grunde gehen" means literally, "to go aground", or "to rack and ruin". Hegel uses it in the sense of something showing its essence, so it carries negative and positive meanings, much like the "Aufhebung": Johannes is expressing his mediation of Cordelia.

[28] Johannes is also melancholy, in keeping with his image as Romantic poet and his failure to embrace the ethical. See "Diapsalmata (39-57) and "The Unhappiest One" (209-21).

the one to do it. Where Author A, according to the *Postscript*, "*is* despair", Wilhelm "has despaired" but has come through this to "choose" himself and become "open" (253-4):

> He is a married man [...] and, in direct opposition to the hiddenness of the esthetic [*sic*], focuses on marriage as the most profound form of life's disclosure, whereby *time* is turned to account for the ethically existing individual, and the possibility of *gaining* a *history* is continuity's ethical victory over hiddenness, depression, illusory passion and despair (254).

In retrospect, author A's aesthetic is clearly identified with the hidden and ephemeral, B's ethic with revelation. Judge Wilhelm follows an ideal of personality much like the one at the end of *The Concept of Irony*, striving to accept actuality and the finite, presuming no knowledge, and, while "longing for something higher", not acting to "have the perfect prematurely" (1989, 329)· This sense of the ethical is clearly conceived of on a religious scale, so that its "openness" is not simply a waiting for possible revelation, but an active simulation of the infinite revelation in the temporal sphere. Wilhelm's criticism of "A" is his complete lack of faith:

> Instead of saving your soul by putting everything in God's hands, instead of making this short-cut you prefer an endless detour which may never lead you to your goal. To this you will no doubt say, 'Yes, that means you never need to act.' I would reply, 'Of course you must, when you know in yourself that you have a place in the world which is yours, and where you should concentrate all your activity' (389).

The act of "choosing oneself", of "choosing the Either / Or," seems to be the quest for "inwardness". It resists speculative mediation and admits that such an overcoming of the mortal state of incomprehension is impossible:

> If one were to talk here of a mediation, one might say it was repentance; but repentance is no mediation, it does not look with longing upon that which should be mediated, that thing is consumed in its wrath … (490)

To choose is to resign oneself to the ethical obligation of "constantly separating": to admit and accept the unbridgeable difference between man and God (489). So as well as being a frankness or honesty – a constant revealing of one's task and place in the temporal – it is also a silence; a respect for the unspeakable faith. This again contrasts with the aesthete's confident declarations of achieved totalities which, as Wilhelm points out, are really an empty "detour" of words.

As with the relation with the infinite, so with the relation with the finite. In a repetition of the gender alignments of *The Concept of Irony*, Wilhelm's treatise associates ethical action with femininity as well as (divine) alterity; and with femininity *as* alterity. The relation with another must not be through a conquering mediation, like author A's – the positing of the other in order to recognize one's own self-consciousness – but a recognition of the "otherness" of the other, which also accepts a relation *with* this other, as ordained, by God, over time. Marriage,

> ... highlights the universal, not the accidental. It does not show how two altogether particular people in all their uncommonness could become happy, but how every married couple can become happy. [...] It understands historical beauty (572-3).

Here ends Wilhelm's catalogue of ethical tasks, and the choice for the reader would appear to have been made. If one is to live ethically (or indeed, *live* at all) one must choose the second view in the aut / aut because his view has chosen the aut / aut – and so chosen himself (485-93).

The Ultimatum

However, as one would expect of a book founded on simultaneous difference, the choice is not as straightforward as Wilhelm's elaborations would make it appear. In fact, just as personality proved to be the problem of *The Concept of Irony*, so personality's action in *Either / Or* raises questions about its own status as "choice". Why, if Wilhelm has "chosen" himself at every moment, and manages to "work the accidental and the universal together", does he seem so preoccupied with the aesthetic? Why does he not simply live through his task and reveal the infinitely ordained in the finite in preparation for the final (promised) Revelation (583)?[29] Why, indeed, does he explain himself at such length, if "inwardness" scorns summaries and conclusions about what exceeds verbalization? In fact, is Wilhelm's ethical relation in practice (as opposed to in preaching) really so different from Johannes'? If its translation into finite terms is to be taken as representative of the more universal ethics, then the degree of hiddenness and revelation is remarkably similar to the aesthete's. Wilhelm may describe love and his marriage as a continually

[29] As Wilhelm says in relation to the Last Judgment, "Ethics says it is the meaning of life and reality that man be revealed".

receptive attitude to the other, but he sums up his marriage, defines his wife's task, even presumes to speak for her: perhaps behaviour more fitting of a Hegelian master than for a philosopher-knight (561-2, 574-6). What, according to his described ethics, is necessarily hidden (the constant "unknown" "difference" in the private bond between marriage partners) is revealed in his text, and what must necessarily be revealed (the wife's task according to *her* "choosing" of herself) is evaded. The more Wilhelm explains his "choosing" as the alternative to aesthetic emptiness, the more difficult it becomes to see how and when this "choosing" is going to actually happen, and the more apparent it becomes that Wilhelm's writing shares many elements with the aesthetic he so disdains.

Circumstances are conspiring here for a repetition of the problem of personality we encountered in *The Concept of Irony*. The "choice" suggested by Kierkegaard's text as an alternative to the sameness and hiddenness of mediation, is a denial of "known" beginnings and endings, an ironic reserve which relies on being open to the words of an other, or the revelation of the divine Other. However, to choose this alternative, to posit it, is to run the risk of "curtailing" the irony that enables the alternative, and so curtailing the ethical relation; which is precisely what is happening here. While Johannes' mediating is a form of secrecy (hiding his bypassing of actuality) and Wilhelm's (epistemological) reserve is a way of enabling revelation, his reliance on the event of this revelation – the "one" act in time, the truth-made-flesh – cuts off the ethical possibility, creating another form of secrecy. So that if Johannes refuses to "give birth" for fear of betraying his secret abstraction (509), Wilhelm enters into procreation, but only as a form of parthenogenesis:

> Only when one has taken possession of oneself in the choice, has attired oneself in one's self, has penetrated oneself so totally that every moment is attended by the consciousness of a responsibility for oneself, only then has one chosen oneself ethically [...] only then has one repented oneself, only then is one [...] in absolute continuity with the reality one belongs to. [...] Ethical repentance has but two movements; either it abolishes its object or it bears it (540-41).[30]

[30] This is a far cry from the supportive, midwifely role that Kierkegaard has previously led us to expect from the ethical-ironist. Commenting on birthing analogies in a different context, Wanda Warren Berry argues that Kierkegaard's pseudonymous authorship is a "non-authoritarian" and "non-masculinist" writing strategy that encourages his female and male readers to "give birth to themselves" (1995, 117). I would agree with this, but would also want to point out the ethical problems of self-birthing, given the way Kierkegaard characterizes irony's ethical vigilance elsewhere. To "choose" oneself, or "give birth" to oneself may be the way to reach the

Neither of the two views actually loves, actually seduces: Wilhelm seems to be no more of an amorist, no more likely to actually embrace his loved one, than Johannes. His description of the "aesthetic" marriage where the husband directs the relationship in a "circle" of secrecy is surprisingly applicable to his own.[31] Of course, the lack of realization would not matter for Wilhelm if his view were really ironically ethical – he would "delight" in the "aut / aut" – but since realization has become his faith, the never-arriving undermines his posited "choice". Instead of an "either / or" we are left with a "neither / nor." Rather than "choosing" himself "in and out of the world", through repentance, he is chosen out – more by accident than by choice – and cannot choose himself back (447). In the terms of the ironic structure, his "bearing" of the finite responsibility is not responsible enough, so it is "abolished": his correspondence is forgotten and we move to the Ultimatum, with its dictum that "against God we are always in the wrong" (597-609).[32]

This is not a death, however, because we are condemned to repeat, to redouble: the repetition that is the condition of irony in this ethico-religious framework. The infinite repetition of the "aut / aut", which is the infinite openness to the possibility of the other (here a *feminized* other), becomes a repetition that bears a different responsibility: for the *promise* of the infinite entering the finite, the "one event" in (historical) time of Christ's sacrificial incarnation, which delivers man from the "one event" of Adam's sin. The "personality" emulates this movement, "choosing" himself, sacrificing himself, but since he still cannot "know", cannot actually make that movement, he is never realized and never sacrificed. He is condemned rather than resigned to repetition. This must be why the Ultimatum is so preoccupied with recurrence, the "eternal torment of constantly beginning over again yet without being able to begin" (601).[33]

"inwardness" that Kierkegaard wants everyone to achieve, but there will inevitably be a disregarding of alterity in this movement.

[31] Wilhelm also says that the only situation in which one should not marry is if you carry some kind of unmentionable secret; a statement which could be an embedded reference to Kierkegaard's own breaking of his engagement to Regine Olsen (448).

[32] In his "Last Word", Wilhelm claims to have "forgotten most of what was in them," a grand bathos after his extensive writings. The idea that "against God we are always in the wrong" is "edifying", which indicates further that Wilhelm's description of the ethico-religious has not reached it.

[33] Kierkegaard (alias Vigilius Haufniensis) spends a whole book deliberating on the problem of the "one event" of Adam's sin, disseminated through time, in *The Concept of Anxiety*. See especially the ontological confusion of chapter 1: "Anxiety as the

I do not intend to pursue the theological paradoxes and difficulties at this point. For my concern is not with prefiguration and incarnation, but with irony and the difficult meeting of its ethics with its expression or simulation. In Kierkegaard's writings this meeting is initially enabled, but subsequently, and retroactively, it is problematized by the religious paradox of incarnation. It creates an ironic authorship, but one constrained by an impatience with its ignorance, and the guilt caused by this impatience. In attempting to leave behind the dialectical anxiety he has admitted, he is condemned to repeat the pattern of double-bind and double dissimulation: in *Either / Or* where he sacrifices the aesthetic ethical for the religious ethical, only to repeat the aesthetic in the religious; in *Repetition*, where, for all Constantius' attempts to define it, and the Young Man's (poetic) aspirations to reach it, "repetition" is not defined or reached but occurs accidentally, and absurdly, to and through the absent "other" (Kierkegaard, 1983);[34] in the impossibility of resolving methodically the "accidental" nature of hereditary sin in *The Concept of Anxiety*; in the *Philosophical Fragments* where Johannes Climacus' get-out-clause for the impossible conflict of time and "one event" is to faint (1992b, 141); most radically, perhaps, in *Fear and Trembling*, where Johannes de Silentio's desperate attempts to make the "movement" of faith get him nowhere, and he still "cannot understand" Abraham's leap of faith (1983, 34-8);[35] "finally", in *The Point of View*, where Kierkegaard writes and reveals himself *as* Kierkegaard, "ends" his authorship and writes his epitaph, only to write again in *Two Ages* (1939, 100-103). Every time the ironic subject seeks an end, aspires to religious "inwardness", and relies on a promise of "truth" from the infinite, it inadvertently cuts off the ethical responsibility, and so the openness to 'other' possibility, that would enable inwardness. And so it continues, hobbling eternally as an ambivalent ghost in its own structure.

Presupposition of Hereditary Sin and as Explaining Hereditary Sin Retrogressively in Terms of Its Origin" (1980, 25-46).

[34] The lover that the young man has deserted is the one who "achieves" repetition by her marriage to another man. It is through this act that the young man receives "everything" back "double", like Job, who has been Constantius' example of repetition.

[35] The dilemma is about Abraham's willingness to sacrifice Issac, a religious-ethical movement far removed from worldly ethics, yet made in time. It is worth noting that de Silentio describes Abraham's answer to Issac ("God himself will provide the lamb for the burnt offering") as being "in the form of irony" (1983, 118), which again indicates that the infinite ethical movement comes only through the absurd, and a receptiveness to the absurd.

This is why Kierkegaard seems at once to return to Hegel and to transcendentalism; why he is too Socratic and too religious; why he is not "Socratic" enough (in the sense of Kierkegaard's drawing of Socrates as the risk of irony) and not "religious" enough (in the sense of Kierkegaard's figuration of faith as absolute non-knowledge, arbitrariness and otherness). It is also why Kierkegaard's philosophy is at once more "honest" and more "dissimulative" than other considerations of irony and ethics. It persistently reaches a point of irreducibility, where it is impossible to discern whether the anxiety of irony is a marker of the incorporation of the risk and openness by the dialectical temporality, or whether it is a marker of the risk exceeding its incorporation; or even whether as a marker (or symptom) it is between or beyond these two choices. If it were the latter, then the anxiety of irony might be a way of taking account of risk without it becoming a "pure" or oppositional term. Faith, strangely enough, may well be the answer to enabling the risk of irony to hold forth, to discredit its "will to truth", but only a faith which has nothing to do with a sequential exchange of terms and a guaranteed revelation, before or beyond the current structure, of the (infinite, absolute) other. In the eyes of most religious faiths, and certainly the Christian faith that Kierkegaard follows, this is, of course, no "true" faith at all. Kierkegaard cannot maintain this uncertain faith within the dialectical structure without succumbing to an unbearable anxiety. As a result, he reenacts the impotence of his pseudonyms. Like de Silentio in *Fear and Trembling*, and unlike Abraham, Kierkegaard cannot receive the truth because he and his writing are not absurd enough, not premised purely on accident, not utterly open to speak, as Abraham is, in another's words; "in the form of irony". He may describe the movements of swimming, he may even swim – as de Silentio can in his acknowledgement of the absurd (1983, 37-8) – but he cannot swim "out of the sea of argument" as Socrates suggests in the epigraph to this chapter; because even to reduce the ethical "irreducibility" to an unknown promise holds back the rescuing dolphin.

Chapter 3

Unsustainable Change? The Traps of Ironic Femininity

Having explored dialectical feminism and dialectical irony in two separate chapters, we might now begin to discern common preoccupations and patterns of behaviour. My analyses of Kristeva and Kierkegaard have focussed on what I have referred to as the problem of "dialectical anxiety": the tension in the dialectical philosophy between a historical analysis of being and experience which opens idealist concepts and hierarchies to the possibility of change; and the simultaneous desire of this analysis to resolve uncertainty and to know its own origin and destination. While Kristeva and Kierkegaard are vastly different – Kristeva seeking a "revolution" of theoretical terms and Kierkegaard seeking a more chivalrous philosophical method – their negotiations with dialectical anxiety share a desire to maintain the mobility of the dialectic in spite of the structure's desire for closure.

Both writers query a Hegelian structure which ensures its own completion by excluding or incorporating the "other": whatever is contingent; unknowable; absurd; irrational; corporeal; private; particular; or feminine. Kristeva's objections to this completion are political. She believes that the figuration of a *transcendent* "self-consciousness" forecloses the power of the dialectic's alternating movement to destabilize established hierarchies and reveal the material conflict which lies beneath apparently "immutable" categories and subject positions. Kierkegaard has little problem with transcendence *per se*, but considers it unethical for a mortal system to ignore its mutable lot and assume knowledge of the divine purpose from the start. Hence Kristeva theorizes the libidinal, material determination of the subject-in-process and Kierkegaard conceives his "actual", "phenomenal" but unknowable "personality". These refigurations of "self-consciousness" attempt to introduce to the galloping progress of the dialectic a certain flexibility, an openness to risk or diversion, in the hope of creating a less abstract and self-perpetuating evocation of thought and experience.

It is through Kristeva's and Kierkegaard's attempts to refigure Hegelian self-consciousness that we can think about the difficulties of and possibilities for feminist and ironic agency. Their negotiations with dialectical anxiety highlight the baffling complications raised by any challenge to the determination, or pre-determination, of subjective and sexual categories within theoretical and philosophical structures; especially structures which function through a play of oppositions. The convergence of the two writers' work on the figure of the "other" within the play of oppositions, and the anxiety it provokes, are what link their different concerns and what should also bring into focus the problem of accommodating and theorizing difference in a non-essentializing way. It quickly becomes clear that there are connections in the binarist structure between the "other", the feminine, the movement of irony and dialectical anxiety which are more than coincidental. The question is whether the implications of their interrelation will direct us towards other ways of figuring sexual difference and femininity. I will therefore outline the way these forces and categories compose themselves in relation to each other before returning to the question of "agency".

I. Connections

Kristeva, Hegel and the "Negative" Woman

The problem of dialectical anxiety relates in more ways than one to the feminist demand for change in the prevailing hierarchy of terms. To a large extent, on a structural and economic level, feminism operates through the same tension as the dialectic: it interrogates apparently immutable configurations of gender and reveals their historical and cultural foundations, while seeking alternative sexual specifications. The anxiety surrounding this double purpose, which in Hegel's dialectic is what spurs on the mediation of history, is a problem to the feminist dialectic because of feminism's different historical, political and ethical concerns. Once it is accepted that sexual difference cannot be categorized through purely biological factors it is impossible to divorce any new (feminist) delineation of gender categories from the cultural influences surrounding it.

However, the prevailing desire of feminism is to avoid repeating the fixities and hierarchies of patriarchal structures, which means that determinations which are imposed on the feminist configuration by existing philosophies must be interrogated and resisted. Any new figurations of "woman" or "femininity" must be wary of complying with idealized notions of gender and identity if they are not to curtail the agency for change which enabled the feminist demand to be made in the first place.

This is why Kristeva's model of sexual difference upholds Hegel's basic structure while withholding from his anticipated sublation of anxiety through absolute self-consciousness. She treads an impossible balance between her historical theoretical inheritance and the necessity of exceeding its strictures. Her "subject-in-process" perpetuates the ambivalence of dialectical mediation – the tension between "becoming" (through the thetic phase) and "un-becoming" (through the death drive) – so that settled subject positions and categories can never be assumed.[1] This resistance to closure not only aims to fend off sexist figurations of femininity, but seeks to acknowledge the heterogeneous nature of what comes under the name of "identity" in general. Kristeva's highlighting of the different drives and directional movements within the dialectic is meant to be a step towards a more ethical mode of theorizing subjective and sexual relations. Unlike classical, "metaphysical" philosophies, this multi-directional dialectic will not seek a single, certain truth of consciousness at the expense of others. If a "feminist" dialectic is to be thought, then, it must shy away from defining a newly fixed, abstract "essence" of "woman" because any such definition would create a new set of excluded characteristics which are "other" to it. As Kristeva insists in her texts on feminism, such a (re-)imposition of immovable positions and hierarchies is alien to a discourse whose basic motivation is the search for equality and freedom (Kristeva, 1986b, 209-10). Feminism must negotiate with the prevailing ethical order as much as with the political order if it is to instigate real change in the patriarchal mould.

The ethical dimension of the feminist demand feeds in turn into the question of the function and position of "woman" and "femininity" within dialectical philosophy. This question is, of course, tangled up

---

[1] In terms of the dialectical movement towards self-consciousness, which is the underlying model for Kristeva's subject-in-process, the thetic phase corresponds to Hegel's progressive determination of history and consciousness and the death drive aligns itself with Hegelian negativity.

with the broader economic and structural tensions of the feminist dialectic and its attempts to rewrite the historical figuration of "woman" as "other" to the higher aims of masculine power and thought. However, there is a specific problem in effecting this ethical negotiation in the face of Hegel's particular conception of femininity because his ethical order has already figured her as an *essentially reactionary* principle within the dialectic. This figuration threatens to upset the novelty and autonomy of Kristeva's non-transcendent feminist ethics.

Since Spirit is known by Hegel to be the destiny of the dialectic, every individual category, thought or movement is in some way a manifestation of the absolute which is to come. Even those elements which are thought of as external to the purpose of philosophical mediation – negating it, inducing anxiety through their unknowability – are somehow productive. Under the dictation of the law of the universal, that which threatens the unity of the philosophical structure is considered to be external to the purpose of philosophical mediation. However, its externality is simultaneously figured as somehow necessary to the development of the structure's internal purpose; either as something which at some point will be incorporated by the structure or as something which will be rejected permanently by the structure as a means to perfecting its boundaries. In both cases the other element ceases to be independent of the growing dialectical self-consciousness and – strangely enough for something that is "other" – no longer retains the power to be different. Hence the repetitiveness of Hegel's definitions and descriptions: of the force which drives the mediation of knowledge as a "moment" expressed as the "subsistence of independent matters" which nevertheless "remain(s) within itself in the expression" (1977, 81); of universal knowledge as "self-consciousness as self-consciousness, which is the simple unity of knowing" (485); of "ethical substance" as "absolute Spirit realized in the plurality of existent consciousness" (267).[2] Everything is tied up in

[2] Perhaps the most telling of Hegel's circular definitions is his description of contingency – the ridding of which is, he claims, the aim of philosophical enquiry – as an "external necessity" (Hegel, 1975 p. 28). Robert Smith points to the contradictory nature of this definition. As he points out, "to qualify necessity as external is to disesteem its necessity." However, the contradiction is logical to Hegel because he considers the history of Spirit as the *whole* of history, so that any causality cannot ultimately be external to it; including that of the contingency. Its dialectic serves to regulate it "so that its externality effectively signifies *virtual internality*" (Smith 1995, 21-22)

the tight circle of dialectical progression; and this includes the woman, who Hegel sees as the embodiment of negativity.

Hegel's portraits of the position of "woman" place her firmly within the lower strata of being and consciousness. According to his "ethical order", woman is entrenched within the Family (1977, 266-94).[3] The Family is the negative "other" of the Community, concerning itself with the individual, with human law and purely ethical relationships.[4] It is unaware of the divine law and the "life in and for the universal" which the community serves and determines (269). Within this narrow realm, woman, unlike man, is not a citizen and is thus "unaware of the self-conscious power of universality" (275).[5] As the eventual realization of the absolute is considered to be incontestable, these oppositions are all working in the service of universal knowledge anyway:

> … the ethical substance is *actual* substance, absolute Spirit realized in the plurality of existent consciousness; this spirit is the community which […] here has emerged *on its own account* […] as essence *for* the consciousness which here is our object. It is Spirit which is *for itself* in that it preserves itself in its reflection in individuals; and it is *implicitly* Spirit, or substance, in that it preserves them within itself (267).

Nevertheless, as far as *she* knows, woman's place within this universal structure is in the private, human sphere, functioning through negative, individualistic ethical relations rather than the "positive ethical action" of the "*abstract*, pure universal" (271-2).

Thus to privilege the ethical realm (as Kristeva's "herethics" does) is effectively to repeat the disempowered and divided status allotted her by Hegel's epic system, even while it seems to open up its closed

---

[3] Hegel's example for the position of woman within the ethical order is Antigone, which fits with his belief in the "epic" art of the Greeks revealing the absolute through its idealized characters (see Hegel 1993, 80-97).

[4] The "community" through which Hegel defines his ethical order is described as "Spirit" as it is manifested in "existent consciousnesses". Its substance is defined in terms of divine law and its purpose is public and "universal". The "other side" of this community is the Family "which has the form of immediate substance or substance that simply is". It is opposed to the "actual, self-conscious existence" of the wider (national) community, as it concerns itself with human rather than divine law. Nevertheless, it is a "moment" which is necessary to the community insofar as it prepares the "individual" for life and death as a "citizen". In terms of the divine law, the "individual […] is only an unreal impotent shadow" of the "citizen", which is "actual and substantial" (1977, 267-268 & 270).

[5] Hegel is comparing the differing positions of Antigone and her brother in this section.

systemacity. Not only this, but the position's negativity and otherness – unbeknown to the woman, in her state of limited consciousness – is actually dictated by the universal law and helps in the progress towards (transcendent) Spirit-as-consciousness.

This is why Kristeva's negotiation with dialectical anxiety constantly comes back to its own impossibility. Rightly recognizing that she cannot leap out of the prevailing symbolic system, Kristeva follows the logic of the dialectic, seeking out the negative, anxiety producing elements within its oppositional structure as the means to exceeding and disrupting the status quo. However, she cannot effectively battle with the circularity of its logic and the way in which it ensures its possession of and control over "excessive" elements. Every time she makes a further movement towards heterogeneity by tracing the dialectic of more liminal, internal oppositions (from the broad abstractions of symbolic versus semiotic or masculine versus feminine, to the threshold movement of "hainadoration" on the boundary of these categories) the imperative to "know" and "determine" the other according to the law of the general symbolic system takes over, swallowing the rebellious elements up into the equivalent of Hegel's universal consciousness.

If we take Kristeva as a model for the difficulties of surpassing or overturning the masculinist status quo, we can see that to privilege the negativity of the feminine term as a form of *external* agency is as inhibiting as it is momentarily liberating. This realization should alter the terms of the feminist question with which we are dealing. We should now consider if it is possible to employ the negative, ethical movement of the dialectic strategically, as an *internal* agent for altering the predetermined masculine hierarchy and the negative figuration of femininity, even though this movement is already subscribed by the hierarchy and caught up in the overarching teleology of the "progressive" dialectic.

Kierkegaard, Hegel and the Ironic Subject

It is at this point that irony begins to figure, because it takes the form of an internal force of negativity which conforms to the movement of dialectical mediation while upsetting the certain "universality" of its ending. Irony is potentially a force which dispossesses the philosophical "subject" or concept of its authority. Its counteraction denies the possibility of actively positing truth and knowledge because to do this is to assume that there *is* a truth that can be reached through the particular method; and if the subject already had the proper authority to guarantee this path (in the case of Hegel, Absolute Knowledge; in the case of Kristeva, the law of the Symbolic) it would not need to be searching for the knowledge in the first place. In other words, every assertion of knowledge made by a particular structure is at best a guess: real knowledge can only be *received* from some other source – ultimately the Absolute Other – and this source is beyond the determinable reach of the "conscious", present subject.[6]

Kierkegaard's portrait of irony is a variation of the Socratic method of enquiry, which because it questions self-knowledge as well as every other possible knowledge, is far more invasive, more perturbing to positive models of consciousness than a mere "method" could ever be. If there is no verifiable "individual" to begin with because self-knowledge depends on the affirmation of the Absolute that we are searching for, then the starting block for any kind of "method" or "process" is radically destabilized. As far as Kierkegaard is concerned, the questions irony poses about the authority of philosophical assertions ruptures the bond Hegel assumes to lie between the conceptual progress of the dialectic (towards philosophical self-consciouness) and the attainment of universal knowledge as final destination. Irony's reliance on an unknowable, uncontainable "other" makes the balance in the dialectic between "internal" and "external" less regulable. It seems to say that Hegel's dialectic may very well fulfil the promise of its own structural intentions – its own internal purpose – but this is *all* it does. The claim made over "external" elements is contingent, a matter of the desire of this particular structure; rather than a pure necessity dictated by an omniscient, truth-wielding Absolute.

As such, irony holds possibilities as a form of agency for feminism within the dialectic. It shares with feminism its rejection of the authority and "objectivity" of the philosophical structure, and its concern with knowledges other than those presently asserted. Like the "feminine" term within Hegel's dialectic it is considered a negative force, working through the individual rather than the universal and

[6] Of course it could still be argued that Kristeva's "subject-in-process", which acknowledges the division and desires of the unconscious, can never be fully "conscious" in the way Hegel's philosophical subject is assumed to be; because its determination is recognized as being the "desire" of the symbolic. However, I would argue here, as I argued in Chapter 1, that this desire is still predetermined according to a universalized idea of language and consciousness, and that this compromises the potential of the "unknowable" desire to counteract the dialectical, symbolic law.

thus other, or merely instrumental to the conceptual aims of philosophy. And yet its haunting (half-)presence suggests that it cannot be defined and subscribed this easily: its negativity is not simply oppositional and nihilistic because it waits for the chance of receiving the other's truth; but neither does its negativity serve a positive end (in the Hegelian sense) because such an end cannot be predicted. Irony thus stands as an ethical mode of thinking *within* the prevailing dialectic, and as a genuine threat to the enveloping tendencies of dialectical progression.

Kristeva, Kierkegaard and Negative Capability

Sure enough, Kristeva's ambivalent abject *as well as* Kierkegaard's negative "personality" are configurations of consciousness which are interrupted by the force of irony: a sense of alterity which heightens dialectical anxiety, delays its conceptual resolution and marks the contingent and desirous aspects of philosophical determination. What is interesting is that this ironic force and the trace or figure of femininity should appear to behave so similarly in both writers' work. The figurative comparisons are obvious. For Kristeva, the abject is a feminized force, a half-consciousness within the dialectic which defies identity and positionality; a comic, irrational path running between the logical, conceptual terms of the dialectic. Kierkegaard's "ethical" irony is equated with and received by the feminine element in every text. At times metaphorical (as with Socrates' "midwifery") at times literal (as the lover, wife or even "real-life" fiancée) "she" is, like irony, the absurd, unknowable and unspeakable premise of writing; the "other" which prompts a startling subjective / authorial anxiety.

The combined characteristics of irony and the feminine might, then, be thought to create a force of "otherness" within the dialectic which operates as a quasi-subjective quasi-knowledge, holding off the full-circle return of Hegel's sublated self-consciousness. They create a more anxious mediation of "experience" but one which might steer us away from predetermined positioning and allow for a more open reading of (sexual) difference.

However, negotiations with the liminal are never this easy. Although it is clear that Kristeva's and Kierkegaard's "other" dialectics question the predestination of Hegel's dialectical structure, they also seem not to be able to bear for long the perpetuation of anxiety which results. Just as they both trace a different, "risky" movement on the boundary of the dialectical machinations, so this movement seems to slide into something which curtails the potential it might have had for disrupting sameness. As Kristeva's carefully "in between" abject is interpreted as a loss of sanity, meaning and identity, so the "herethical" feminine turns out to be a (re)incorporated "other"; as Kierkegaard's indecisive irony becomes an ethical "choice", so the "woman" who received the absurd repetition is disengaged from the text in the name of "communication".[7] In each case some structural imperative seems to kick in which induces an extreme fear of the radical unknowability of the other movement and provokes a blundering, hyper-Hegelian reaction. What was pursued as a redefinition of the determination of being and knowledge is suddenly perceived as an absolute threat to any kind of ontology or epistemology. Kristeva's reaction is more exaggerated than Kierkegaard's. Abjection was initially considered as a means of examining the "want of the (Lacanian) object of want", but it is suddenly disregarded as the "muddy canals" of potential psychosis (Kristeva 1982, 247). This is, no doubt, because Kristeva's Althusserian and Lacanian register is more resolutely Hegelian, more insistent on "positivity" and "determination". Unlike Kristeva's, Kierkegaard's narrative style does seem to treat ironically the epistemological desire which overruns his considerations of contingency and absurdity; thus extending the time in which irony's potential subversion can exist.[8] However, both of their negotiations with the dialectic's strict oppositional boundaries do seem to lose their conviction. When they do, the figures of the ironic and feminine other fall back into repeating Hegel's depiction of them as negative moments on the path of dialectical progression. Their indeterminable, singular status is abstracted once again, becoming the "essential", "internal enemy" of the universal: "womankind – the everlasting irony in (the life of) the community" (Hegel 1977, 288).

[7] This is the case with Kierkegaard's staging of his broken engagement to Regine Olsen. This event is figured as the prompt for his early texts (*Either / Or; Repetition*) and is the implicit subject of his philosophical musings. However, references to this "cause" are erased and denied by the time he writes his "final" text, *The Point of View*.

[8] The pseudonymous authorship of his texts is the most obvious example of the way in which Kierkegaard sustains his irony. This "strategy" is also revealed as a means to expressing the "immanence" of temporal experience in the *Concluding Unscientific Postscript*, (1992c, 625). However, given the fact that this final "revelation" of his trickery is not in actual fact final at all – Kierkegaard's authorship did not end with his "Final Declaration" – it is tempting to think that irony, once unleashed to the extent it has been with Kierkegaard, cannot be wholly re-contained.

II. Directions

Risk and Curtailment

The relations between irony, the feminine, and feminist agency are thus as fraught as they are complicated. The ironic feminine, or feminine irony, function at once as prompters of risk and difference within the dialectic and as agents for curtailing risk. Their alterity and their double movement acts as a kind of negative capability. To follow this action, as, to different extents, Kristeva and Kierkegaard do, is to mark the contingency of dialectical determinations without altering the dialectic's fundamental laws. What we might call the Hegelian "circle" of dialectical logic – Absolute Spirit as self-consciousness arrived at through the battle with an other which was always already a manifestation of Spirit – is toyed with and delayed, so that while it does still return to itself it is no longer quite the same. To maintain this analogy; rather than being a perfect circle drawn with a steady line, it is elongated, irregular and not immediately recognisable as a circle. The whole dialectical process has lost something of its purity and its power to satisfy.

This trajectory is most clearly encountered – and the challenge to the dialectic most sustained – in Kierkegaard's work, with its hobbling Hegelian repetitions and ghostly half-returns to self-consciousness as the "incarnated" individual.[9] The paradoxical temporal situation surrounding and perpetuated by these repetitions appears to be where his figuration of (feminine) irony as negative capability is staged; and is thus the stage for the curtailment of his initial privileging of riskiness and alterity. It is therefore worth pausing over this temporal paradox for a bit longer and considering it through the lens of the "other", if we are to pursue the question of feminist agency through irony.

Two lines of enquiry are of particular relevance to this pursuit: how far can Kierkegaard's ironic repetition of dialectical logic be taken towards altering Hegel's configuration of "woman-as-eternal-other"; and is there any way in which this manifestation of irony as a form of negative ethics can be rethought and refigured so that it will better tolerate the anxiety it provokes, thus causing a less shame-faced interference in the "legal" structures that encircle it?

---

[9] As I argued in Chapter 2, the "actualization of force" never quite takes place in Kierkegaard's structure.

I intend to spend the remaining part of this chapter examining these two questions. In analysing the status of "woman-as-other" I will touch on psychoanalytic ideas on (sexual) alterity and anxiety, and in considering the ethical structure I will turn to the work of Levinas, Irigaray and Derrida, who place a radically different slant on the ethical significance of alterity.

Kierkegaard's Other

Kierkegaard's temporal paradox operates within a mimetic structure which cannot tolerate the sense of contingency which irony introduces. The difficulty which Kierkegaard's subjective irony faces up to is how "individuality" can be experienced, thought, known or written of in the present, as a phenomenon or manifestation within history. "Individuality" refers to any singular knowledge, idea or object, as well as the existential "subject" which perceives or knows it. Not only can the subjective individual only be known through the other, but this other must be acknowledged as totally other and not as some sub-clause of a predestined path towards subjectivity. Self-knowledge, which precedes all other knowledge, can only be attained by recognizing the otherness of the other, and this otherness necessarily resists all phenomenality at the *present* time. The way in which the present philosophical mediation of experience operates, then, is paradoxical because there is a fundamental disjunction between the desire or motivation which propels the mediation (the retrieval of a lost or awaited absolute, with which the present mediation assumes a mimetic relation) and the possibilities of the present (blind guessing, contingency, mutability). This is why the paradox finds its expression in the model of the "incarnated" individual, Christ. He bridged the gap between eternity and history and vouched for the existence of truth, but a mere mortal cannot hope to emulate his example. The other may be longed for or anticipated but never predicted because in its singularity it has no *demonstrable* connection with the present.[10] Whatever threads the two "times" together to make the time of Kierkegaard's philosophical narrative can only be a matter of absurd belief or faith: the moment in which the

[10] Hence Kierkegaard's obsessive returns to the subject of the "one event" in history; particularly in *The Concept of Irony* and *Fear and Trembling*.

subject and his "knowledge" is asserted is a "moment of madness" (1992b, 52).[11]

As long as this "madness" lasts in Kierkegaard's writing, the alterity of woman is not circumscribed into an *essential* category or position. She is beyond the "present" theorizing of the (masculine) subject and holds the power to disrupt this theorizing by reminding it of its contingency. This is why Kierkegaard spends so much time narrating the unknowable specificity of the female characters in his various ironic-dialectical tales of seduction and betrayal. The "Shadowgraphs" of *Either / Or* would epitomize this tendency. They describe in detail the love affairs and suffering of individual women in famous literary examples of romantic betrayal, before the narrator insists that "nothing visible had appeared" through his descriptions (1992a, 207).[12] The singularity of the "other" women cannot be sufficiently "known", possessed and presented as it is by the speculative aesthete of "Papers A" or by Hegel's categorization of woman as the negative element within the public sphere.[13] It is only through realizing this impossibility that the (masculine) subject can step beyond the vain self-projections of his desire – for her, for knowledge, for reconciliation between eternity and history – into a properly ethico-religious mode of thought.

There is, of course, still a marked element of objectification in this figuration of woman which verges on the fetishistic. Woman's singular otherness also functions as a secular substitute for the long-awaited revelation of the absolute knowledge of the absolute Other (God). The romantic tales are ultimately displaced representations of man's aspiration to this revelation; and thus the mimetic relation with the first and final "truth" is always simmering beneath. This side of the ironic representation means that Kierkegaard's figurations of the

---

[11] The Danish word "*Daarskab*" is translated here as "foolishness", but I am using an alternative translation of the word, in order to correspond to the French translation of the word ["*folie*"] which Derrida uses. I will be analyzing Derrida's reading of this "madness" later in the chapter.

[12] The narrator focuses on the torments of Marie Beaumarchais in Goethe's *Clavigo*, Donna Elvira in Mozart's *Don Giovanni* and Margrete in Goethe's *Faust*. Highlighting the unknowable specificity of the women's experiences the narrator adds: "only someone who has been bitten by snake bites knows what the victim of a snake-bite suffers!" (208).

[13] Kierkegaard's recasting of Antigone as a "modern" tragic heroine is another example of his resistance to the generalizing speculative categories of gender. His Antigone suffers the secret, internalized, "ambiguous" pain of her father's guilt rather than the "external" suffering of the pattern of destiny which fits the purely "epic" model so beloved of Hegel. See "Ancient Tragedy's Reflection in the Modern" (139-161).

"other" woman can be read as denials of her subjectivity as well as problematizations of the authority of (masculine) subjectivity.[14] However, this repetition of the speculative is partly due to the lack of intention left in Kierkegaard's dialectic – it cannot overcome the Hegelian structure as Hegel would overcome the "past" in his dialectical progress – so is not left unmarked and unquestioned. Indeed, the continual thwartings within Kierkegaard's romantic tales; the fact that the "ethical" universal is never adequately "chosen" and only rarely, and arbitrarily, received means that the parallel between the historical and eternal is always troubled. Even when a Kierkegaardian personality makes the inevitable movement of religious aspiration and chooses himself or "receives" himself "back" by sacrificing the female other (and thus curtailing her other possibilities), a guilty half-consciousness of this objectification and appropriation remains; and it disables the completion of the repetition.[15]

Given that the most adequate description of Kierkegaard's woman-as-other is as a displaced and ironized fetish object, the most illuminating comparison to be made is perhaps a psychoanalytic one. I am thinking once again of Lacan's figuration of the feminine, which in spite of his complex elucidation of desire, is more fetishistic than Kierkegaard's. "She" is in an *essentially* ironic position. Negative capability in Lacan's structure is a movement of utter freedom and

---

[14] Feminist readings of Kierkegaard also pinpoint other misogynist tendencies. Leslie A. Howe, for example, argues that while Kierkegaard's model of selfhood is built on a balance of "the different (sometimes opposed, sometimes complementary) aspects of our existence" (1994, 154), and while women and men are equal before God, there is a clear sense in which woman's self-consciousness is less individuated, on a "lower" synthesis, than man's self-consciousness (131-57).

[15] This is drawn most subtly in *Repetition* where although the Young Man "receives himself back" and experiences a "repetition" which is described in universal (Hegelian) terms, "he himself understands repetition in another way […] as a secret he cannot explain" (1983, 229). This "secret" haunts the apparent, rhapsodic conclusion of the text's "psychological experiment" in the form of a final, ironic letter from the pseudonymous author, Constantin Constantius. Constantius calls himself a "vanishing person" and "midwife" before passing the responsibility for *final* interpretation onto the reader of the text: "You will understand the variety of the transitions, and even if now and then you wonder a bit at suddenly getting a shower bath of moods, you nevertheless will subsequently realize how everything is variously adapted […] so that the particular mood is fairly correct, which is a primary point here where the lyrical is so important" (230-231). This seems to suggest that the "lyrical" or "poetic" irony of subjective experience (of "moods") cannot be resolved by the philosophical repetition.

utter conscription, beginning and ending with the internal law of the dialectical structure: the so-called "indivisibility" of the signifier.[16] Such is the degree of feminine negativity within this structure that it acts as the very limit of existence and knowledge, the structure's founding moment and that which lies beyond it.[17] Thus "woman" cannot be referred to, not because we cannot "know" the categorical or conceptual (although Lacan's ironic style of lecturing suggests this) but because "she" is the site of both the founding and unfounding of the categorical and the conceptual; the negative moment of otherness that is the condition for psychic mediation. This is why the "*jouissance*" of ~~the~~ woman (in effect her only signification) is both sexual and mystical. It points to the "copula" in both senses of the word: as both the proliferation of the symbolic structure (the negative / negated "other" which supports the fantasy of identity) and its instigation (the primary and primordial Other which began the fantasy, and is thus in some sense beyond it). That her "non-essence" is essential also ensures that "she" remains a "pure" other or "pure" negative. Her negativity is an idealized concept, which explains the

[16] I refer here to Lacan's "Seminar on the *Purloined Letter*", (1972, 38-72); and to Derrida's analysis of this text in his essay "Le Facteur de la verité", in *The Post Card* (1987b, 414-96). Lacan's analysis of Poe's story revolves around a lost letter. Its trajectory as it is tracked down by the detective (alias, "analyst"), Dupin, is interpreted by Lacan as a metaphor for the sliding movement of the signifier. As the locus of (displaced) desire it is a "symbol only of absence" (1972, 54). However, Lacan also says that its "materiality [...] [will] not admit partition" (53) and remarks that "since it can be diverted, it must have a course which is proper to it: the trait by which its incidence as signifier is affirmed". It "sustains" itself through "the alternating operation which is its principle, requiring it to leave its place, even though it returns to it by a circular path" (59-60). Derrida picks up on this "indivisibility" of the letter and Lacan's description of its predestined "return" to itself, reading them as the refusal of the risk or loss that would at first appear to be Lacan's subject. For Derrida, Lacan's signifier closely resembles an absolute limit or law which operates in the same circular, sublating way as Hegel's.

[17] See Lacan 1982a and 1982b. Time and again in these texts, "woman" is figured as the origin and limit of the signifier's desire, through her "pre-symbolic" unity with the child, through her symbolic status as castrated "lack" and her resulting "otherness" to symbolic Law. Derrida outlines in detail the way in which the essential negativity of the Woman in this model effectively operates as a repetition of the metaphysical / fetishistic pairing of Woman with (absent but revealable) Truth, even though the claim is of the absence of (her) Truth: "He gives to Woman or to Femininity a capital letter that elsewhere he often reserves for Truth. [...] Femininity is the Truth (of) castration [...] because in the logic of the signifier it has always already been castrated" (Derrida, 1987b, 441-2).

easy slippage in Lacan's writing between "other" and "Other", woman and God.[18]

It is thus interesting to note that Lacan's conclusion to "God and the *Jouissance* of ~~The~~ Woman" takes Kierkegaard's repeated tale of failed seduction as a model for "existence" itself, for unlike Kierkegaard's repetition, Lacan's version of the tale unanxiously incorporates the risky and indefinite negativity of the feminine into a truth of abstract universality *from the beginning*:

> In other words, *it is not by chance* that Kierkegaard discovered existence in a little tale of seduction. It is by being castrated, by renouncing love that he believes he accedes to it. But then, after all, why shouldn't Régine also have existed? This desire for a good at one remove, a good not caused by a *petit a*, perhaps it was through the intermediary of Régine that he came to it (1982b, 147-8, my emphasis).

"Kierkegaard" (note that we are taking the stories of *Repetition* and *Either / Or* as a *literal* autobiography) gives up his desire for symbolic power – the system's fantasy of a stable identity – and assumes the position of lack, the non-knowledge of "feminine" irony. In doing this he receives a "true" existence back: "a good not caused by *petit a*." No matter that in Kierkegaard's ironic communication this "good" can only be received by chance according to the time of the communication. For the figural *is the essence* of the structure for Lacan, the big Other and universal Truth revealed through negative "moment" of feminine *jouissance*. Lacan's Symbolic is thus its own other, its own cause, while pretending that there is another other – the "good which bypasses *petit a*"; the "more than one God" – which may be "known" in the abyssal silence of the negative feminine.

Conversely, in the "Concluding Letter" of *Repetition*, Kierkegaard's pseudonymous author, Constantin Constantius, explains the movement of the story, after its completion, in less decisive terms. The categories he employs are very Hegelian: the "universal" aligns

---

[18] As in "God and the *Jouissance* of ~~the~~ Woman" where there is an ironic indication of a link between the two: "[…] naturally you are all going to be convinced that I believe in God. I believe in the *jouissance* of the woman in so far as it is something more, on condition that you screen off that *something more* until I have properly explained it. […] Might not this *jouissance* which one experiences and knows nothing of, be that which puts us on the path of ex-istence? And why not interpret one face of the Other, the God face, as supported by feminine *jouissance*?" (1982b). Lacan makes it clear here that the other side of the face of the Other is *signifiance* itself, which is obviously prior to the *jouissant* God face, since the latter "comes about thanks to the being of *signifiance*." For an ironic, feminist reading of this mystification of the feminine see Luce Irigaray's, "Così Fan Tutti" (1977 85-93; 1985b 90-96).

with the figure of philosophical knowledge and the "exception" parallels the poetic, as represented by the young male lover in his pursuit of the woman. While Constantius portrays the existential aim of the story as being the attainment of the universal – which would fit Lacan's Hegelian depiction of the symbolic – the point for Constantius is more importantly that the attainment of the universal cannot be predicted. As he says, mouthing Kierkegaard's ironic jibe at Hegel's progressive "order", "one tries in vain to say 1, 2, 3" (1983, 226). Thus,

> If heaven [the universal] loves one sinner [the exception] more than ninety-nine who are righteous, the sinner, of course, does not know this from the beginning; on the contrary, he is aware only of heaven's wrath until he finally, as it were, forces heaven to speak out (227).

Although the woman in *Repetition* is, in the end, the negative term through which the lover "receives [himself] back" (much as if he has "forced heaven to speak out"), this is an unexpected event and not *necessarily* the case throughout the course of the narrative. The anxiety provoked by her alterity is not domesticated; a point backed up by the uncertainties of authorial "intention" in the pseudonymous writing of the piece. This is a very different repetitive movement to Lacan's, where the circular logic still works according to the "1, 2, 3" of the Signifier. Kierkegaard cannot quite make the return of this perfect circle because the otherness of the other has been recognized as non-essential, and its refusal to coincide with the determination of the present symbolization haunts the repetition.

Strangely enough, it could be argued that the "legal" status of Kierkegaard's feminine "other" bears a closer resemblance to the role it plays in Freud's delineation of anxiety than to its role in Lacan's delineation.[19] In "Inhibitions, Symptoms and Anxiety", Freud identifies anxiety as the projection of a "sense of danger" which stands in line with his other central neuroses as a signification of the loss or separation from the mother (1993b, 309).[20] However, he also

[19] It is interesting to note the frequency with which Freud devotes whole paragraphs to discussing the various nuances in the meaning of the German word "Angst". See the editor's appendix to Freud 1993a 64-5; also 1993b, 324-5 and 1991a, 281-282.

[20] Initially, Freud had identified anxiety as a manifestation of a sense of danger which in its neurotic form is driven by a sexual aetiology; and also pointed to a "normal" form of anxiety, where the sense of danger would come from a real threat or fear, for example the threat of physical attack. See 1993a, 45-49. "Inhibitions, Symptoms and Anxiety" places anxiety further back in the psychic topography.

defines its specific quality as "the quality of indefiniteness and lack of object" and distinguishes it from a general feeling of fear by this lack (325). It is both a harking back to the mother origin, and a defiance of such certainty or literalness which casts itself as a plural, unprescribable "fear".[21] As Freud says, "on the one hand [it is] an expectation of trauma, and on the other a repetition of it in mitigated form" (326). Of course, unlike Lacan, Kierkegaard does not share Freud's specification of the lost object as the "mother"; although the figurative parallels with the "origin" and the "source" of meaning are the same in Kierkegaard's "other" women. However, the blurred link between desire for an object and its indirect manifestation as anxiety remains less determinable and determining in Freud's and Kierkegaard's structures, than in Lacan's model.[22] It represents the mark of the ambiguity and uncanniness that arises with the attempt to posit the "cause" of anxiety, rather than the regulating Law of anxiety's symbolization.[23] The other is thus not determinedly positioned as the cipher of the symbolic Law.

I have digressed through psychoanalytic models of anxiety and desire not in an attempt to retrieve Kierkegaard's religious "choice" from its problematic relinquishing of the ethical and the feminine, but to emphasize that his figuration of ironic femininity as an unknowable, undeterminable "other" is significantly different from Hegel's, Lacan's or Kristeva's dialectical "others". It is also worth restating here that as a way of acknowledging alterity, the reconfiguration of philosophical determination as "belief" or "faith" in

---

[21] Indeed Freud seems suspicious of pinpointing the loss to being the loss of the "mother". He is resistant to Otto Rank's hypothesis that anxiety is the result of birth trauma because it is too literal in its linking of material / actual event with the affect of anxiety. He is also careful to point out that the manifestation of anxiety is more often than not a sense of the loss of the object incurred *indirectly* (1993b, 301-302 & 309).

[22] Freud states that he "gave up the theory of abreaction which had played such a large part in the cathartic method" because "it did not tally with the facts" of anxiety (309). The "facts" are that the indeterminable nature of the repressed material of anxiety neurosis means that the ego "cannot undo its repressions" and is condemned to the "automatic rule" of the compulsion to repeat (312).

[23] Remember that Freud characterizes the "uncanny" ("*unheimlich*") as "a doubling, dividing and interchanging of the self" and "the constant recurrence of the same thing – the repetition of the same features or character-traits or vicissitudes…"(1990, 356). The "uncanniness" of Kierkegaard's philosophical determination may explain why the margin drawn in *Repetition* between simply repeating and "really" repeating – receiving repetition, achieving a repetition "forwards" instead of repeating the same old self-projecting patterns – is almost indiscernible, and certainly inexpressible.

an awaited instant of revelation is perhaps preferable to the habitual dialectical insistence on (predetermined and determining) "knowledge". It introduces a higher degree of risk and uncertainty and is thus not as quick to (re)incorporate difference.

If my footnotes have been gesturing towards Derrida's deconstruction of Lacan's "phallogocentrism", Kierkegaard's problematic irony points to it again. Writing of the fetishistic equation drawn in conventional philosophy between "woman" and a hidden (veiled) or revealed Truth, Derrida writes that "should th(e) veil be suspended, or even fall a bit differently, there would no longer be any truth, only "truth" – written in quotation marks" (1979, 58 & 59). Is this not what the mark of Kierkegaardian anxiety does, even while it does not escape the demand of its mimetic, dialectical structure to go beyond, to reveal truth and receive itself back? If the feminine in Kierkegaard's writings is an absurdity which receives the truth through her non-presence; if she is ultimately perceived as a negative moment on the path to selfhood; if eventually she returns to being "the eternal irony in the life of the community", she is also these things "falling a bit differently", marking these figurations as the mutable desire of the (historical) philosophical structure rather than as its eternal truth. This mark leads the way to other ways of tolerating, without pacifying, the anxiety of the other.

The Asymmetry of Levinas

If Kierkegaard's structure *could* bear the undecidable aspect of its anxiety, we would be approaching the terrain of what Emmanuel Levinas calls the "*il y a*": an irreducible otherness which disrupts the proprietorship of the other under most philosophical conceptions of the other (Levinas, 1969). Levinas is similarly concerned with forging an ethical register of philosophy which does not assume to stamp out the contingencies and irregularities of "experience". As far as he is concerned, the whole possibility of any "experiencing" subject depends upon a radical alterity which simply cannot be reconciled with the idea of a complete presence reached through progressive reasoning. According to Levinas, the fundamental mistake made by philosophy since Plato has been to conceive of the time of Being as a long line of "nows"; discrete moments of full presence which are presumed to lead from the still point of the beginning to the still point at the end.[24] It should rather be accepted that time is a constant movement which exceeds such linear and spatial metaphors and which is characterized by the unknowability of its future. The determination, or "intentionality", of Being-in-time does not lie in an absolute unity of "moments" (as it does in the mimetic side of Kierkegaard's dialectic) but in the indiscernability or melting away of such "moments".[25] This means that the other in Levinas' terms cannot be defined in the terms of a "being" or "thing" because it is that which *gives* the possibility of "beings" and "things" and so cannot be swallowed up by their "experience" and logic.[26] Levinas comments:

> The Being which we become aware of when the world disappears is not a person or a thing, or the sum total of persons and things; it is the fact that one is, the fact that *there is* [*il y a*] (1978, 21.)

The fact that the "there is" of Being bears an excessive, even extravagant relation to phenomenal time means that it works less as a cipher or mediator of positive "events" (such as the realization of self-consciousness) than an interruption of such "eventfulness".

---

[24] As Levinas says, Plato constructed "a world without time" as his ideal, and thus portrays the world of beings as an impossible pursuit of "an ideal of fusion" (1979, 88). His rejection of the philosophical definition of time as a series of "nows" is close to Heidegger's critique of the same, although he considers Heidegger's more ontological definitions of Being and time to replicate Plato's emphasis on fusion or unity. For an illuminating account of the differences between Levinas and Heidegger, which focuses on Levinas' notion of time as "*il y a*" and "instant", see Chanter 1990, 137-154.

[25] As Tina Chanter says, "it is an excess or extravagance of being that Levinas is concerned to describe [...] in the fact that one instant dissolves into the next, fading away, becoming indiscernible, merging into time" (1990, 141, note 6).

[26] The defining characteristic of ethics for Levinas is gratuity. In "The Trace of the Other" he identifies ethics with the Greek word "liturgy", whose sense he gives as being the readiness to "put out funds at a loss" (1986, 350). The importance for Levinas of writing a gratuitous philosophy links to the ongoing exposition of the significance of the "gift" in modern theory and philosophy; and in particular in the work of Derrida. See Derrida 1992a, 1992b and 1995. The idea of the "gift" is inspired mainly by Nietzsche's and Heidegger's reevaluations of metaphysical hierarchies and categories. Nietzsche expounds the "gift-giving virtue" in *Thus Spoke Zarathustra*, as an affirmation of human / bodily creativity which counters the other-worldly (ie. Christian) models of evaluation because they provoke feelings of resentment and greed. Heidegger's deliberations over what he calls the "es gibt" of Being (translating literally as "it gives") focus on that which brings "Being" about in time as something which, unlike most "metaphysical" configurations, is neither a transcendental law of determination nor an already determined individual consciousness. For an illuminating introduction to the different modern theoretical discussions of the gift, see Alan D. Schrift 1997. I will return to both Nietzsche's and Heidegger's ideas of the gift in the second part of this thesis.

Consequently, the anxiety that it provokes is less about the necessity of making a choice between an ontology of immanence and an ontology of transcendence than about the necessity of marking or naming the excess of both, while acknowledging its phenomenal absence.

In accordance with this sense of excess, the naming, or "Saying", is necessarily a non-reference, a recognition of something unrecognisable within the present terms of philosophy. Levinas signals its lack of currency by writing in the prophetic register traditionally associated with religion. The "beyond" or "*il y a*" "does not intend to win its civic rights within the domain of thought by being assimilated to a philosophical evidence" (1969, 22) For Levinas, this means that some notion of transcendence is crucial to his ethical framework. The relationship to the Other – what Levinas calls the "face-to-face relation" – is one which exceeds and precedes any individual being and any account of Being:

> It is a relationship with *a surplus always exterior to the totality*, as though the objective totality did not fill out the true measure of being, as though another concept, the concept of *infinity*, were needed to express this transcendence with regard to totality, non-encompassable within a totality and as primordial as totality (22-3).

The beyond is, however, apparent. It is not simply divorced from philosophical "totality" as an abstract law or condition, because it is "reflected *within* the totality and history, *within* experience" (23).[27] In fact, the excess is the very experience of Being, and this is why the transcendent ethical "moment" or "instant" of the individual's interaction with the Other cannot "be described in a purely negative fashion". Neither is it positive, of course, because to actualize it would be to ignore its excessiveness, its primacy; which is why the "evidence" of the ethical relation to the other is always in some degree yet to come. We end up (and indeed begin) in the paradoxical position of accounting for what totality has forgotten in a revelation which has yet to be seen:

---

[27] However, this experience resists the ego-centred ontology of phenomenology or even existentialism. See "There is: Existence without Existents" for Levinas' poetic evocation of the horror of the experience of nothingness and absence, which is necessarily described in the "impersonal form" of "there is" ["*il y a*"] (1989, 29-36). Sean Hand points out in his introduction to the essay, that this evocation contests the Sartrean *en-soi* and the Heideggerian *es gibt*, which do not sufficiently describe the otherness or uncanniness of the experience.

> … ethics is an optics. But it is a "vision" without image, bereft of the synoptic and totalizing objectifying virtues of vision, a relation or an intentionality of a wholly different type (23).[28]

While the language may still be reminiscent of dialectical specularity, the interruption of the unfigurable Other in the ethical structure is a far cry from Hegel's negatively capable moments or Lacan's veiled (m)Other of "signifiance", or even the "negative freedom" of Sartre.[29] The language springs from the paradox and the anxiety of this "not yet" revelation. If there is a necessity to speak, to figure, it is not *under the intention* of the philosophical subject returning to itself – not as a "choice" – but *in response* to the call of the Other, as "a choice of what ha(s) not been chosen" (254). The point of subjective return, the "instant" of decision is therefore not definitive in any way, and has never held the authority to curtail the unsettling (non-)presence of the Other. Its (self-)projection relies on the trace of "a future never future enough, more remote than the possible" (254-5). Thus it is that Levinas speaks of the asymmetry of the face-to-face relation and of the never-ending responsibility of the subject to the other.[30] His ethics "redefines subjectivity as [a] heteronymous responsibility in contrast to autonomous freedom" (1984, 63).

This exaggerated sense of responsibility, which concurs with the excessiveness of the other, means that while Levinas addresses the other in specifically *feminine* terms, "she" is not clearly defined as a presence whose antithetical status battles with the masculine subject and has to be "known" and overcome. Nor is her relation to the masculine subject one which enables a return to complete self-consciousness. She is completely other and unknowable, always exceeding whatever desire the subject may have to possess her. The relation he speaks of does not affirm a "neutral" (in other words "universal" and presumed-to-be-masculine) category of consciousness but is constituted by *difference*. The asymmetry and the responsibility of being lie in the unbridgeable nature of this difference – with all its

---

[28] This unseen optics is reminiscent of Kierkegaard's portrait of the "light and shadow" of irony which cannot be actively seen.

[29] Levinas uses a violent and militaristic vocabulary, similar to Kierkegaard's, to describe the way in which Hegel's ontology consumes any possibility of otherness. See Levinas 1969, 37-38. This imagery is analyzed in Cornell 1992, 96-97.

[30] The excessiveness of the Other and the futurity of its arrival mean that it can never entirely be accounted for, and one can never be ethical enough in encountering it. See Levinas 1977 for a description of this ethical "vigilance" as a kind of "insomnia".

connotations of desire, expectation and equivocality – and is epitomized by the erotic relation between the two sexes.[31]

Thus while his depiction of the asymmetrical relation to alterity resembles Kierkegaard's analogy between the absurd, longed-for instant and the feminine, Levinas' other cannot be curtailed and sacrificed. Whereas Kierkegaard's structure ultimately tries to resolve the anxious / erotic tension by incarnating it into an impossible philosophical "present", Levinas' structure accepts that the negative capability of both never "happens". It remains an anxious possibility which is yet to be embraced.[32] If the relation between the "*il y a*" and the "instant" is figured in transcendent terms it is because it disrupts the conventional reading of (universal) Being and (historical) existence through the lens of phenomenal time; and not because it is anticipating some revelation of the absolute. Rather than awaiting rescue from the "sea of argument", like Socrates and Kierkegaard, Levinas' ethical register works by resisting this desire for resolution:

> Language as *saying* is an ethical openness to the other; as that which is *said* – reduced to a fixed identity or synchronized presence – it is an ontological closure to the other (1984, 65).

As the temporal paradox loses its belief in an original, phenomenal "essence" – the first Truth or Idea that philosophy seeks to retrieve – the feminine other is no longer fetishized as a substitute object of truth. Instead, she is the "not-yet" presence which cannot be possessed and thus behaves as a reminder *before* and to the existential "subject" of what is beyond itself. Through their endlessly shifting erotic relation is found a "way of remaining in the no-man's-land between being and not-yet-being" (1969, 259).

Levinas' rereading of time and existence turns the Kierkegaardian paradox inside out, and makes an ethical structure which revolves

---

[31] Levinas says that it is "in eros that transcendence can be conceived as something radical", in other words as what exceeds and redefines the conventional notion of time and presence (1978, 96). Levinas always refers to the face-to-face relation in erotic terms (the "caress"; the "tender" etc.).

[32] The contrast in Levinas' attitude towards "existence" is made clear in his analysis of Heideggerian anxiety, where existence is built on the promise of nothing: "Existence itself, as through the effect of intentionality, is animated by a meaning, by the primordial ontological meaning of nothingness. It does not derive from what one can know *about* the destiny of man, or *about* his ends; existence in its very event of existence signifies, in anxiety, nothingness, as if the verb to exist had a direct complement" (1985, 39-41). The (anxious) asymmetry of the face-to-face relation is the whole point of Levinas' structure, rather than its embarrassing failure.

around – is even rescued by – the anxiety of alterity.[33] No longer agitating for resolution and return, it is defined through a relation of difference where the singularity of terms is affirmed without becoming essential. Irony is thus a perpetual condition of the structure – the constant recognition of the asymmetrical relation to the other – without being objectified and curtailed. Similarly, the feminine maintains her power to rattle the closure of the masculine philosophical subject without being defined possessively as its negative opposite. It might, then, be possible to say that the temptation to "leap" out of the anxious predicament of the philosophical dialectic, as Kierkegaard does, has been mitigated.

The Other Hierarchy

There *is*, however, a difficulty with Levinas' radically ethical writing, which arises from his insisting on the transcendence of the face-to-face relation. If the Other is *always* beyond the realm of beings and the relation between the Other and this realm is inherently asymmetrical, it is difficult to see how the status of the Other can be as transformed by the encounter, as is the "existent" subject. While the transcendence of the relation eases the pressure to reveal a (self-) presence and thus appropriate the Other, does it not perpetuate a certain idealization of the Other which inhibits the realization of its own, independent specificity? Does this not mean that the "ironic feminine" still lacks any individual agency with regard to existential / historical time, other than in its somewhat passive relation to the (masculine) subject?

Derrida has something to say about this. Although his deconstructive project is very similar to Levinas' in its exploration of the anxiety of the other, he is suspicious of Levinas' continued reliance on the language of (religious) revelation and its connotation with the idea of the absolute.[34] Derrida agrees with Kierkegaard that

---

[33] The "tenderness" of the face-to-face relation is based primarily in its ability to rescue the "existant" from the solitude of closed subjectivity. Levinas calls the "manifestation" of the face "the first discourse" and says that to speak this discourse is "a way of coming from behind one's appearance, behind one's form – an opening into the openness" (1986, 352). It can thus be interpreted as the means to a certain form of freedom; but one based in taking responsibility.

[34] For a more detailed reading of the relation and differences between Levinas and Derrida, which is supportive of Levinas, see Critchley 1992.

"the instant of decision is madness" and defines the "experience" of the "subject" in relation to the Other in a similar vein to Levinas. It

> … remains irreducible to presence or to presentation, it demands a temporality of the instant without ever constituting a present. If it can be said, it belongs to an atemporal temporality, to a duration that cannot be grasped: something one can neither stabilize, establish, grasp [prendre], apprehend, or comprehend […] Understanding, common sense, and reason cannot seize [begriefen], conceive, understand or mediate it; neither can they negate or deny it, implicate it in the work of negation, make it work … (1995, 65).

However, he fears that Levinas' transcendent terminology may allow the "unsayability" of this "Saying of the unsayable" to become the universal condition of any "saying" at all; and thus hold back from the acknowledgment of risk and contingency that is such an important part of his privileging of the ethical.

While the religious register is important to Levinas because it cannot be divorced from the existent / historical, and because it pushes philosophical determination away from epistemology and ontology, to Derrida it still risks repeating the (Kierkegaardian) sacrifice of temporal ethics for the sake of the religious Other. Paradoxically, this is because of the way in which Levinas insists on the singularity of the instant as that which is as much within the sphere of human interaction and expression as in the singular encounter with the absolute, infinite Other. This is not to say, of course, that Kierkegaard's division between the absolute and singular responsibility in the situation of divine revelation and the merely "general" responsibility of human ethics (which repeats the same) is a preferable structure for Derrida.[35] Derrida unravels this separation throughout *The Gift of Death* [*Donner le mort*], and both Derrida and Levinas are concerned with a singularity which is not simply reducible to Being. But Derrida points out that since Levinas maintains the idea of God (insofar as there is an Infinite "event" of Otherness, an encounter that comes from the direction of "Illeity") as well as the many historical, human others, and since the historical others are as singularly Other as God, then these others may slip into being seen as absolutely other to philosophical totality; their infinite

---

[35] Derrida comments succinctly on the problem of this separation, highlighting its mimetic relation to an original "presence". Analysing its occurrence in *Fear and Trembling*, when Kierkegaard speaks of the (impossible) need for this singular faith to be repeated historically, Derrida comments: "It […] describes the non-history of absolute beginnings, which are repeated, and the very historicity that presupposes a tradition to be reinvented each step of the way, in this incessant repetition of the absolute beginning" (1995, 80).

otherness may become an absolute identity.[36] While Kierkegaard cannot "distinguish so conveniently between the ethical and the religious" – at least, not without resorting to the dissimulative "strategies" of his dialectic of inwardness – Levinas is "no longer able to distinguish between the infinite alterity of God and that of every human. His ethics is already a religious one" (1995, 84). Of course, Levinas would readily admit that his ethics is religious, but religious in this context means something more theological than Levinas would assume his ethical structure to be. It suggests a conception of religion which is at more of a remove from the existent / historical realm than Levinas' purposely anxious ethical description should be; one which behaves as a law or limit, initiating the whole system. If this is the case, the ethical subject will be subjected or called to account by an alterity which is *determinedly* other, other in the face-to-face relation *as a rule*. Ironically, then, the extreme responsibility and non-violence of Levinas' ethical structure (which never forces "choice" or "presence") carries with it a different threat of violence by effacing the *specificity* of the other in its equation with absolute otherness. It risks creating another abstracted "position" for the Other, where its rôle within and possible interruption of the existent / historical order will always be secondary to the *law* of its otherness.

It is at this point that the debate over the anxiety of alterity and the temporal order has clear implications for feminism. For while the feminist project is all about making room for the other, admitting the risk of difference in the structure, its search for agency is also necessarily based in the specificity of the individual experience or subject of "woman". The specificity of the feminine other does not seem possible in Levinas' structure in a form which upholds his questioning of idealized conceptions of Being-as-presence. Indeed, in texts such as "En ce moment même dans cet ouvrage me voici"

---

36 Levinas' ethical emphasis explains his use of the word "Illeity" to describe the individual's non-conceptual relation with the infinite. It is less possible to associate it with an onto-theological conception of God and yet it is bound up with the singularity of the ethical encounter: it derives from the trace of the Other (the "Pro -nom" "il") which the ethical subject encounters in its subjection to the Other. See Levinas 1974 and 1981. Levinas is trying to avoid the Heideggerian notion of the "given" of Being (*Dasein*] as "Being-with-Others", because he considers this to be too ontological, too close to the Platonic emphasis on "social fusion". Derrida is less suspicious of Heidegger because he reads *Dasein* as a double movement of presentation to the world and *withdrawal* from it; so that it is a *differentiated* notion of ontology. For other discussions of the differing attitudes of Levinas and Derrida to these questions, see Critchley 1992, 108-120 Cornell 1992, 62-90.

(1987c), Derrida highlights the tendency of Levinasian ethics to write the specificity of femininity as that which comes second to (masculine) spirituality, even while the (masculine) ethical "subject" only "is" in its meeting of the call of an Other (thus challenging the metaphysical dichotomy of immanence and transcendence).[37]

From an explicitly feminist perspective, Luce Irigaray echoes these remarks on the "secondariness" of woman in her otherwise sympathetic engagement with Levinasian ethics. Irigaray's perpetual problem is the permanently negative "position" assigned to the feminine in philosophy and psychoanalysis, and like Levinas she challenges the Hegelian figuration of the feminine other as the "negative capability" of the dialectic. Yet while in response she adopts a Levinasian register to write an ethical account of sexual difference – as a way of remembering what is walled up, like Antigone, in the dialectic – she also realizes that the ethical respect for the Other as *transcendent* Other leads to a failure to "recognize the feminine other and the self as other in relation to her" (Irigaray 1991a, 181).[38] The radical nature of the perpetual "beyondness" of the Other and its lack of "definition" surrounds it with a mystery which strongly resembles the way in which the negative, excluded feminine has been figured throughout the history of philosophy. Irigaray asks

> … how to define this Other which seems so self-evident to [Levinas], and which I see as a postulate, the projection or the remnant of a system. […] Who is the other, if the other of sexual difference is not recognized or known? (181)

That this mystery is the basis of the erotic and ethical relation to the feminine other negates the tenderness or closeness that Levinas claims is reached through it (Irigaray calls it an "autistic, egological, solitary love") and denies the feminine term the subjectivity which the masculine term already seems to possess (180):

> The feminine other is left without her own specific face. On this point, his philosophy falls radically short of ethics. To go beyond the face of metaphysics would mean precisely to leave the woman her face, and even to assist her to discover it and to keep it (183-4).[39]

---

[37] Derrida comments on this text in the context of a discussion on sexual difference in the interview, "Choreographies" (1985, 176-179).

[38] Irigaray writes her own version of Levinasian ethics, with a heightened sense of the question of sexual difference, in "Fécondité de la caresse: lecture de Lévinas, *Totalité et infini*, section IV, B, 'Phénomenologie de l'éros'" (1984, 173-199); translated as "The Fecundity of the Caress …", in Irigaray 1993, 185-287.

[39] Irigaray is adopting and altering Levinas' vocabulary: her usual catachrestic strategy. This signifies that her own writing is (historically) implicated in the

Like Derrida, Irigaray blames this lack of feminine specificity on Levinas' failure to distinguish between philosophy and theology; and more precisely, his failure to interrogate the "sexual attribution [*caractère sexué*]" of the theological model he uses (185). Although Levinas' ethical register challenges the phallic solipsism of the metaphysical subject, the transcendent, theological aspect of this register is still "monotheistic. It still roots itself in a singularity which is assumed to come *before* (sexual) difference; but which is nevertheless always figured as "God-the-father". The ethical relation is thus founded on a patriarchal, sexually *indifferent* spirituality which separates itself from a corporeal relation to the other. Irigaray continually points to the conspicuous absence of physical, bodily metaphors in Levinas' descriptions of the "erotics" of the face-to-face relation. The feminine other, her different, sexual body, and the erotic relation to her, thus always seem to come second.

Levinas' wholehearted embracing of ethics thus seems to bring about less of an interruption in the Hegelian "circle" – at least as far as the question of sexual difference is concerned – than one might have hoped. His model takes ethics as far as seems possible in subjecting the conventional philosophical subject to perpetual reminders of its indebtedness to and responsibility for the other. It is like Kierkegaard's ironic structure of existence without the (comforting) possibility of incarnation; or Kristeva's "herethics" without the need to determine (her) "knowledge". Yet there is still a residual

---

patriarchal structures she is tackling; especially since "she" is denied an independent subjectivity by those structures. In the case of Levinas she is also signifying her closeness to his basic ethical principles, if not with their practice. The catachresis is more marked in "Fécondité de la caresse" (1984), where Irigaray is working out her own ethical register. Here she uses the active term "l'amante" to indicate the role of the female lover in the erotic relation, as well as the passive term "l'aimée," which Levinas employs. As she explains, "I wanted to signify that the woman can be a subject in love [*un sujet amoureux*] and is not reducible to a more or less immediate object of desire" (1991a, 185). While it could be argued that Derrida's attempt at catachresis is rather awkward in comparison to Irigaray's, "En ce moment même dans cet ouvrage me voici" uses a similar strategy to mark the silenced singularity of the feminine in Levinas' texts. Derrida explains his adoption of a feminine "voice" as an effort to write "a choreographic text with polysexual signatures" as a contrast to the "mono-sexual discourse" which threatens "to immobilize (in silence), stop or unilateralize [...] what remains no doubt irreducibly dissymmetrical" (1985, 183). He is careful to point out that the dissymmetry to which he refers "is still [...] not symmetrical in turn", by which he means that the dissymmetry does not always follow the same order: the feminine other always coming second; the masculine relation to her "never ethical enough" (184). I will return to this notion of a "double dissymmetry" in the next chapter.

idealization of the other which seems to *place* her, rather than free her possibilities and difference. However, the limitations of this ethical approach may allow us to redirect our thoughts about ironic and feminist agency once again. The specific problems of Levinasian ethics also prompt a more general question about the transformatory possibilities of an ironic ethical agency. For if *even* Levinas repeats to a degree the static idealization of the other, we might be forced to ask if this repetition is inevitable within an ethical structure? At least in an ethical structure which understands its responsibility to difference as deriving from a transcendent phenomenon (God, the Other, Illeity); even if its transcendence is not absolute and its phenomenal arrival is never assumed? Even if it disrupts dialectical circularity, does the notion of an ethical "subject" within such a structure always necessitate the sacrifice of the potentially radical *specificity* of the other?

Irigaray and Derrida

Beyond their critiques of Levinas, the differences between Irigaray's and Derrida's portraits of sexual difference and sexual ethics bring these questions into focus.

Irigaray's response to the "facelessness" of Levinas' femininity is to demand a feminine version of the ethically obliged subject to match Levinas' masculine one. Irigaray believes that by creating a positive, subjective figuration out of the feminine characteristics that have been habitually negated by theories of masculine subjectivity, the first step is taken towards disbanding the sexually polarized systems of Western thought.[40] As long as woman is perceived as the other of the male rather than as a positive element in her own right, the *difference* of sexual difference – indeed, the difference of being – will remain unthought. For Irigaray, difference is that which "lies *between* what is already identified and what has still to be identified" and its "full

[40] Irigaray attributes this polarized view to "Aristotelianism and the philosophical systems which are derived from it" (1984, 17; 1993, 10). Tina Chanter writes interestingly on Irigaray's double relation to Levinas. She emphasizes the importance of Levinas for Irigaray in "his refusal to submit the otherness of the other to the demands of logic" which leaves a "space" in which "to think difference without reverting to sameness" (1995, 221). However, she also points out that Levinas' figurations of the feminine figure are confined to the traditional dualisms of the erotic and the maternal: "It is not, perhaps, too extreme to accuse Levinas of expressing the traditional denigration and deification of the feminine in the restricted possibilities he extends to the feminine" (199).

dynamic reserve" can only be realized once the temporal, spatial, spiritual, corporeal and mental attributes of individual beings have been dissociated from the positive / negative values of their sexually divided positions (1984, 15-16; 1993, 8).

> If there is no double desire [ie. for woman as well as man], the positive and negative poles divide themselves among the two sexes instead of creating a chiasmus or double loop in which each can go toward the other and come back to itself (1984, 16; 1993, 9).

The ethical system which Irigaray seeks to construct maintains Levinas' emphasis on the shifting relations of difference, but roots this relation in the subjectification of the feminine other as much as in the interrogation of the (already-subjective) masculine term. The "not-yet-being" of the ethical relation thus becomes something more phenomenal; a space or "envelope" which resembles the physical connection of sexual coupling but without its usual connotations of consummation and possession.[41] This "communion" of difference should be conceived of as the primary event of "Being" – coming before any abstract categories of existence – but should always maintain the gap "*between man and woman*" (1984, 20; 1993, 13).

> … it must […] welcome the advent of difference, […] think of itself as waiting on this side of difference, rather than as existing already on the other side of difference, most notably as an ethics. The phrase *there is* usually upholds the present but postpones any celebrations. There is not and will never be any sense of that wonder conjured up by a *wedding*, an ecstasy that none the less remains *agency* (1984, 21; 1993, 14).

Eventfulness is continually emphasized in this description, revealing Irigaray's impatience with Levinas' transcendent asymmetry of terms. She sees no reason why if (masculine) subjectivity can be opened up to its (feminine) alterity through its relation to transcendence, (feminine) alterity should not also be opened up to its (masculine) subjectivity through a relation to the phenomenal and physical. Hence she speaks of "the opening of a *sensible transcendental* that comes into being through us, of which *we would be* the mediators and bridges" (1984, 124; 1993, 129).

And yet, oddly enough, her figurations of gender do not seem much less idealized than Levinas', and she still seems to rely on the idea of a

---

[41] This "envelope" is an alteration of what Irigaray considers to be the historical metaphor of femininity as a cipher or "threshold" for the active male principle: "the maternal-feminine […] serves as an *envelope*, a *container*, the starting point from which man limits his things" (1984, 17; 1993, 10).

divine incarnation as being the only way in which the new ethics can be brought about. The "mystery" and "wonder" of the sexual relation, which is so crucial for the mutual connection-without-consummation, is called "a love so scrupulous that it is divine" (1984, 25, my translation); and Irigaray notes that "certain figures of gods become men, of God become man, and of twice-born beings indicate the path of love". Moreover, the corporeality or carnality of her ethics relies on the actualization of female sexual characteristics which, while challenging the Aristotelian or Freudian model of them as "absence", does not seem any more open to difference; whether to the male sex, to other sexual characteristics or to their possible non-heterosexual function. The "active" sexuality of feminine morphology consists of the "*half-open* threshold" of her labia which "serve neither conception nor *jouissance*", but whose significance nevertheless comes about through a simulation of procreative copulation (1984, 24; 1993, 18). In "The Fecundity of the Caress" Irigaray describes the new ethics as a symbolic birth through love-making which precedes actual conception:

> If she comes back to herself, to herself within herself, to him within herself, she may feel responsible for another parousia. She may need to create, engender, give birth to the mystery she bears – prior to any conception of a child ... The lover would assist her in this parturition, provided he does not simply send her back to the depths. The one for the other, messengers of a future that is still to be built and contemplated [...] The one for the other, mediators of a secret, a force, and an order that also touches on the divine (1984; 184; 1993, 199).

While the echo of Levinas' register in this writing is clearly part of Irigaray's ironic, catachrestic method, this does not quite seem to be the radical displacement of habitual sexual configurations that Irigaray's prophetic tone anticipates. It is highly questionable whether a mime of a conventional marriage, which simply attributes a more positive role to the physical marks of female sexuality, really alters the "monosexual" parameters of the religious hierarchy. Although her irony succeeds in challenging Levinas' restricted figurations of femininity, it upholds his prophetic register, so leaves the polarizing structures in place.[42] Irigaray's ethics reads as an inverted repetition of

[42] The feminist debate surrounding Irigaray's mimetic / ironic rewriting of male philosophers is a fraught one. Arguments usually run along the lines of one side claiming that Irigaray's emphasis on figuring a "positive" female term is a crucial marker of political agency within her deconstructive critique of "phallocentric" traditions; while the other side claims that her figuration of this positive term through corporeal imagery panders to the "phallocentric" tradition of figuring femininity as "matter" rather than "mind" or "spirit". See Margaret Whitford's introduction to *The*

the Levinasian model rather than as a disbanding of its religious and sexual divisions. The "asymmetry" of the ethical relation is still reliant on a mysterious something which is yet to be revealed, but rather than being a non-actualisable alterity it will be a physically present alterity. This does little to disrupt the residual idealization of the absent other under Levinas' ethics: it simply translates it into a residual idealization of the other's possible presence. While it does not quite return us to the metaphysical notion of being as a fully "present" phenomenon, it does create a too-ontological reading of sexual difference where the (future) physical "experience" of the feminine gives the most truthful account of Being. Not only does this establish another kind of unhelpful sexual polarity (between a natural, "elemental", physical sexuality and the false sexual abstractions of patriarchal culture) but it does not address the ethical difficulties of the subjectification of the other: for there is no logical reason why the immanent arrival of a feminine, physical, or spatial presence should be less consuming and possessive than the old masculine subject, just because historically it has been other to this presence.[43] What we end up with is a slightly more phenomenal version of Levinas' sexual hierarchy: a pair of lips as the (awaited) present otherness of the feminine other; rather than the never-to-be-present otherness of the feminine other:

> Is this the mystery of the feminine identity? Of its self-contemplation, of this very strange world of silence? Both the threshold and reception of exchange, the sealed-up secret of wisdom, belief, and faith in all truths? (1984, 24; 1993, 18)

Irigaray Reader, where she claims that Irigaray's "positive" femininity "point[s] to the dangers for women of embracing postmodernism too hastily or too uncritically" and "warns against displacing the male / female binary before the female side has acceded to identity and subjectivity" (1991, 13). On the other side, see Judith Butler's criticism of Irigaray (1993, 36-55), which centres on her "idealizing and appropriating [of] the 'elsewhere' as the feminine" (49). I would argue that Irigaray's obsession with the physical manifestation of femininity is not "essentialist" insofar as it is an ironized repetition of the traditional excluded "position" of femininity and demonstrates that Irigaray is (rightly) suspicious of the notion of an *external* feminist agency. However, Irigaray's irony curtails its own potential for subversion because it does not interrogate its own dialectic of immanence.

[43] Both of these problems indicate that Irigaray is still caught in the mimetic movement of negation followed by revelation. The "god" she conceives of who would take "us" "beyond the circularity of discourse, of the nothing that is in and of being" is one which "refer[s] back to a time before our space-time was formed into a closed world by an economy of natural elements forced to bow down to man's affect and will" (1984, 123-4; 1993, 128-9). This is a clear idealization of some natural "other" space. I will return to this difficulty with Irigaray's work in chapter 5.

In spite of its rhetorical uncertainty, or because its irony does not go far enough in interrogating its own faith in the future revelation of its "mystery", this description reinscribes the idealization and fetishization of the feminine other as much as it decentres it.

Derrida's response to this problem is ironic, insofar as it doubles and undermines the hierarchy of terms within the dialectical circle. However, he lays an even greater emphasis on the anxious undecidability of the "present": to such an extent that the established notion of ethics – as a non-violent, non-consuming respect for the other – is dislocated.

While Irigaray believes that a new, non-violent relation between the philosophical "subject" and its other, and between masculinity and femininity, is possible by marking the potential subjectivity of the other as well as the alterity of the subject, Derrida believes that to think of the other in terms of its possible "presence" is to destroy its specificity. If its power to challenge the prevailing hierarchy of terms lies in its *difference* to the self-determined, fully "present" subject, then to evaluate it phenomenally is to curtail its power and to repeat the dialectic which repositions it as the possession of (subjective) being:

> To *insist* upon thinking *its other*: its proper other, the proper of its other, an other proper? In thinking it *as such*, in recognizing it, one misses it. One reappropriates it for oneself, one disposes of it, one misses it, or rather one misses (the) missing (of) it, which, as concerns the other, always amounts to the same. Between the proper of the other and the other of the proper (1982a, xi-xii).[44]

The significance of this pun-laden statement to sexual ethics is not, perhaps, immediately apparent. However, the syntactical complications are what convey his point. In trying to "think" the other from the position of an essential being (as philosophical subject, author or even the system as a whole) it is inevitable that the other will be thought of as another such entity or being, since it is the other *of* being. As such, it cannot entirely be the other because in a sense it still belongs to being. Hence the play on the French word "propre",

[44] Derrida is not writing here about Irigaray or Levinas, but this general comment about philosophy's tendency to define and "fix" its own identity by thinking the other, is the tendency which Derrida believes is perpetuated by Levinas' and Irigaray's (residual) idealizations of the Other.

with its connotations of (self-) possession, purity, propriety and legality.[45]

This paradoxical statement reverberates with Kierkegaard's paradox of the instant and Levinas' and Irigaray's asymmetrical "experience" of time and being. However, it is far more unsettling because it suggests that as long as the two poles of "self" and "other", "subject" and "object" exist as categories which represent "presence" – even residually – no real difference can be realized. This is why Derrida finds Levinas' (residual) religiosity problematic: it upholds the sense of immanent revelation and of an *absolute* alterity, both of which imply a continued association with the language and logic of (in this case divine) "presence". As Derrida says,

> In order to reject the Kierkegaardian notion of subjective existence Levinas should eliminate even the notions of an *essence* and a *truth* of subjective existence (of the Ego, and primarily of the Ego of the Other) (1978a, 110).

It is the sense in Levinas' ethical structure of the Other having an "ego" that most worries Derrida. This also means that a response such as Irigaray's, which replaces Levinas' disjunction between infinite Being and being with the physical / sexual differences of being, is fooling itself if it claims to have decentered the established sexual and ethical hierarchy.[46] Any order which leaves the belief in the other as a revealable "presence" intact does not change the pattern of the dialectic, with its positive / negative, sublating movement. In Levinas' terms, the generosity of the "*il y a*" of Being will fall back into a tit-for-tat exchange. The potential difference of Irigaray's ironic, mimetic analysis will thus be curtailed by a too certain sense of what is "beyond" its current uncertainty.

---

[45] This play on the different meanings of "propre" (as "proper", "clean", the possessive pronoun indicating ownership, and as the root of "appropriate / appropriation") recurs throughout Derrida's writing, and is often connected to the "moral" fear in Western philosophy of the feminine's "impropriety" in not being known and defined by the masculine term. For an example of Derrida tracing such a fear – in Lacan's "fixing" of feminine sexuality – see "Le facteur de la verité" (1987b, 480-82, n. 60).

[46] This is especially the case with Irigaray's ethics, whose prophetic register and emphasis on physicality is sometimes suggestive of a space "before" or "beyond" language. Levinas' language is more careful not to suggest such a thing. As Simon Critchley points out, Levinas' writing "enacts […] a 'spiralling movement' […] in which language oscillates enigmatically, or undecidedly, between the Saying and the Said. […] It is not a question of simply overcoming language in the name of some irreducibly ontic 'beyond'" (Critchley 1992, 123).

There is, of course, a very fine-line distinction being drawn here, as all three theorists intersect on different levels. Derrida and Levinas are more wary of phenomenology than Irigaray; Irigaray and Derrida feel Levinas' religious structure needs further interrogation; Irigaray and Levinas seek to emphasize the *possibilities* of an ethics – even if it is flawed – rather than interrogating the idea of ethics as Derrida does. However, in terms of their different depictions of the force of irony in relation to the feminine other, Levinas' and Irigaray's continued use of an irony which still operates through a dialectic of presence and non-presence is what separates them from Derrida, and what he objects to in their rewritings of the philosophical hierarchy. It is also what divides Irigaray's and Derrida's ironic readings of Levinas; for while Irigaray's catachrestic method in "Questions to Emmanuel Levinas' and "The Fecundity of the Caress" marks the absence of an active female "lover" in Levinas' structure, Derrida's text, "En ce moment même dans cet ouvrage me voici" ironizes sexual dissymmetry *as it results from* Levinas' assumption of the inevitability of the philosophical subject. Derrida's catachresis in this piece is thus double, as it performs both the (permanent) absence of the feminine term and the undesirability of making her present as a "subject": hence the irony of the title.

Derrida is concerned above all to deconstruct the belief in the end of uncertainty. For him it parallels the constant refrain of the "logocentrism" of Western metaphysics: the measurement of everything according to idealized categories of "centre" and "presence" which extinguishes anything "peculiar".[47] Any claim to jump beyond into a "new" political, ethical or sexual structure will always bear the imprint of this belief, as

> … a *relève* of the binary oppositions of classical idealism, a resolution of contradiction into a raising up, while idealizing, while sublimating into an anamnesic interiority (*Erinnerung*), while *interning* difference in a self-presence. (1987a, 43)[48]

---

[47] Derrida cites several examples of Hegel's exclusion of "peculiarities" from the philosophical body as the epigraph to "Tympan", where he makes his point about thinking the "proper of the other" (1982a, ix). Elsewhere Derrida summarizes "logocentrism" as "a series of substitutions, of center for center, as a linked chain of determinations of the center". Its "matrix" is "the determination of Being as *presence* in all senses of this word …" (1978b, 279).

[48] "Relève" is Derrida's French translation of the Hegelian term "Aufhebung", which retains the German sense of "preserving", "negating" and "lifting up" to a higher, spiritual realm.

The process of acknowledging alterity must instead be undertaken as something which will forever *disrupt* the sense of ending, transcending, and incorporating which comes with the logic of (absolute) presence. As such, the process can no longer be initiated from the *position* of subjective presence, or under some category of "present" identity. Neither can it simply overcome the logic of presence with a wholly "new" logic which "presents" itself as being uncontaminated by the oppressive one it resists. As with Kierkegaard, the irony of such a movement will always return. Derrida points out that Levinas' Ethics manages to write itself beyond the legal and conceptual resolutions of the Hegelian *relève*. As the "saying" rather than the "said" it is not a "*theory* of Ethics" but an "Ethics of Ethics", "the essence of the ethical relation in general" (1978a, 111). However, because the "beyondness" of this Ethics remains generalized, and its relation to the logic it exceeds is not sufficiently signalled, the Ethics might not be beyond all laws but be the "Law of laws": "a coherence which breaks down the coherence of the discourse against coherence – the infinite concept, hidden within the protest against the concept".

Beyond the Ethical

In order to think the otherness of the other, then, a continual movement must be made which exceeds the logic of presence and its circularity, while interrogating in an equally excessive way the determination of its own excess. Derrida outlines such a movement as a "double gesture" or "double writing": a mode of analysis which upsets, dislodges and overturns philosophy's "hierarchy of dual oppositions" while recognizing that this movement is one of an "interminable analysis" (1987a, 42). Thus it is not part of "a chronological phase, a given moment, or a page that one day simply will be turned in order to go on to other things" (41-2).

The gesture is very close to Levinas' "saying of the unsayable" insofar as it recognizes the other as something utterly different to what is "present", and which challenges its insularity and closure, rather than as an opposed "exteriority" which helps to develop an initial self-presence. The difference with Derrida's "gesture" is that it claims to avoid the idealization of the other's absence by marking what is other to the apparent *necessity* or law of its otherness. Breaking with the personification of the other, Derrida describes what he calls "undecidables" within the textual field:

> … that is, unities of simulacrum, "false" verbal properties (nominal or semantic) that can no longer be included within philosophical (binary) opposition, but which, however, inhabit philosophical opposition, resisting and disorganizing it, *without ever* constituting a third term, without ever leaving room for a solution in the form of speculative dialectics (43).

These "undecidables", it seems, are the force of alterity working within *every* localized decision or determination; whether it be theoretical, conceptual, textual or experiential. So localized are they that to cast them as phenomena, categories or even as an absence of Being is to miss their singularity completely (or "miss" the "missing" of them). They exist, but not in the sense of the word that denotes a concrete entity. They are not the generalizable Other of abstract philosophical Law, but contingent forces which inhabit the boundary of even the smallest "instant" of determination.[49] Their excessiveness lies in the fact that they may *interrupt* laws and determinations – including their own determination – at any moment. Their alterity can thus be neither regulative (as it is in Kristeva and Hegel) nor messianic (as it is in Kierkegaard or, ultimately, Levinas and Irigaray). As such they even "resist" and "disorganize" the determination of the "new" writing, even if it is an open, ethically-responsible one. This explains the "doubleness" of Derrida's "double gesture", which accepts that a new structure or hierarchy will not overcome the old one completely.

Derrida's reinterpretation of the force of alterity through these "undecidables" is an obscure and unexpected manoeuvre which will inevitably require further explanation. Its relevance to the question of how to write a new sexual order, which is open to otherness, lies in the fact that Derrida seems to be writing of the necessity of "saying", but of saying without being able to fully determine what is said. He writes of a

> … madness […] acting in the night of non-knowledge and non-rule. Not of the absence of rules and knowledge but of a reinstitution of rules which by definition is not preceded by any knowledge or by any guarantee as such (1992c, 26).[50]

---

[49] In fact, according to Derrida they are a means to writing "an inscription of the relations between the philosophical and the nonphilosophical, in a kind of unheard of *graphics*, within which philosophical conceptuality would be no more than a *function*" (1978a, 110-11).

[50] Referring to Kierkegaard in the same passage, Derrida states that this madness "is particularly true of the just decision that must rend time and defy dialectics", which is an apt description of the practice and purpose of deconstruction. Note that the word used is "rend", which is expressive of interruption rather than negation.

Derrida realizes that some form of decision, even a "reinstitution of rules", is necessary if one is to speak at all: the alternative to this would be nihilism. He also realizes that it is impossible to make such a decision without there being some curtailment of "other" possibilities. Any decision, any textual or conceptual mark "never proceeds without a certain dissymmetry and some quality of violence". What is important to Derrida is that this dissymmetry does not attain the status of a permanent rule. Derrida's "decision" admits the violence of its own "saying" and the necessity of this violence if any "other" singularity is to be figurable. Yet he insists that this does not signify a return to Hegelian immanence, or even to a Kierkegaardian repetition: far from it. For the "undecidable" aspect of the decision interrupts any sense of authority, rationality or permanence behind it:

> the moment of *decision, as such*, always remains a finite moment of urgency and precipitation, [...] since it always marks the interruption of the juridico- or ethico- or politico-cognitive deliberation that precedes it, that *must* precede it. [...] it no longer responds to the demands of theoretical rationality (26-7).

The decision is thus read as something which occurs unpredictably, contingently, rather than as the culmination of a proscribed path; a necessary "stage" in a larger plan. This applies as much to decisions about the other as conventional philosophical decisions, and thus extends to any "new" intervention – any agency – which seeks to be more responsible for what it excludes. The problem with Levinas' "Ethics of Ethics" and Irigaray's sexual ethics is not so much that they commit a violence against the other in naming "her" as Other, as that they do not admit that this violence is implicit in any such naming. Their languages of revelation (Levinas' religious revelation, Irigaray's physical revelation) risk leading them "too quickly to a *neutralization*" of philosophy's "violent hierarchy", which is itself a violation of the possibility of further, "other" interruptions (41).[51] In order that the singularity of these interruptions be respected, it is necessary that the ethical "decision" should also be interruptible, at least as anything that can be spoken of in the abstract:

---

[51] For an illuminating account of the "decidability" of ethics in this context, see Elam 1994, 105-120. Elam says that she "would strongly suggest that ethical consequences are precisely *not* decidable – calculated once and for all; statistical inference should not be understood as a final judgment" (118).

> The concept of responsibility, like that of decision, would thus be found to lack coherence, even lacking identity with respect to itself, paralyzed by what can be called an aporia or an antimony (Derrida 1995, 84).

Note the shift in register and terminology, from something that suggests resolution, revelation (paradox) to something that suggests no resolution (aporia). The significance of this shift cannot be over-emphasized, because it is through the specific *style* of writing that Derrida defines the "undecidable" elements of philosophical, amongst other, decisions. How he does this is something I will tackle in the next chapter. For the time being it is sufficient to remark that Derrida echoes, while altering, the styles of the theorists whose ironic / ethical displacements of dialectical sublation we have looked at in this chapter. It retains the shocking absurdity and comedy of Kierkegaard's writing (a gesture which recognizes the difficulty of leaving behind the violations of the dialectic), and the expressive, beyond-conceptual styles of Levinas and Irigaray (a gesture which recognizes that the otherness of the other cannot be contained by conventional logic). However, the "moment of madness" can no longer be read as the shock of an identifiable Other impacting on an existential subject. Instead alterity – and its madness – is drawn as a force which interrupts the determination of "present" identity, "present" time, and even its own non-presence. The paradox, or aporia, now revolves around the question of how the radical intrusion of the other can ever have been conceived of as an abstract category or identity, including a "feminine" identity; and secondly, how the *specificity* of the other can now be signified in a way which both addresses the "violent hierarchy" of its own philosophical / linguistic history and avoids subscribing it as another regulated identity.

To be "responsible" to the other, to realize its specificity, one must interrogate or ironize twice: first by marking the ethical possibilities in what is violent and then by marking the violent possibilities in what is ethical. What bearing does this claim have on the idea of woman-as-other, or the feminist "other"? What of its impact on the connection we have been tracing between the feminine and the ironic, their movement of negative capability; and the simultaneous demand, if one follows an ethical, or "ultra-ethical", structure to repeat old hierarchies in a "new" way and to speak an "unsayable" beyond? I intend to answer these questions in the next chapter, in a sustained analysis of Derrida's deconstructive rewritings of dialectical philosophy. In the process, I will pay particular attention to his use of the "double gesture", not because it claims to move beyond, to reveal, to resolve the problem of finding a feminist agency, but because it promises to perform the anxiety of the system and the "paradox" of the ironic feminine in a radically responsible way.

Chapter 4

"Irony and Something Else": Jacques Derrida

> "If God is (probably) a man in speculative dialectics, the godness of God – the irony that divides him and makes him come off his hinges – the infinite disquiet of his essence is (if possible) woman(ly).
>
> The remain(s) here suspends itself
>
> Let us give ourselves the time of this suspense. For the moment time will be nothing but the suspense between the regularity and the irregularity of the morsels of what remains."
> Jacques Derrida (1981b, 263a & 316a; 1986b, 188a & 226a).

I. Suspension

The new problem for feminism and the new approach to the problem will, then, be a repetition. In previous chapters we have moved from woman as "the eternal irony" to woman as "determinate nothingness" to woman as necessarily sacrificed ethical "other", to woman as infinitely-awaited other. All these figurations have repeated the structural position of the feminine, or the actual manifestation of "woman", as a form of negative capability, while claiming to move beyond or break free from the prevailing system to figure something new. At the same time, these repetitions have gradually moved inwards, from considering the possible agency of the (feminine) other as being a matter of "knowledge", to being a matter of "faith", to something far less certain.

Derrida appears to follow and repeat this pattern. In his essay *The Gift of Death*, which undertakes among other things a close reading of Kierkegaard's *Fear and Trembling*, the figure of woman seems at once expendable and something which provokes uncertainty or change. Having analysed the apparent "necessity" in Kierkegaard's work of subscribing and sacrificing the other, of disregarding the human ethical in order to be supremely, religiously, ethical, Derrida asks two questions:

> Would the logic of sacrificial responsibility within the implacable universality of the law, of its law, be altered, inflected, attenuated, or displaced, if a woman were to intervene in some consequential manner? Does the system of this sacrificial responsibility [...] imply at its very basis an exclusion or sacrifice of woman? A woman's sacrifice or a sacrifice of woman, according to one sense of the genitive or the other? (1995, 76-7).

In response he says, firstly, "Let us leave the question in suspense", and secondly,

> Perhaps irony would permit us to find something like a common thread in the questions I have just posed and what Hegel said about woman: that she is "the eternal irony of the community".

This double response seems at once to be a repetition of Kierkegaard's anxious paradox, of Levinas' iteration of the paradox in a way which challenges the dialectical negation of the other, and something else altogether. It is not entirely clear what is being posited about "woman" and the "law", and what is being left "in suspense". Is the suspension of the question a suspension of the possible "intervention" of a woman, or a suspension of the necessity of the sacrifice of woman? Is either suspension conditional on the other one? Is the suspended question a repetition of "the logic of sacrificial responsibility" or an interrogation of the law of this logic? And what is the relation of the suspended question to the "common thread" of irony Derrida finds between these possibilities, and to Hegel's assignation of woman's ironic place? The duplicity of Derrida's response would seem to allow for all these possibilities, while disallowing the certainty of any.

Why this should be is what I want to analyse in this chapter. According to Derrida, it is his performance of the anxieties surrounding the "law" of intervention and decision which makes his repetition different; and as he says, "inventive".[1] As I hope to show, this is not an attempt to sublimate the anxiety, as was Kierkegaard's repetitive "indirect communication." Derrida's repetition is far more

---

[1] Derrida asserts that deconstruction "is inventive or it is nothing at all ... its writing is not only performative, it produces rules – other conventions – for new performativities ..." (1987d, 35).

willing to accept anxiety's "undecidable" nature. As a result it may seem more violent and less mindful of the ethical demand to account for the other, than most of the writers analysed in the last chapter. However, it is because Derrida does not deny the contingent determination of writing, does not avoid or generalize the specificity that is inherent to the time of this writing, that he does not simply redouble the prevailing, dialectical structure and its sacrifice of the feminine other.

The Time of Writing

It is this time of writing that is so different in Derrida's work. In Kierkegaard's writing, the ironic communication lay in not knowing its own determination in the present, and this indeterminacy was crucial for allowing the ethical relation of "love" of what was other to the abstract system. Yet the "not knowing" of the present still relied upon a linear relation to the unknown Other[2] – the religious promise of certain revelation – which meant that determination was only possible through the leap into the unknown, and a leaving behind of the temporal and the ethical. As I discussed in the last chapter, this was an impossibility in the terms of the ironic logic of the communication, which is why Kierkegaard's writings suffered the ghostly return of its own paradox. Like Levinas, Derrida radicalizes the "unknown" of the ironic communication and recognizes the impossibility of making the "other" that is its determination present. Thus the ghostly paradox is already the condition of the communication, and has lost its linear temporality. We are "speaking" or "writing" as something which happens beyond or after its determination, without this determination ever being conventionally present, either in the past or future, or in a space of revelation outside of time:

> Thus, at the moment when the question "How to avoid speaking?" arises, it is already too late. There was no longer any question of not speaking. Language has started without us, in us and before us. This is what theology calls God, and it is necessary, it will have been necessary, to speak. This "it is necessary" [*il faut*] is both the trace of undeniable necessity – which is another way of saying that one cannot avoid denying it, one can only deny it – and of a past injunction. Always already past, hence without a past present. (1989a, 29)

---

2 By "linear" I mean the causality of the "communication" depends on a certain, singular origin, which projects a sequence of events. This "linearity" can also be circular, as it is in Hegel's dialectic, where the origin of events is revealed as the end point as well.

The different structure of tenses here is of great significance The "past injunction" or "il faut" is other in a transcendent sense which can be compared to the God of theology, not because there is a linear relation between the determining "Other" (divine creator, originary source) and the time when language occurs, but precisely because there is no connection, no line of authority.[3] The "truth" of the Other has never been and never will be simply and completely present. However, neither is the Other beyond the time of speaking, which means that the "communication" is permanently interrupted, or has the potential to be interrupted, by its possible presence. The determination ("il faut") of the necessity to speak cannot thus be construed as an originary, and originally present, source of speaking: it is a "trace" which is "always already past, hence without a past present".

We are already some way from the paradox of the instant. Not only is the ground of the "deciding" moment unknown, but its unknowability seems to be the (internal) drive behind the necessity of the "communication", and the law of its repetition. Given this, it is difficult to speak of a "law" or a "repetition", or even of "communication". If the "law" is subject to (the possibility of) interruption by its own (other) determination, it cannot be transcendent in the sense of a true imperative, because it cannot have the power to regulate.[4] Similarly, the sequence in which speaking – no matter how paradoxical – has its foundation, and the linear direction that is the assumption behind the idea of communicating, are inapplicable. There is, simply, no originary presence, no primordial point of reference, from which to spring into a journey towards truth or being, knowledge or identity. This means, in turn, that truth, being, knowledge or identity cannot be the (pre-)determined end of philosophy. The "instant" is always already divided and extended by the time of its "speaking" (figuration), and thus its occurrence does not run as a straight line of mediation from "a" to "b". Derrida seems to be in the middle of the uncanny anxiety of "writing" that Kierkegaardian irony approached but could not withstand because of its (dialectical) need of return and revelation.

---

[3] Relating this to the act of reading Derrida, Nicholas Royle, calls this the "double-bind of deconstruction, in other words the necessity and impossibility of deconstructive reading. It demands and dissolves the strange time, which is never proper, never *on* time, of reading" (1995, 162).

[4] If we were speaking in Kantian terms, this would mean that the "principle of reason" has no reason of its own. For an analysis of Derrida in these terms, see Bennington 1994, 259-73.

This is not simply perversity on Derrida's part. It forms his attempt to challenge the idealized notions of "presence" and "otherness" which are perpetuated in dialectical thought, by recasting the determination of the philosophical structure through the time of its writing. Rather than striving for conceptual purity in the face of the contingencies and ambiguities of representative language, he accepts the unpredictability of philosophical "mediation" as an inherent part of its determination. Rather than assuming that whatever is not subsumable or totally figurable in the mediation of philosophy must be from a different domain altogether, Derrida takes the "other" philosophy as being, quite simply, the unsubsumable or unfigurable aspect of the mediation itself; in other words, what remains after "mediation".[5] The complicating factor with this remainder is that it is not simply left behind while philosophy continues on its destined path: it is not negated, as the teleology of the dialectic would presume. Instead it constitutes an active part in the creation and maintenance of that "destiny". The remainder, the other, to the dialectic is also its injunction; yet it is an injunction without the purity or authority of an external (atemporal) force. The position from which philosophy thinks and speaks is thus neither an incomplete precursor to completion (Hegel) nor the accidental predicament instituted by a mercurial God or Law (Kierkegaard). Instead it is determined by the divided time of the repeatable, alterable language of the "mediation" itself.

Iterability

This property of mediation and repetition which is without the teleological law of mediation and repetition is what Derrida calls "iterability". The term iterability, whose derivation, as Derrida points out, "comes from *itara*, *other* in Sanskrit [...] may be read as the exploitation of the logic which links repetition to alterity" (1982c, 315). It does not signify "simply [...] repeatability of the same, but rather alterability of this same idealized in the singularity of the event". (1988, 119) We can see in this phrase the impossibility of an *Aufhebung* or an *either/or* which I have just been tracing. The risk of otherness does not occur as the consequence of the mimetic relation between an "origin" and its "copy", but at the very point of origin. It is with iterability that Derrida's deconstructions always begin, as his

---

[5] I am purposely using the term mediation here, both to relate Derrida's notion of writing back to Kierkegaard's and because the majority of Derrida's deconstructions focus on dialectical structures.

first principle is always the impossibility of a unified and wholly present first principle:

> … iterability prohibits *a priori* (and in principle) the full and rigorous attainment of the ideal plenitude such exclusions purport to isolate. These hypothetical exclusions cannot be formed. They are illegitimate and impossible inasmuch as they suppose the self-identity of an isolated element – i.e. an element constitutive of the hypothesis – divides at once. (1977, 201-2)

Such singularities are always infused from the start with what is other to them. This is not to say that the premise of communication is total absence, but that the condition of continuing to speak, write or philosophize is as much the possibility of no presence as the possibility of presence. We are always already in the position of substituting for, prolonging or anticipating "complete" presence. Hence the "undecidable" elements Derrida speaks of repeatedly intrude upon every linguistic, textual, conceptual and categorical determination; supplementing any sense of origin and deferring any sense of end. This is the logic of "*différance*".[6]

This logic follows a double causality; or more accurately, a contaminated causality. According to Derrida, the language of philosophy is divided by an unknowable, unrevealable otherness, which means that a single meaning or identity is forever deferred. Because this meaning is deferred, the otherness cannot be captured by a conceptual idea or category and made present; and vice versa. "Condition or effect – take your pick – of iterability" (1977, 190) It is because this breaking is "something like an *originary* différance" that a repetition of the same is not (and never was) possible, and yet it is important to remember that this is also what drives and conditions any possibility in the first place (1982b, 9). Thus Derrida may seem to be repeating the logic of the "instant" when he writes of the "singularity of the event", but is in fact crossing this event through with the movement of its representation and the possible interruption of, and alteration by, what it excludes: "Neither / nor, that is, *simultaneously* either *or*; the mark [*marque*] is also the margin [*marge*], the march [*marche*]" (1972b, 59; 1987a, 43).[7]

---

[6] Unravelling the Platonic idea of the mimetic relation between original "idea" and the sign which describes it, Derrida says that in "attempting to put into question these traits of the provisional secondariness of the [sign as] substitute, one would come to see something like an originary *différance*; but one could no longer call it originary or final in the extent to which the values of origin, archi-, *telos*, *eskhaton*, etc. have always denoted presence – *ousia*, *parousia*" (1982b, 9).

[7] The punning connections between the words in the original version emphasize the "undecidability" of linguistic and textual decisions.

Simply put, presence of any kind is conditioned on alterity: not only the presence of origin, truth or meaning as received and transcribed by the philosopher / speaker, but the present consciousness of the philosopher / speaker himself, which metaphysics (invariably) figures as the instant of self-identical speaking. This alterity calls for a recognition that,

> … the intention which animates utterance will never be completely present in itself and its content. The iteration which structures it a priori introduces an essential dihiscence and demarcation (1982c, 326).

This pattern of the "idealized" singular cut by its own alterability repeats throughout Derrida's work in different guises: as the sign; as the speech act; as the philosophical subject; as the historical moment; as the ethical decision and the legal judgment; even as the "moment" of sexual differentiation. In each case the whole possibility of the "event" or "decision" depends on "an experience of the undecidable" at the very core of its determination (1988, 148).

Affirmation and Ruination

As far as the figuration of the feminine "other" is concerned, the most important aspect of this different conception of time and "communication" is that what would be interpreted as "negativity" by dialectical repetition becomes affirmative. "Iterability" is, importantly, not a negation of the singular event, or a denial of the possibility of deciding "being" or "meaning", but something much more fertile, as Derrida's description of "dehiscence" suggests:

> As in the realm of botany, from which it draws its metaphorical value, this word marks emphatically that the divided opening, in the growth of a plant, is also what, in a *positive* sense, makes production, reproduction, development possible. Dehiscence (like iterability) limits what it makes possible, while rendering its rigor and purity impossible. What is at work here is something like a law of undecidable contamination … (1977, 197).

That the division is the potential for proliferation – a kind of cross-fertilization rather than a definite absence – begins to explain why, when Derrida writes of an aporetic and contaminating law, it is a creative law, founded on an aporia which is not entirely empty. Derrida frequently emphasizes that a lack of foundation beneath the law of "decision" does not necessitate a negative or negated action:

> On the contrary, it operates so much better, to the extent that it serves to obscure the abyss or fill its absence of foundation, stabilizing a chaotic process

> of change in what are called conventions. Chaos refers precisely to the abyss or the open mouth, *that which speaks* as well as that which signifies hunger (1995, 84, my emphasis).

In fact, deconstruction is a form of writing which focuses on remains and ruins precisely because it is the remains which are considered to be the fecund force of language and philosophy. No laws, systems, institutions, monuments, events or acts (including speech acts) are immune to the "law of undecidable contamination", to the possible spoiling of their "purity", to their own mutability, but this risk of ruination is also the condition of their own and of other possibilities. This means that "ruin is not a negative thing" (1992c, 44; 1994a, 105).[8] It also means that the remains, remnants and deviations of these laws, systems and events should be cherished and remembered rather than banished, because they are irreducible and productive elements of the laws, systems and events.

The need to affirm these "other" elements has inevitable implications for the way Derrida writes and philosophizes. Plato's hierarchical distinction between "pure" and "mimetic" language, between "speaking" and "writing", cannot hold in the face of *différance*: the "risk" of deviating from the "originating" norm of language is not only present as a rule but is what promises further possibilities and creativity.[9] The "logical" philosophical register therefore gives way to something less "decidable" and more "literary", which why Derrida's own "style" of writing seems to hold off from making certain assertions. This is no longer a demonstration of crisis,

---

[8] Derrida asks "How can we love except in this finitude? Where else would the right to love, indeed the love of right, come from? [*D'où viendrait autrement le droit d"aimer, voire l'amour du droit*?]" and suggests that one could write a treatise on the love of ruins. Throughout this text there is a clear association drawn between (ethical) responsibility, (legal) right and a love of the ghostly, which draws attention to the impermanence and instability of any ethical or legal decisions and foundations. This association is similar to the one found in Kierkegaard's *Concept of Irony* in moments when the emphasis is on love as the indeterminacy of the personality rather than the necessity of its sacrifice. For further consideration of deconstruction as ruination and love (of ruination), see Royle 1995, 124-142.

[9] Plato considers writing as a "mimetic" form which works through intellectual recollection (*epistemis*) rather than sensual imagery, and is thus untrustworthy because it lacks the authority of the present speaker, verifying the image (1973, 276a). This criticism is linked to Plato's famous discrediting of poetic (mimetic) forms of narration as compared with the "purer" form of diegesis, on the basis that the former involves the narrator speaking as someone else, whereas the latter involves the narrator speaking as himself. See 1987a, 392 d & 394b. For a more detailed analysis of Platonic ideas of speech, writing and mimesis in relation to post-structuralist ideas, see Melburg 1995 and Sallis 1995.

of anxiety in the face of the (negative) "unknown", but a sign of the writing remaining open to "other" textual possibilities and alive to its own uncanny interrupted time.[10] Derrida performs a kind of serious play or comic anxiety which takes account of the impossibility of pure positions and oppositions – including "positivity" and "negativity" – in the singular time of writing.

The "law" of the feminine

Derrida's apparently small shift in temporality makes a profound difference to the philosophical figuration of the feminine and ironic "other". There can no longer be the purity of position which would permit an "eternal" or "essential" law of either; and if they are other as excess or remainder to the prevailing philosophical structure, neither of these things is purely negative. This is not to say that "femininity" or "woman" have suddenly been admitted as the central position or conceptual focus of Derrida's structure. Such a gesture would be at once too epistemological and too phenomenological, even though avoiding this gesture risks a repeating "her" exclusion. However, we have already established that iteration – more specifically, the time of iteration – means that there is never simply repetition. And just as iteration contaminates the choice between immanence and transcendence, presence and absence, so its contaminates the position of any other as "other", including the "otherness" of the feminine. The feminine is necessarily other only to the extent that her exclusion has become the habit of a "phallogocentric" tradition of philosophy whose central truth is an apparently "pure" and "neutral" but actually masculine presence.[11] Her "otherness" is not essential and "otherness" is not the eternally negative condition for positive presence.

This strange, "undecidable" position of the feminine is highly complicated and requires further elaboration. A more concrete

---

[10] The debate conducted between Derrida and John Searle about J. L. Austin's speech act theory is an appropriate case in point. Derrida equates speech act theory with a philosophical tradition which takes as its base an impossible norm of "serious", "ordinary" language which excludes from consideration all that is "non-ordinary", "non-serious" or "parasitic"; even while acknowledging (as did Plato) that the risk of these deviations is present as a rule. Derrida challenges the notion that the riskiness of language can be considered as something separate or external to each "performative" speech act (1982c, 307-30; 1977, 162-254).

[11] "Phallogocentrism" is the word Derrida employs to describe the way in which Lacan places the phallus in a transcendental position in his signifying system (1987b, 476-83).

example of her "other" determination may be useful here. Derrida's essay "La loi du genre" ("The Law of Genre") focuses on the question of what constitutes and marks out different categories and classifications. Derrida is ostensibly writing about literary genre, but makes it clear through his play on the multiple meanings of the French word "genre", that his discussion extends to the classification of "type", "genus", "species" and, significantly, "gender" (1986c, 252-3; 1992d, 224). The question of "genre" has a legal resonance insofar as the act of drawing boundaries suggests a formal and enforceable prohibition of certain characteristics. However, Derrida's text shows how the "force" of this law may not be as pure and complete as might be imagined.

Derrida begins by stating "Ne pas mêler les genres", which translates as "Not to mix genres" or "Genres are not to be mixed" (1986c, 251; 1992d, 223). The ambiguity of this statement is somewhat lost in translation, but its gist seems simple enough: it is a constative description of the discretion of genre. However, read in another way, it can also sound like an imperative: "Do not mix genres". Derrida reads this as the universal injunction:

> as soon as genre announces itself, one must respect a norm, one must not cross demarcation, one must not risk impurity, anomaly or monstrosity (1986c, 253; 1992d, 224-5).

In other words, it is also a legalistic statement which demands obedience. Yet such obedience is difficult to give when one considers the ambiguity of the statement. Is it a neutral declaration of an already-established fact, or something more intentional and prescriptive? The answer is both, or either, depending on the specific context. As in "Signature Event Context", Derrida does not interpret this ambiguity as an accidental, one-off occurrence, but reads it as the condition for the classification of "genre". If a "genre" is going to be determined, its boundaries must be marked, and this marking consists of stating what the genre is not. However, because of the "risk" of mutism – some of the elements making up one "genre" also constituting another, or a "genre" signifying something else in another context or "textual field" – this marking cannot be made only once. It must be repeated, re-cited.[12] As far as Derrida is concerned, this re-citation alters the legal certainties of generic definition, because it

[12] Derrida plays on the French word "récit" throughout his text because it holds several, contradictory meanings; most notably a "fictional narration" and a "factual account."

means that the mark of "otherness" (what the genre "is not") remains on the boundary of the genre. It cannot simply be excluded as "other" because its mark is necessary to the formative reiteration of the genre. Neither can it be absorbed by the "genre" because its alterity is what marks (and makes) the boundary. Derrida describes this as "a sort of participation without belonging – a taking part in without being part of, without having membership in a set" (1986c, 256; 1992d, 227).
It is "precisely a principle of contamination, a law of impurity, a parasitical economy," which he calls "the law of the law of genre".

What is most significant about this "law of impurity" is that it alters the accepted teleos of generic determination and the positive and negative evaluations which accompany it. Rather than a genre "announcing" itself, and establishing a certain position for itself by permanently prohibiting its "other", the "other" – specifically its contamination of the closed law, its recitation of other generic possibilities – is what enables the position to be drawn; even though it also rules out the permanence of that position. What was unproblematically positive is contaminated with what its "law" would regard as negative, and what was negative now affirms all possibilities by "participating in without belonging to" what was posited.

If we think about the "law of the law of genre" in relation to "gender", we can see how Derrida's reiteration of the "telos" of decision and citation – whether of species, literary genre, concepts, speech acts or subjective / objective "presence" – carries profound implications for the categories of "femininity", "masculinity", "woman" and "man". Indeed much of his analysis revolves around the different possible "genres" of "gender" and the way in which each decided gender is affirmed "through a random drift that could always render it other" (1986c, 280; 1992d, 245).[13] Neither can it be accidental that Derrida chooses the term "invagination" to describe the double movement or "folding" of the "other" mark on the boundary of the law (1986c, 256 & 271-2; 1992d, 227-8 & 239). The "otherness" of the mark of genre shares something with the historical status of the feminine term (and the womanly body) as the "other" of philosophical law. Habitually negated and apparently excluded, it is in fact a constitutive part of the law.

Any categorization of sexual identities and the characteristics which denote them (biological, phenomenal, behavioural, socio-economic

---

[13] Derrida's text plays out the transformation of orders and hierarchies in a close reading of Maurice Blanchot's "La folie du jour", which is itself of uncertain genre and stages an encounter with the "law" in several guises.

etc.) works according to the same "parasitical economy", "where the trait that marks membership inevitably divides, the boundary of the set comes to form, by invagination, an internal pocket larger than the whole" (1986c, 256; 1992d, 227-8). There is always an *excess* to the category or boundary which is "other" to that category or boundary, while enabling it to be drawn. Not only does this render impossible any "absolute" or "eternal" category of gender, but it also problematizes the habitual, dialectical figuration of the feminine "other" and her supposed "negativity". For if the "law" of her "otherness" is itself contaminated by another "other", and if, legally speaking, her facilitation of the dialectical realization of "self-consciousness" lies in her "otherness" being an internally-marked "excess", then her "otherness" is neither legally pure not purely negative. Her negatively-capable status as the "eternal irony" in the community is under threat.

If the implications of this threat are to be investigated further it is important that Derrida's questions about legal purity are sustained. This means that we should be wary of letting the feminine "other" become the representative model of Derrida's treatment of the other in general. Neither should "otherness" sum up the figures of femininity and irony, or the two categories be viewed as being interchangeable. In fact, what "La loi du genre" seems to demand is that more questions be asked about the *specificity* of such tropes, identities and sub-sets; particularly about the way in which they have become *general* generic categories in fixed topographies.

Derrida undertakes his most sustained analysis of irony and the feminine in his massive textual encounter with Hegel, *Glas*. I wish to use this encounter to demonstrate how Derrida's premises of "undecidability" and the impossibility of legal "purity" not only displace the habitual dialectical figuration of "woman" and "irony" as forms of negative capability, but dethrone them from the idealized positions which they risk occupying when they have been recognized as "disruptors" of the philosophical status quo. The ethical concerns which were debated in my last chapter haunt this analysis; particularly with regard to Derrida's apparent "suspension" of the question of woman's exclusion and sacrifice. I hope they will illuminate the way in which Derrida's approach to alterity and sexual difference radically alters established notions of textual responsibility and agency.

The godness of God

Glas revolves around the remains of "absolute knowledge" – in French "savoir absolu" – which Derrida abbreviates to "SA" (1981b, 1a; 1986a, 1a). To be more precise, it revolves around the remains of "absolute knowledge" as it manifests itself in Hegel's historical model of society: through the family and through religion. According to Hegel, both of these structures are the means by which the absolute, "Spirit", is revealed; and as philosophy's aim is to reach a "mediated" knowledge of revealed Spirit, a dialectical analysis of the laws of both structures is the proper means of explaining how Spirit determines itself in its "essential" form. Derrida, in turn, analyses the legal and ethical movement of Hegel's dialectical analysis.

Hegel's systematic analysis and Derrida's deconstructive reading of it are vastly complicated, and my analysis of both necessarily restricts itself to aspects which are relevant to the figuration of the feminine and irony. (I have sketched the dialectical structure of Hegel's family, and of "woman's" ironic function within it, in my Introduction and in chapter 3). What is important to me, as it is to Derrida, is that Hegel's religious and familial "laws" follow the same dialectical pattern.

Hegel believes that the purpose of the family is to bring up the individual in such a way that he is fit to join (bourgeois) society, and take up a public role within it. In the process, the individual shifts from being a private and "indeterminate" individual, living by "human" law, to being a "universal self", where he exists, as a citizen, only as a function of the "laws and customs" of the nation of which he is a part (Hegel 1977, 282-3). The path of this journey is from indeterminate "consciousness" to determinate "self-consciousness" and ultimately to a state of "simple universality", which for Hegel is "pure being, death" (279). Death is the "fulfilment and the supreme 'work' which the individual as such undertakes on [...] behalf" of the community. It is through the life and death of individuality that "Spirit" is mediated, moving from consciousness to (ethical) self-consciousness, before being sublated into pure concept: Being "in-and-for itself".

Hegel's structure of religion parallels the family structure, as it is defined as the "consciousness of absolute Being" (410). Religion begins and departs from absolute Spirit, and is manifested across history, first as "natural" religion, then as aesthetic or "artistic" religion, and finally as "revealed" religion. This "true shape" is not the end of the matter, however, because according to Hegel, the shape is still the "unvanquished aspect" from which Spirit must be resolved into the pure form of "the Notion", where the shape or the element of [Spirit's] existence […] is Spirit itself".

It is at this point of "resolution" and sublation that Derrida stages his analysis of Hegel's dialectic, because the sense of this process does not seem to tie up as neatly as Hegel's circular logic would imply. Derrida is puzzled as to why, if revealed religion is the "unity" of all other religions, it must lose its "shape" in order to become Spirit "in-and-for-itself"? Similarly, why, if Spirit is manifested in the community through the (ethical) life and action of the individual, should the true purpose of this action only come about in his death? How, if the absolute is in its essence *revealed*, can the pure, conceptual truth of Sprit only be truly knowable and revealable to itself by disappearing back into its initial state as "an absence of figure, irrepresentable moment"? As Derrida remarks, Hegel's God "shows himself neither at the beginning nor at the end of times, but that is in order to show himself the whole time through his figures and in an absolute light" (Derrida, 1981b, 351a; 1986a, 237a).

Derrida's response to these questions links religion and family by centring on the significance of the Holy Family in Hegel's *Phenomenology*. In terms of the dialectic, it would seem that the "necessity" of the final "relève" in Hegel's structure stems from the fact that Hegel's "absolute religion", manifested in Christianity, remains divided. According to Hegel, Spirit "in-itself" develops "self-consciousness" by being alienated from itself, and this alienation is most completely represented in God's incarnation in human form.[14] It thus feeds itself through the Holy Family, Father becoming Son, God made flesh, through an actual mother (Mary). The problem for Hegel, starting from his premise of a complete philosophy and an absolute knowledge, is that in this manifested form as Christ, Absolute Spirit and self-consciousness are not reconciled. Absolute knowledge of the Absolute Spirit may be anticipated through His presence but is not *actually* made present:

> Through the death of the mediating term, the reconciliation still remains affected by the adverse opposition of a beyond (*Gegensatze eines Jenseits*), remains distant, in the distance of a future (the Last Judgment for the religious community) and in the distance of a past (the Incarnation of God). The

---

[14] Derrida, summarizing Hegel's chapter on religion in the *Phenomenology*, says "Christianity, absolute religion, develops itself according to the following syllogism: (1) The spirit within itself: the Trinity. (2) The spirit in its alienation: the Kingdom of the Son. (3) The spirit in its plenitude: the Kingdom of the Spirit" (1981b, 131a; 1986a, 94a).

> reconciliation is not present. Present in the heart, it is cut off [*coupé*] from consciousness, divided in two (*entzweit*) (1981b, 131a; 1986a, 94a).

Even in its absolute form, Spirit is divided from its "own proper truth, the *Sa*", and must be *aufgehoben* if "*Sa*" is to be realized.

According to Derrida's reading, this division is a family drama which "has the form of an inequality between the father and the mother". Hegel clearly attributes the division between absolute religion and absolute knowledge to the alienation of the (Holy) mother from conceptual knowledge. Not only this, but as the "universal" or conceptual model of the incarnated subject, the "community" must necessarily follow the same pattern of division and sublation.[15] Thus Christ has a "father existing *in (it)self* – Spirit in its pure form, holding the promise of self-consciousness – but has a mother who is "only [...] actual"; and the community,

> ... has for its father its own [proper] doing and knowing, but for its mother, eternal love which it only *feels*, but does not behold in its consciousness as an actual, immediate object (1981b, 131a; 1986a, 94a, quoting Hegel).

The hierarchy is clear. The "actual" enables "self-consciousness" by being the cipher for the incarnation of Spirit, but itself has no consciousness of Spirit's trajectory from *in-itself* to *in-and-for-itself.* The mother divides and disrupts the purity and "self-containedness" of the paternal "concept" – stands opposed to its absolute purpose – and thus provokes the dialectical transition from the merely represented to the absolutely known. The feminine element functions as a form of negative capability for the philosophical process.

Thus the familiar Hegelian pattern is established whereby philosophy stands at / as the beginning and the culmination of time, the promise and fulfilment of (self-)consciousness; while the immediate, the actual, the ethical, the feminine are its "eternal irony", the necessary opposition to the concept "in itself" which enables and is then consumed by absolute knowledge. Form and content tie up neatly and the familial divisions are "relieved".

Derrida, however, does not see things so simply. His response is similar to the complaint made by Kierkegaard in his *Concluding Unscientific Postscript*, which Derrida inserts into the main text of *Glas*:

---

[15] For Hegel, Jesus represents the "*individual* divine Man" – the historical manifestation of God – while the community represents the "universal divine Man" as the (possibly) present manifestation of Spirit (1977, 478).

> Speculative philosophy removes every difficulty, and then leaves me with the difficulty of trying to determine what it really accomplishes by this so-called removal [aufheben] (1981b, 279-80a; 1986a, 200a).

What is left after the "removal" and "relief" is the anticipation of removal and relief. As long as philosophy takes the form of the "actual", and is represented in time – which, clearly, it still is – it is not complete and "Sa" has not arrived. Moreover, even if it anticipates a philosophy written for the dead, at the end of time, this philosophy would not be known in any "form" recognisable to the current philosophy. Kierkegaard interpreted this as the paradox of the "instant" in history: the unknowability of the absolute in the present; the division between essential "Being" and the subjective individual. For Kierkegaard, this paradox can only be resolved by the return of the "one event" of incarnation and not under the jurisdiction of a human system like philosophy. However, Derrida takes his cue from Hegel's own insistence on philosphy's purity and "self-containedness" to show how the strange circularity of Hegel's dialectic is rooted in the same idea of a revealable absolute which bolsters his claim to philosophy's supreme authority, and gives Kierkegaard his faith in incarnation. If philosophy is the essence of the absolute in its manifest "knowability"; and if, in order to fulfil this essence, it must materialize in the "actual", "represented" form which contradicts this "knowledge"; and if the journey and end of this fulfilment are determined from the beginning; then the form which contradicts "Sa" must be "present" at the beginning, as a constitutive part of the determination. This makes philosophy somewhat less "pure" and self-sufficient than Hegel's logic would have us believe:

> Philosophy's need is not yet philosophy. There is a *not yet* of philosophy. Philosophy – already – is announced in it. Now, reason's and thus Hegelian philosophy's essential proposition: philosophy has its beginning only in itself. Philosophy is the beginning, as the beginning of (it)self, the posit(ion)ing by (it)self of the beginning. How are these two axioms to be reconciled: philosophy only proceeds from / by itself, and yet is the daughter of a need or an interest that are not yet philosophy? (1981b, 134a; 1986a, 95a).

The "remaining" conflict which Derrida highlights is not "caused" by Hegel's historicism, or by the pre-ordained irreconcilability of the historical "realm" with the pure conceptual one; but by the fact that there is an impossibility about the complete separation of these two realms, and their subsequent reconciliation. The separation is only necessary as a means of fulfilling the desire of a structure which has assigned itself divine status and wishes to achieve final, absolute authority. If the dialectical process is followed as closely as Derrida follows it, it quickly becomes clear that historical and conceptual realms contaminate each other *as part of* their very "law" of being. Neither precedes the other and neither outlives or absorbs the other. Thus philosophy "as reason" exists somewhere *between* the already posited and the "not yet"; somewhere *between* father and daughter.

The sexual confusion in Derrida's version of Hegel's familial law confirms its "phallocentrism" as well as its "logocentrism". Hegel's dialectic desires to keep the "pure" male concept, "Sa", undivided at the centre of all (familial) relations. While Hegel insists that sexual differentiation is a central part of the dialectical process, the difference exists only as opposition and only in order to serve the completion of a masculine self-consciousness (1981b, 234a; 1986a, 167-8a). The principle of "Sa" is exchanged from father to son though the "actual" mother – who herself lacks the "objective" principle – and is raised to completion by the realization of her "lack" and the negation of her actuality: "what denies and cuts [*coupe*] subjectivity of / from itself is also what raises and accomplishes it" (1981b, 17a; 1986a, 12-13a). The Oedipal resonances here are not accidental, for Derrida sees in the dialectical process something approximating a model of (sexual) repression. It roots its reason in what it "does not permit itself to be thought" and seeks possession of a single, all-powerful "thing".

Just as Derrida recognizes the already-divided nature of philosophy, so he questions its singular sexual origin and end. For if the "feminine" element in the dialectic necessarily divides the male principle from itself, and if this division reveals the essence of the principle then, legally speaking, the dividing "mother" was part of the original principle "before" it was ever meant to be divided, and continues to divide after sublation, as part of its conceptual determination:

> As irony, the woman is at once a *moment to be passed* and the very *form* of *Sa*. Double mark and double place. (1981b, 265a; 1986a, 190a).[16]

Thus it is that even from the beginning of his reading (which marks the beginning of Hegel's quest for "savoir absolu") Derrida describes "IC" – the Immaculate Conception – as an equivalent "siglum" to

---

[16] In terms of the typography that distinguishes the different "narratives" of *Glas*, this quotation comes from a passage which immediately precedes the Kierkegaardian insertion about what remains after the Hegelian Aufhebung. This suggests that Derrida's problematizing of Hegel's "sublatable" ironic woman could also serve as a comment on Kierkegaard's sacrifice of his "feminine" ethical irony.

"Sa", saying, "let's note this already since the two staffs represent each other" (1981b, 1a; 1986a, 1a). The feminized divisions spoken of dialectically as "moments" to be overcome are not simply a part of, but a *condition* of, the whole dialectical sequence. They are *already* participating in the self-contained determination of Spirit, dividing before and within its law. The pure "staff" of the father-concept is already divided into the feminine; and both are already "represented" in temporal, human form. This sentence indicates epigramatically the ironies which intrude upon "Sa's" "immaculate" perfection, once the undecidable elements within its own law are pursued rather than repressed or subsumed. Like the "principle of contamination" in "La loi du genre", these "undecidables" founder the final authority of Hegel's dialectic.

Derrida radicalizes the force of undecidability in his reading of the position of Antigone in Hegel's philosophy of the family. For Hegel, Antigone exemplifies "ethical", "ironical" femininity,

> … as principally the law of woman, […] the law of the inward life, a life which has not yet attained its full actualization; as the law of the ancient gods, "the gods of the underworld"(Hegel, 1942, 115).

She keeps "family law" by burying her brother and thus stands "as a law opposed to public law, to the law of the land" and the state. However, Derrida notes certain singular characteristics in this exemplary figure, which cannot be contained by the universal law her "opposition" and "irony" are supposed to serve. Most notably, Antigone is not properly a part of the erotic relations which, for Hegel, define the interaction of family members and the relative positions of the sexes. As sister and brother, Antigone and Polynices do not desire each other, and unlike spousal and parent / child relations their relationship is not based in a "mutual recognition" which "represents" the higher, "objective" ethical duty of the community (*Sittlichkeit*).[17] Rather, it is "linked to the equilibrium of the blood" (Hegel 1977, 275). This means that Antigone's defining state of being is not immediate and contingent in the way the wife's or

---

[17] Hegel determines that because the husband / wife relationship is based partly in desire, the self-recognition involved is a "natural and not an ethical one, it is only a representation, an image of Spirit, not actually Spirit itself" (1977, 273). It thus has its "actual existence" or "objective reality" in the something other than itself – namely the child – which, in becoming independent will negate the family. This is the necessary step which provokes the final "aufhebung" of the ethical life into Spirit. The children have similar relations to their parents, "by the fact that they … have their essential being in what is other than themselves and passes away" (274).

mother's is, even though she remains without objective consciousness. She "has the highest *intuitive* awareness of what is ethical" (274). Her relation to her brother is in a sense already universal and thus does not operate according to the logic of "replaceability" which makes other relations individually insignificant.[18] Antigone's sisterly relationship is irreplaceable; her self-sacrifice inimitable. She is at once more singular and more universal than her other "womanly" counterparts:

> The sister, she holds herself in singularity, but in a singular singularity: purely universal at one stroke [*coup*], without cutting [*couper*] herself from the natural bond of consanguinity (Derrida 1981b, 229a; 1986a, 163a).

Derrida remarks upon the oddity of a situation where the representative model of the "law of woman" does not only not fit the criteria for this category, but does not properly oppose her apparent "opposite", the universal. Antigone, it seems, is "other than the other" she is meant to represent, according to the dialectical law, even while she serves to facilitate this law. She enables her brother to gain "proper" universal subjectivity and bring about the (necessary) disintegration of the family which anticipates "Sittlichkeit". Nevertheless, there remains about her something peculiar, contingent, which cannot be reduced to a generalized category. She participates in, without quite belonging to, the determination of the law and its *aufhebung* of conflicting terms into "Sa". A "vertiginous insistence of an unclassable", Hegel's Antigone troubles both his own gender laws and the (masculine) purity of the dialectical concept, by already being involved in the universal and the absolute at its conception ((1981b, 211a; 1986a, 151a). She is both the system's "space of possibility" and its "impossible place":

> If God is (probably) a man in speculative dialectics, the godness of God – the irony that divides him and makes him come off his hinges – the infinite disquiet of his essence is (if possible) woman(ly) (1981b, 263a; 1986a, 188a).

Derrida's reading of Hegel in *Glas* seems to have destabilized the authority of the dialectic without attempting to overturn its law

---

[18] Because other relations are made up of particular individuals, and are both in the form of immediate, natural desire and the anticipated negation of that desire, the individuals are themselves replaceable. In terms of the (universal) "ethical household" it is the ethical relationships *in general*, not the individuals within them, which matter. For Hegel, this is particularly the case with the relationships of the woman, because she is simply an individual and has no consciousness of the universal realm. As Derrida remarks, "the woman always marries just a bit concept (man); she always conceives just a bit concepts (children). In general" (1981b, 229a; 1986a, 163a).

completely. Indeed, the destabilization is brought about through Derrida's recognition of the impossibility of a fully intended, (pre)determined overturning or sublation. He exposes the laws, hierarchies and categories of dialectical logic to the undecidability of their own determination by highlighting that this determination lies in the very contingency and mutability of their representation which they would appear to overcome. Hegel tries to suppress this instability, controlling the manifest "essence" of the concept – the "form of 'Sa'" – through the movement of sublation, and claiming it is preserved in a realm "beyond" representation. Derrida's writing inhabits the "form of 'Sa'" and by following its undecidable style, marks within it a force of alterity which cannot be relieved or possessed by a universal law; even though it plays a fundamental role in creating decisions and laws. As a result, what the dialectic categorizes as *its* other, *its* negative, sublatable opposite, ceases to be purely this. The "immediate", the "actual", the "unconscious", the "representable" form, and the "feminine" are "other" to their categories. "Woman" (as Antigone) seems "eternally ironic" in a less discrete, less negatively capable way.

Suspended agency

It is at this point in Derrida's reading that the issue of "suspension" returns. Derrida's careful reiteration of Hegel's ironic feminine might trouble the permanence of its categorical status, but does it really displace it? Is it not possible that Derrida's "undecidable" version of Antigone simply acts as another double negation, at once preserving her "suppressed" status as "ethical" hand-maiden and sacrifice, and negating her position altogether? Derrida himself seems to hint at such a possibility; for in the same paragraph as his comments on the woman(ly) godness of God he warns, "let one not go and see in this, precipitantly, the end of phallocentrism, of idealism, of metaphysics".

Such a comment could be read as a suspension of the whole question of the possible agency of irony, which would, in turn, be highly problematic for any political, let alone feminist, engagement with Derrida's text. Is he, then, simply employing the alterity of "woman" as trope through which to negate Hegel?

There are two responses to be made here: one concerning the "end" of idealism to which Derrida refers; and one concerning the difference between sexual "identity" and sexual specificity in Derrida's text.

The difficulty which Derrida's deconstructive style faces and stages, is how to *avoid* endings in the sense of the word which conforms to the universal "idealizing" law of Western metaphysics: its insistence on defining things *essentially* and *finally*. This is to lose or suppress the element that for Derrida as much defines the specificity or singularity of a thing as its legal, political or existential category: namely its resistance to (the) decision, which is the immanent risk of otherness. So if Derrida's tracing of the "remains" of dialectical speculation is to be considered an ironic "strategy", it cannot be said to share the conviction of other "new" philosophies, of moving "beyond" the system it is undermining. It cannot assume that it is as fully determined, independent, or completely "conscious" as a structure which maintains a belief in the integrity of its (own) boundaries. Not only does this distance Derrida's deconstructions from Rortyesque accusations of his championing a purely "private" irony – it cannot remove itself so easily from the "public" realm – but it (at the very least) doubles any complications of "saying" and the site of "saying" that we have already encountered in more messianic conceptions of irony; particularly in relation to the other which disrupts and enables this "saying". In order that his consideration of sexual difference avoids repeating the preordination of the speculative dialectic and the messianism of the transcendental, there has to be some residual element of these "anchorings of Western rationality" (1985, 171). Every decision, even those which apparently parody the orthodoxy, carries the other *in and as* its very determination. This explains Derrida's reluctance to state the "end" of phallocentrism, even as he undermines it. It also accounts for his reluctance to portray the ironic status of the feminine – even his contingent version of it – as the agent for a more ethical, differential strain of philosophy who will "save" it from its absolutist ambitions.[19] Derrida maintains that it is an indication of the *resistance* to "mastery" that old appropriations, abstractions and idealisms cannot be determinedly banished; for it admits the uncontrollable, unconscious element of his own writing that is its creative, even emancipatory, possibility.[20]

---

[19] This leads me to disagree with Simon Critchley's reading of *Glas*, in which he views Antigone as a figure who "marks a place [...] within the Hegelian system where an ethics is glimpsed that is irreducible to dialectics and cognition, what I would call an ethics of the singular". He associates this ethics with Antigone's ironic status, reading it as a form of transcendent agency: "*Whatever the community might do to repress the singular, there always remains the everlasting possibility of irony. Irony is the genre of ethical discourse.*" (1998, 210-211). This reading fails to take account of the degree to which feminine irony remains complicit with the community in Hegel's structure.

[20] See "Psyché: Invention de l'autre", which upholds the connection between the utter otherness of the other and the "inventiveness" of writing as its running theme. Derrida

This is of consequence to the question of the political responsibility of deconstruction. As Ernesto Laclau points out in his delineation of the political importance of deconstruction, to write of the indecision surrounding the structure at *the* point of its revealed inception (which in dialectical mediation is both experiential and categorical) does, in fact, highlight the political to a peculiar degree. First, it questions the logic of the usually naturalized link made between the political idea and its social institution, thus revealing that "that which makes the political possible – the contingency of the acts of institution – is also what makes it impossible, as ultimately, no instituting act is fully achievable" (Laclau 1996, 48). Secondly, it recognizes that within this analysis of "the field of structural undecidability" there arises the possibility of forming "a theory of the decision as taken in an undecidable terrain". In other words, there arises the possibility of creating a structure which acknowledges its own impossibility and madness as and within its recognition that something at least simulating decision and closure will always necessarily take place. Derrida's resistance to the logic of mastery maintains its fundamental concern for emancipation precisely *through* the logic of supplementarity which haunts any potential models of knowledge, even those of deconstruction, with possible interruptions of otherness. To stage this resistance at the "heart" of the dialectical structure – its opposition of the immediate and the absolute at the limit of mediation – is hyperpolitical, as it contaminates the foundations of its categories and oppositions, leaving no level of the structure unaffected.

As for the sexual nature of Derrida's ironic resistance, it cannot conform to the order of division and opposition that constitutes dialectical "identity". It also recognizes that this sexual economy cannot simply be negated and discredited. Thus, while it disallows the abstract categorization of femininity as "Otherness" (or of masculinity as true consciousness), there is not an obvious alternative "beyond" such a figuration which would comply with what one might immediately think of as an autonomous feminist agency. Any "other" sexual structure or "identity" will be subject to other sexual possibilities as a rule, and this includes the possibility of a return to "old" sexual configurations.

---

describe the "logic of supplementarity" as a "fabulous complication" which may, "through a merging of chance and necessity produce the new of an event". It does this by "bending […] rules with respect for the rules themselves in order to allow the other to come or announce its coming in the opening of this dehiscence. This move consists in defining and exhibiting the precarious structure of its rules, even while respecting them, and through the mark of respect that it invents" (1987d 59; 1992e, 340).

According to some feminist critics, Derrida's problematizing of sexual-agency-as-identity is tantamount to suspending possibly "different" figurations of sexual "difference" altogether. Gayatri Chakravorty Spivak accuses him of taking up the fetishist's position in relation to the Hegelian / Freudian sexual economy (Spivak 1983, 169-95). She notes the continual images of "replacement" and "substitution"; in particular, Hegel's feminized family and, in the text which reiterates Genet, the references to his "illegitimate" birth and dildo-filled sex life.[21] Given the way these references dance between the two columns of the text, and given what Derrida says about the "two staffs" of "Sa", she concludes that Derrida's own undecided stance in relation to these two columns resembles the position of the son who sides with the phallic mother. In other words, he is appropriating certain feminine tropes or elements and using them to rebel against the father figures in his text (and their "truth" of castration). According to Spivak, *Glas* is

> … the classic case of fetishism, a uniquely shaped object (his bicolumnar book) that will allow the subject both to be and not to be a man – to have the phallus and yet accede to dissemination (177).

Such a strategy, even if it challenged logocentrism, would hardly constitute a challenge to phallocentrism. It would leave the ironic "substitute" truth of the woman in place, without attending to her "own" specificity. As Spivak asserts,

> … deconstruction looks for a mother who can change her phallus indefinitely and has an outcast homosexual son. Crudely put, a quarrel of sons is not the model for a feminist practice (178).

However, this accusation only sticks if one believes that Derrida's "undecidability" is limited to the established bipolar economy of fetishism, which, I would argue, it is not. Derrida resists what he calls the "economy of truth" in the idea of fetishism, as it is expressed by Freud and Marx, remarking that,

> Despite all the variations to which it can be submitted, the concept fetish includes an invariant predicate: it is a substitute – for the thing itself as center

---

[21] Derrida makes much of Genet's "criminality" in the eyes of both (Lacanian) psychoanalytic and Hegelian "law". As a homosexual, Genet does not complete the "normal" procession through Oedipal complex to become part of the symbolic order. As an illegitimate child, his name is matronymic rather than patronymic, so that he does not fit into Hegel's ideal, ethical family. He refuses the "name of the father" in more ways than one.

> and source of being, the origin of presence, the thing itself par excellence, God or the principle … (1981b, 292a; 1986a, 209a).

To think in terms of substitution is, of course, to work against the very notion of "not deciding" that fetishism is usually taken to represent. It is this reading of the undecidable in terms of a "thing" or "truth" which is already decided, which Derrida finds problematic and seeks to displace; not because he is seeking a "pure" experience of undecidability but because the possibility of difference can only be maintained if decisions can be decided *otherwise*. By marking the already divided nature of the economy's "essential moment", Derrida's writing puts the "substitute" of the "moment" at the heart of its determination, but it also refuses the idea that it is a substitute for, or representative of any single, essential "thing" at all. Spivak regards this interruption as an attempt to de-fetishize philosophy through the logic of fetishism – "the thing itself becomes its own substitute" – but does not believe that this challenges the sexual economy of the fetish because the "fake", "to qualify as a fetish, must carry within itself a trace of the thing itself that it replaces" (Spivak, 1983, 178). This response is a strange curtailment of the logic of displacement which Spivak would seem elsewhere to support, because it fails to acknowledge that any "trace" of the "thing itself" in its deconstructed form will have lost the authority and autonomy that Hegel, Freud or Marx would give it.[22] If the very "origin" of the thing is already divided (or divisible *before* the divisions of dialectical mediation have taken place), then what comes subsequently will not necessarily order itself according to the dictate of the "thing"; and this includes the way in which it divides itself sexually. Far from mimicking a "conventional" fetishism, then, Derrida's writing suspends its phallocentric logic and points to a form of sexual decision-making which is reached through the experience of the undecidable; *without* this undecidable being the opposite, or negative substitute, of a pre-determined sexual category. It multiplies rather than evades sexual and gendered possibilities, so that "Sa" is not only inhabited by its feminine form "sa", but by its homonym "ça" ["*it*"], which does not fit into the sexual "economy of metaphysics".[23] Likewise, the two columns of the text of *Glas* are not self-contained representations of

---

[22] In fact, having teased out her (half) sympathetic relation to deconstruction, she "overcomes" the problems she finds within it by returning to a Marxist / Hegelian model of dialectical antagonism between the sexes. See 1983, 192.

[23] The homonyms repeat across the two sides of the text throughout *Glas*.

one sex or the other, and the text on Genet's "criminal life" upsets the heterosexist balance of both Freud's and Hegel's family laws.

> The economy of the fetish is more powerful than that of the truth – decidable – of the thing itself or than a deciding discourse of castration (pro aut contra). The fetish is not opposable. It oscillates like the clapper of a truth which rings awry [*cloche*] (1981b, 317b; 1986a, 227b).

Derrida's undecidable form of fetishism repeats, while ironizing, the phallic economy of philosophy (the "ironic" woman, the ethical "other", the phallic mother), then displaces the pure, categorical position of this irony (as the substitute for the "truth", the lack *of* determination, the eternal other *of* the universal). The ironic agency of the other is displaced through the (recognition of the) différance of its determination so that it is no longer the possession of the thing it opposes / displaces, and it may be determined according to the economy of other others.

It is thus highly appropriate that woman should be at the point of "suspension", not because her identity is suspended, or because she is the forgotten, transcendental "cause" of suspension, but because the whole question of the instability of identity (both epistemological and ontological) is caught up with an internal illegality which the ambiguous status of the feminine reinforces. Her status *is* to some extent emblematic of Otherness – it is "quasi-transcendental" – because the deconstructive "path" carries contaminating residues of the prevailing structure, in its refusal to feign being a simple leap beyond. Yet "she" also represents the possibility of an identity or decision taken without the full presence of phallogocentric "consciousness" or "knowledge", and without its memory or anticipation.[24] If the woman of the Hegelian or Kierkegaardian framework is the "eternal irony" and the "infinite disquiet of [the] essence" of Godly and subjective consciousness, then the woman of Derrida's framework is the radically contingent irony that remains possible after (and hence as the unremembered, un-sublated *before* of) the negative movement of the dialectical exchange. Which means that

---

[24] This interlinks with the running theme of "contraband" throughout *Glas*, which plays on the French slang verb for having an erection ["*bander"*]: "The matrix in question constitutes the excluded as transcendental of the transcendental, as imitation transcendental, transcendental contraband [contra-band]. The contra-band is not yet dialectical contradiction. To be sure, the contra-band necessarily becomes that, but its not-yet is not-yet the teleological anticipation, which results in it never becoming dialectical contradiction. The contra-band remains something other than what, necessarily, it is to become" (1981b, 340a; 1986a, 244a).

"she" (as irony) is never quite negative and the sublation of "Sa" is never quite executed.[25] If "she" is the other which is necessarily sacrificed (even in Levinas', even in Irigaray's writing) so that the primary moment of consciousness may be an ethical one, then in Derrida's ontology "the remain(s)" of a legal, categorical and absolute Otherness "here suspends itself": thus being as (im)possibly and (in)completely self-determining as the ethical subject (1981b, 315a; 1986a, 226a). All that remains, then, is "the time of this suspense"; for the remainder of "Sa" itself is not a proper [*proper*] remain and its impropriety upsets the direction of all familiar structures:

> What remains of the "remain(s)" when it is pulled to pieces, torn into morsels? Where does the *rule* of its being torn into morsels come from? Must one still try to determine a regularity when tearing to pieces what remains of the remain(s)? A strictly angular question.
>
> […] For the moment time will be nothing but the suspense between the regularity and the irregularity of the morsels of what remains.

The "suspense", or suspension, of the remains of the negative woman-as-Other is a crucial deconstructive manoeuvre. It sits within the parameters of the conventional philosophical question, with its "angular" demands for categorization and generalization, but is too contingent, too *writerly*, to be known by it or answerable to it. Its logic of undecidability bridges, while disabling, the two movements – from "subject" to "object", "regularity" to "irregularity" – which form the dialectical sequence and thus precipitate the "inevitability" of the Hegelian *Aufhebung*. What is left behind – the "morsels of what remains" – replays the fetishization of the lost and desired (phallic)

---

[25] I am using the word "executed" with all its deathly and well as effective connotations here. Derrida repeatedly plays with the element of "pure" negativity which accompanies and enables the recognition of self and essence in dialectical mediation. The big question is how the pure essence of "sa" can come out of a process which begins and ends with an abstract indetermination, a God which "withdraws at the origin and end of religion, before and after religion: whose becoming literally describes a consuming destruction of the figure, between two suns" (1981b, 331a; 1986a, 237a). Derrida epigrammizes the problem in the question; "How can the self and the for-(it)self appear? How would the sun of the all-burning breach/broach its [*sa*] course and its going down [*déclin*]?" (1981b, 334 a; 1986a, 239a) Hence the constant sounding (son) of the death knell (glas) in the text, and the playful figuring of the remains – a feminized "*sa*" – somewhere between the pure essence/absence which is the conflated beginning/ending of Hegel's dialectic: "The triumphal moment of mourning. […] At the angle of the phenomenology of spirit and Sa (of the greater logic), at the hinge [*charnière*], the tomb [*tombeau*] of the Son" (1981b, 322a; 1986a, 231a).

mother as the remembered trace of différance within the founding "moments" of philosophical law. In so doing it founders the monumental status of this law and its concomitant monosexuality: "l"érection tombe" (1979, 104). It is thus possible to see how the "suspension" of the dialectic's temporal limit, through Derrida's double gesture, is always already a "feminist" gesture.[26]

The question which I posed at the beginning of the chapter concerning Derrida's "suspension" of the feminine can now be approached again. Derrida's "suspended" question, in *The Gift of Death,* about the necessity of the "sacrifice" of the feminine within dialectics is not a repetition of this sacrifice, but a deconstruction of the idealization implicit in this sacrifice. It "suspends" the presumption of an indivisible origin on which the dialectical "mediation" depends. It "suspends" the fetishistic positioning of the feminine term as the opposite of (self-)presence and thus the paradoxical substitute for (and means to) self-consciousness. This, in turn, "suspends" the idealized form of "negativity" which dialectical irony embodies, which not only makes the completion of the Hegelian *Aufhebung* impossible, but also the movement of anticipated mastery or revelation that is implicit in most other ironic "strategies".[27] Hence the "common thread" between Derrida's suspended question and Hegel's comment about woman being the "eternal irony". Hegel's proclamation, his "law", returns as a reminder of the impossibility of "finally" overcoming all laws, including the dialectical one, but "in itself", as an absolute determination, it returns decimated.

---

[26] I am referring to Geoffrey Bennington's discussion of the link between naming and responsibility in the context of the feminine, in *Jacques Derrida* (1993, 228). Bennington too, sees the responsible action of deconstruction as being the non-linear temporality of its repetition, which prevents a final ethical decision without preventing judgement. Deconstructive "naming" is thus affirmative whilst interrupting any prospect of essence. This means that the feminine cannot be accounted for as essence in the mark of affirmation, but that this mark is "already a feminist gesture" in deconstructing the fundamental oppositions of metaphysics which determine femininity as a negative opposition. The determination of sexual difference, like the thought of writing, is "beyond good and evil". As in *Glas* and the preface to *Glassery*, Derrida performs an ironic, one might even say invaginated, version of Bennington's expository text in his "autobiographical" "Circumfession" which runs beneath the main text in a similar way to Kierkegaard's footnotes in *The Concept of Irony*.

[27] I have Kierkegaard and, to some extent, Irigaray in mind here.

II. Beyond Suspension

Questions remain around the time of suspense, however, and most of them concern the possible "future" of the remains. Derrida's "double gesture" is hyperpolitical and "always already feminist" insofar as it displaces dialectical phallocentrism; but the feminist imperative concerning the specificity of the feminine remains. What does the feminine in Derrida's writing signify, *beyond* the displacement of her own fetishism? Can she emerge differently as a result of her post-dialectical remaindering? And what is her relation to the wider definition of "sexual difference" which seems to intrude on categories of "man" and "woman" in *Glas*?

These questions may seem too assertive for a style of writing whose temporality resists the stroke of mastery and says that the only time is the time of the remainder. However, Derrida is insistent that deconstruction is "inventive", that its ruins are not negative, that the time of writing is "affirmative". All of these gestures indicate that his "other" configurations of alterity and femininity must at least make a tentative promise of something "new". Indeed, it is important here to reemphasize that having explored the experience of the undecidable, and remembered the residual in the "present", we cannot view the (suspended) current structure of writing as a space defined by lack; even by the lack of anticipation of future structures or identities. It is precisely in this lack of lack that whatever is "new" can be traced; for in refusing permanent positionality it also preserves the multitude of other possible determinations. Derrida speaks of the founding "aporia" of decision as a *resonance* as well as an absence or hunger because once the idea of a "pure" source or origin has been displaced, the decisions of the future are not limited to the dialectical "choice" between essence and absence.

The question of what is new in this logic can thus only be tackled if it is phrased within the aporetic, double style of writing. For this reason I will spend a little more time elaborating the style in the context of its relation to the other as it lives "beyond" the battle with its dialectical negation, before outlining Derrida's treatment of the other in more specifically "feminine" and "feminist" terms. In the process of analysing these sexual questions I will touch on Derrida's interaction with two of his key influences – Heidegger and Nietzsche – both in order to show how the question of "sexual difference" is central to his readings of other theorists, and to reveal the way in which Derrida copes with their sexual legacy; and outlines his own.

The "New" Style

Perhaps the first thing to remark upon is that the "newness" or "excessiveness" of the "new" style and time has in a particular sense already "been". What emerges from the ruins of the dialectic is a form of writing whose life depends on the ghost of supplementarity and différance. Its intention and determination are riddled with the possibilities of other times and other decisions. This "otherness" is "present" or will be "present" as the trace of iterability. As this trace cannot be fully "present" – indeed, is what interrupts the idea of full presence – it was itself a possibility even before the current writing was written; and remains a possibility even if nothing is spoken of:

> Even if one speaks and says nothing, even if an apophatic discourse deprives itself of meaning or of an object, it takes place. That which committed or rendered it possible *has taken place*. [...] This call of the other, having always already preceded the speech to which it has never been present a first time, announces itself in advance as a *recall*. [...] The most negative discourse, even beyond all nihilisms and negative dialectics, preserves the trace of the other. A trace of an event older than it *or* of a "taking place" to come, both of them: here there is neither an alternative nor a contradiction (1989a, 27-8).

Thus writing cannot help being affirmatory, but its affirmation comes through the reiteration of alterity. It takes the form of a promise which does not expect result or revelation in the sense of phenomenal presence. Instead, its promise arises out of the possibilities which remain because the "here and now" is conditional on the other: what could have been and could again be decided (differently). As this other could never have been simply originary – was always "in advance" of present speech or writing – the affirmation calls forth its own repetition. What is promised, what emerges from the time from the remainder thus functions as a double affirmation:

> Having come already from the other, in the dissymmetry of the request, and from the other of whom it is requested to request a *yes*, the *yes* entrusts itself to the memory of the other, of the *yes* of the other and of the other yes (1992f, 305).

It speaks a "Yes to emancipation" – twice – by recalling its (own) alterity and the alterity of the other (1996, 82).

The chain of allusions which spirals out of this yes is almost too long and complex to describe here. Most obviously, it follows the parodic braying of the ass in Nietzsche's *Thus Spake Zarathustra*, and

Nietzsche's own affirmative response to the "eternal return".[28] However, its literary allusion is of more immediate relevance to the emergence or "emancipation" of the "feminine" other: to Molly Bloom in James Joyce's *Ulysses*. Derrida explores the double affirmation most explicitly in his text "Ulysses Gramaphone", in which the "yeses" of Molly's monologue dominate his discussion of chance, necessity, repetition and "new" directions.[29] His careful variation on the theme of Ulysses' (Bloom's) wanderings in Joyce's book traces and laughs at the inevitable returns: the circularity of scholarly and literary attempts to encompass past ventures and systems and move onto new ground. Yet, following Joyce's plot, it also traces the way in which these same returns throw open the path for something new precisely through the chanciness and supplementarity which is implicit in their circuits and "meetings".[30] A particular assertion by someone – a "self-positing" as Derrida calls it – is thus already a response to this possible meeting, this chance, and thus a response to and affirmation of the (wholly) other.[31] Molly's "monologue" is the case in point here: she is ostensibly alone, talking to herself, and yet this "self-positing" – "like a dispatch" sent to herself – works through recollection and repetition, so "*both never leaves itself and never arrives at itself*" (303). Molly's "self-positing" ends Joyce's book. Yet as a recollection of a response to another's request for marriage, which is spoken by one who at once wallows in and is dismissive of her status as the fleshly "other" of the masculine

---

[28] See Nietzsche 1969, 319-25. The braying of the ass ("Ye-a") interrupts the new-found religion of the "higher men", but also echoes Zarathustra's joyful "saying yes" to the "eternal return of the same thing". This suggests that it is never as easy as one imagines to escape the "law tables" of religious thinking. I will analyse Nietzsche in greater detail in my final chapter.

[29] This is most obvious in his parodic scholarly computation of the number of "yeses" spoken by Molly: 79 out of more than 222 in the whole book (1992f, 305-6).

[30] Derrida refers to these meetings as "écheances", which, as the editor, Derek Attridge, notes, "combines the sense of necessity as in the "falling due of a bill" and chance ("*le cas échéant*" means "if it should happen")" (258). The issue of translation is important here, as, like "the law of the law of genre" it must be repeated, thus opening up "the space for a *re-marking*", and, retrospectively, for deviance or alteration of the translation.

[31] Derrida compares this to the double "yes" involved in answering a telephone: the first affirmation (picking up the receiver) is a "yes without a word" (296). In French, "to say yes" ["*oui dire*"] also translates as "hearsay", so that the act of "saying yes" is always already transferred through another.

spirit, this monologue-which-is-not points to the potential fecundity of recirculation when it keeps an ear open to the other.[32]

Clearly, then, a wholly "other" register is needed if we are to speak properly of this newly recalled "other." It should be a register which acknowledges the necessity of "self-positing", signing, deciding, without forcing this decision into a fixed *place* which would subscribe and incorporate the freedom of the trace of the other. This register *would* be ironic, but not ironic in the sense that the philosophical tradition has left us with. It would be due to an anxiety, but not to a negative anxiety. It would avoid final determination, but not out of a sense of having lost knowledge and in anticipation of its return. It would be comic and parodic in relation to the prevailing structure not in order to negate it, but with the intention of taking responsibility for the otherness that was already the condition for the structure's existence. This is why when Derrida speaks of the manner in which he has tried to think "an experience of the secret and of singularity" he insists that "There is irony and there is something else" (1996, 81). Derrida describes this "something else" as the "issue of philosophical responsibility", as the need to take seriously the injunction, inherited from philosophy, to endlessly "renew transcendental questioning". Indeed, this statement brings into focus the difficulty of speaking of the difference of deconstructive thinking and its potential for an other register and other future in the "here and now". Phrases like "philosophical responsibility" and "transcendental questioning" seem to conform to the "seriousness" of the "history of philosophy". Irony then seems reactive and its risk seems to be incorporated. However, the context of these statements makes it clear that Derrida's irony and the "something else" are disrupting each other and their established positions within the history of philosophy. Derrida also says that the "issue of philosophical responsibility" is "a question of memory" and that the transcendental questioning

> … must be renewed in taking account of the possibility of fiction, of accidentality and contingency, thereby ensuring that this new form of transcendental questioning only mimics the phantom of classical transcendental

---

[32] See Joyce 1993. In her editor's introduction, Jeri Johnson points to the textual facility of Molly's monologue as much as to its corporeal or libidinal resonances: she is not quite as defined as "*Weib ... der [sic] Fleisch der stets bejaht*" as Joyce might at first have us think. Johnson asserts that the weaving of "Penelope's textual strategies point the way back to a necessarily endless and endlessly rewarding rereading of *Ulysses* and forward to the infinite, and definitely material, play of *Finnegan's Wake*" xxxvii.

> seriousness without renouncing that which, within this phantom, constitutes an essential heritage (81-2).

"Memory" in this context *is* the legacy of the serious history of philosophy, but it is also the trace of the other in the "mediation" of history which undermines that history's presumption to have completed its destination; acknowledging the possibility of "fiction", "accidentality" and "contingency". The serious undertaking of philosophical responsibility is thus the end of this history in the sense that it ends its completion. Its authority and seriousness become a "phantom" and its injunction to question is a mimicry of that phantom. Having said that, the phantom *is* the serious and responsible element of that history – the "essential heritage" that must be maintained – because it is the *différance* of the time of the other in the "present" philosophy which was the very enablement of the injunction to question and to decide. Irony and seriousness cross and contaminate each other and their own historically-established effect. While not moving beyond the inherited register of questioning – in fact, by purposely *avoiding* a leap into a newly configured, "wholly other" register – Derrida suggests "serious" irony takes responsibility for its own historical register, and recuperates an affirmative gesture out of the positive / negative destinations and "positions" of "classical transcendental" teleology. It is, ironically,

> … an apocalypse without apocalypse, an apocalypse without vision, without truth, without revelation, *dispatches* [*des envois*] (for the "come" is plural in itself, in oneself), addresses without message and without destination, without sender or decidable addressee, without last judgment, without any other eschatology than the tone of the "Come," its very difference, an apocalypse beyond good and evil (1984b, 34-5).

Feminism, Pragmatism, Responsibility

All of this may seem purely theoretical and very far removed from any kind of alternative figuration of "femininity" or "sexual difference". However, Derrida's accommodation of the "recall" of the other speaks clearly to any feminist project which seeks to avoid the presumptuous assertions and inequalities of the past. On an obvious level, any such feminist writing must try to come to terms with what "remains" of old structures and prejudices within its "new" structure. This is particularly true in the case of the remains of the "old" figuration of Woman-as-generalized-Other; not simply because it risks (re-)subscribing "her" as an ahistorical, permanently alienated figure, but because it excludes other sexual and cultural "others".[33] Feminism as a "discipline" arises from the patriarchy it criticizes; not only as a reaction against its oppressions, but in some respects as a continuation of its discursive structures and their biases.[34] This complicity must be continually re-marked if feminism is to live up to its emancipatory hopes. It is only by acknowledging its own "risk" of oppression in every specific context, in relation to every specific decision, that the heterogeneous and changing specificity of what historically has been "Other" will "come" to be written.

Derrida imagines this process as a "maverick" form of feminism (resembling the irony "gone awry" of *Glas*) which, in addressing the risks of its own alterity, breaks with the "history" of "revolution", with its "continuous progress" and orientation "towards a notion of women's truth" (1985, 167). Instead, it will think through

> … a completely other history: a history of paradoxical laws and non-dialectical discontinuities, a history of absolutely heterogeneous pockets, irreducible particularities, of unheard of and incalculable sexual differences.

This notion of an "incalculable" sexual difference throws into focus the issue of history's continuing responsibility for sexual alterity. According to Derrida's logic, this responsibility is limitless. In fact, it is so far-reaching that it cannot be interpreted as an *ethical* responsibility (as it is in the work of Levinas): ethics is a code of

---

[33] By which I mean two things. Firstly, that it fails to take account of other alienated "identities" which the "Other Woman" blots out: for example, women of other cultures, of other colours, of other sexual orientations than the predominantly white, Western, middle-class, heterosexual, academic "tradition" with which this category is associated. Secondly, that it perpetuates a fixed and singular notion of "identity": the idea that an individual "subject" is a constant category, summed up by a determinable set of characteristics ("white" "gay" "woman"). While such characteristics and "identities" are important to political agency, of equal importance is the recognition that they signify different things in different historical / cultural contexts, and that the context of the "subject" is forever changing. See Elam 1994, 69-81, for a succinct analysis of the fraught relationship of feminism and deconstruction to "identity politics".

[34] Elizabeth Grosz writes of the necessity of a "double affirmation" in feminism; both of patriarchy and of feminism. She explains: "the ways in which feminist self-help projects and equal opportunity commitments must negotiate with patriarchal institutions of the capitalist state for funding, the implication of Western feminism in neocolonialism, indeed the very investment of all of us in the West to a kind of cannibalization of the imperialized other – all illustrate our necessary, indeed constitutive immersion in the very systems from which we seek to distance, and against which we seek to position, ourselves. Without both moments in this affirmative investment, however, feminism remains in danger of repeating and being unable to recognize the very implications it believes it has repudiated" (1997, 76).

human "subjects", and Derrida claims the "source" of the call of responsibility "is not yet a divine or human 'subject'" (1991, 110). In describing this, Derrida also indicates why his "new" style does not try to actualize a figure of alterity which would be compatible with a (feminist) "identity politics" or a theory of "woman-as-subject":

> Something of this call of the other must remain nonreappropriable, nonsubjective, and in a certain way nonidentifiable, a sheer supposition, so as to remain *other*, a *singular* call to response or to responsibility. This is why the determination of the singular "Who?" – or at least its determination as subject – still remains problematic. And it *should* remain so. This obligation to protect the other's otherness is not merely a theoretical imperative (110-11).

In saying that the preservation of the other's otherness is "not merely a theoretical imperative", he is reaffirming deconstruction's ironic relation to the purely "logical" or "rational". Yet he is also talking about the more "pragmatic" implications of the "recall", because it creates an obligation to the other which cannot simply be met on one occasion. Philosophy's debt to the "feminine" other cannot be paid off like a legal settlement and then scrubbed off the records. It is a continuing debt, and one whose remembrance impinges on every decision and category, refusing their autonomy.[35] Strangely, it is the inexhaustability of this obligation, and the refusal of the other to appear as a calculable, "economic" object, which transforms the relation of sexual terms into one of possible affirmation and multiplication. The sexual hierarchy is no longer a finite "exchange" between (decidable) "subject" and "object". Like a gift, it is partly "aneconomic", and "must not circulate [...] must not be exchanged [or] exhausted [...] by the process of exchange" (1992b, 7).[36]

---

[35] Diane Elam cites this inexhaustability as a key element in what she calls the "groundless solidarity" between feminism and deconstruction: "This means a deferral of concensus but *not* at the cost of political solidarity or ethical judgment. [...] the infinite displacement brought about by feminism and deconstruction: the displacement of the subject, of identity politics, of the subject of feminism and deconstruction" (1994, 25 & 105-120). While I would qualify her use of the word "ethical" here, her description of mutually affirmative but abyssal relation between the two discourses is convincing.

[36] Derrida's definition of the 'gift' plays on the German meaning of "Gift" – "poison" – as well as the definition meaning "present". Once again, the implication is that of a contaminating, foreign body, which is somehow necessary to any affirmation.

III. Sexual Difference, Ontological Difference

While this emphasis on incalculability and dissymmetry pushes the engagement with sexual difference beyond the domain of ontology, the call for the "new" sexual specificity, which constitutes the recall of the other, still has to be constantly negotiated in relation to more conventional orderings of sexual difference as "sexed" and "opposed" beings. The double movement between ironic undecidability and contingent responsibility must necessarily be reiterated. Derrida has rarely attempted this in a context which concerns itself predominantly with the "question of sexual difference" or the "question of woman" – primarily because he seeks to resist the too-easy assimilation of specific (sexual) marks and contexts into a general schema.[37] However, the texts which do attempt this reveal Derrida's double style, and the risks involved in making its sexual decisions, more clearly than perhaps any other texts. For this reason I will devote the final section of this chapter to a brief reading of two such texts: Derrida's "Geschlecht I: Sexual Difference, Ontological Difference"; and *Spurs: Nietzsche's Styles*. The first text centres on Heidegger, and treats the problems of negotiating a *différantial* idea of sexuality within the ontologically-obsessed philosophical tradition. The second text concentrates more closely on the relation of this negotiation to issues concerning "feminine" subjectivity and "feminist" agency. Taken in combination these texts demonstrate both the power of deconstruction to transform the dialectic of sexual opposition, and the limits of its strategic relevance to feminism.

---

[37] See in particular "Fourmis" (1994b), for such a reluctance to translate in the context of sexual difference. Derrida's reading of Hélène Cixous affirms her evocation of sexual difference(s) as both "'reparation' and 'separation'", by engaging in an exhaustive analysis of every double meaning in her text which points to connection and giving or dislocation and decision. In particular, Derrida plays on the idiomatic French phrase for "both of them" – "tous les deux" – which, translated literally, can also mean "all the twos." His aim is to imply "everything that can happen *to* sexual difference or *from* sexual difference", [...] "all the couples, the duals, the duos, the differences, all the dyads in the world: each time there are two in the world" (78). The difficulty of translation is of course a common theme in Derrida's work, but is of particular relevance to the question of sexual difference if that difference is considered to be that which "unhinges" dialectical speculation. Thus Derrida calls the typographical punning in *Glas* an explanation of "untranslatability", a "round trip without circularity and without perfect specularity" (1986b, 20).

"Geschlecht"

"Geschlecht" is concerned with teasing out a marked sexual specificity which is not forced to conform to a generalized "law" of divided sexual "being". In taking as its prompt the word "Geschlecht", Derrida is gesturing towards the profound difficulty of positing where and when sexual difference should be decided, and what this decision means in terms of "being" a particular sex. Derrida's notion of the "gift" is similar to Heidegger's conception of Beings as "thrownness", so Heidegger might reasonably be expected to share Derrida's concern with "the otherness of the other."[38] Indeed, Derrida's marked reluctance to translate the word "Geschlecht" announces a mutual suspicion of generalization in the two philosophers. The written context of the word "is not irrelevant" to the elaboration of its significance in Heidegger's path of thought:

> I leave it here in its language for reasons that should become binding in the course of this very reading. And it is indeed a matter of "*Geschlecht*" (sex, race, family, generation, lineage, species, genre / genus) and not of *the Geschlecht*: one will not pass so easily toward the thing itself (the *Geschlecht*), beyond the mark of the word (*Geschlecht*) (1983, 115).

The alterity and specificity of every context must be accounted for, which means that what the word signifies as "being", concept, or proper noun, should not be generally assumed.

However, in Heidegger's reluctance to "pass so easily toward the thing" there is a point of difficulty; namely his apparent effort to keep *Dasein* – the "given" of his structure – sexually "neutral", or to avoid mentioning sex at all.[39] It is this neutrality which is the focus of Derrida's text. It suggests two possible readings of Heidegger: one which implies a *différantial* model of sexual difference which resists binarist or oppositional orderings; and one which relegates sexual difference to a secondary position in relation to the ontological order.

"Geschlecht" centres on a ruling question: why does Heidegger ignore the question of sexual difference in his early texts, only to

---

[38] See chapter 3, footnote 26, for a brief description of Heidegger's relation to ideas of "the gift".

[39] It is impossible to fully explain the meaning of *Dasein* here as it could easily take the whole chapter. However, its literal translation – "there being" or "being there" – indicates that Heidegger's basic category of Being is neither a transcendental law nor a phenomenal "thing": it is already part of the world without yet being actualized.

make a point of the asexuality or neutrality of *Dasein* in later texts?[40] Derrida believes this double response stems from the "double" status of *Dasein*. In *Being and Time* "Being", in the existential-ontological sense in which it is being read, is more primary than structures of reading such as anthropology or ethics with which questions on sexuality are naturally associated: "the existential analytic of *Dasein can* only occur within the perspective of a fundamental ontology" (1983, 68). At first glance this would suggest that Heidegger considers sexuality to be irrelevant to his elaboration of the order of being; that *Dasein* has a certain transcendent quality about it which might make it a "pure", metaphysical determination. Heidegger's ontology would then be of little interest to a feminist or deconstructivist reading, other than as another example of (phal)logocentric thinking. However, Heidegger's delineation of *Dasein* also suggests that his ontology cannot be traced in isolation of structures such as anthropology or ethics, since the latter are within the realm of determinate beings – including the philosophers who form questions – which the "Being" of Heidegger's ontology becomes. Although Heidegger says that "Being" is the fundamental category of existence, and prior to any existent "being", he insists that "Being" cannot be thought of as any entity itself: it is only in its apparentness in the world of things that it can be deemed to be present. In itself, therefore, Being is nothing, even as it is the predicate of existence which is in some sense always already present.

> Neutral *Dasein* is never what exists; *Dasein* exists in each case only in its factical concretion. But neutral *Dasein* is indeed the primal source of intrinsic possibility that springs up in every existence and makes it intrinsically possible (Heidegger 1984, 137).

That the relation of Being to itself is as it is already revealed in the world (and is thus also nothing in itself) means that Being is immanent without being self-identical. It reveals itself and makes itself present in and as its *withdrawal* from being (present). Thus while Heidegger may, in the language of existentialism, call the "there-ness" or "throwness" of Being (*Dasein*) the "exemplary being",

---

[40] In "Geschlecht", Derrida analyses the absence of the question of sexuality in *Being and Time* and the explanation of Dasein's neutrality in a course given by Heidegger at the University of Marburg / Lahn in the Summer Semester 1928. "Geschlecht II: Heidegger's Hand", reads Heidegger's later work on the order of being and sexual / generic marking in his analysis of Trakl's poetry (1987e).

its directionality is determined as much by its non-presence as by its presence.[41]

This "ontico-ontological difference" is clearly similar to Derrida's différantial non-ontology, in being an already disseminated and yet never *present* structure.[42] Indeed, elsewhere Derrida calls Heidegger's "process of truth … the ambiguity or duplicity of the presence of the present, of its *appearance* – that which appears *and* its appearing – in the *fold* of the present participle" (1981a, 192). As such it troubles any simple notions of the primacy and purity of Being, either as metaphysical category or phenomenal essence. The only "unity" which is a constant is the present / absent time of (re)presentation, which is presumably why Heidegger ascribes a "privileged constitutive function" to language in *Being and Time* (1962, 400), and concentrates much of his later work on the disclosure of Being through *poetry*.[43]

The question Derrida asks now is why, if Heidegger holds proto-deconstructive ideas about "presence" and the temporal order of Beings, should he want to evade or erase sexual difference? *Dasein's* appearing / withdrawing movement implies that the apparently "asexual" Being which sits "in bare relation to itself", is already marked with the "internal possibility" of becoming sexual; divided … by sexuality toward a determinate sex" (1983, 75). In fact, while Heidegger names "neutral *Dasein*" as "the primal source of intrinsic possibility", he also says that *Dasein* "harbours the intrinsic

---

[41] Heidegger describes an existential-ontological anxiety provoked by the disclosure of *Dasein* in terms rather like Kierkegaard's and claims it "belongs to Dasein's essential state of Being-in-the-world". However, his emphasis is more "uncanny" than Kierkegaard's: he insists that this state of mind is "never present-at-hand" and that the "not-at-home" should be considered as "the more primordial phenomenon" (1962, 234).

[42] It also resembles Levinas' *il y a* but maintains less of an anticipation of revelation.

[43] For a remarkably lucid explanation of Heidegger's privileging of poetic language see Clark 1986. According to Clark, Heidegger believes that poetic language *is* not present but gives presence, as proximity. It does not simply imitate or represent something that is already there, but *discloses* the apparent. The sense of "disclosure" used by Heidegger in this context retains the idea of withdrawal. As Clark says, "being *qua* disclosure is precisely that which does not appear in that which is disclosed (entities)" so that "in what is *disclosed disclosure* itself is erased" (1009). This means that poetic language, in its simultaneous referentiality and ambiguity, most closely evokes the "unveiling" of being, which "becomes present as an appearance that tantalizingly conceals" (1011). It also means that Heidegger uses the language of ontology in a way which is not necessarily "digestive", as Levinas would maintain.

possibility for being factically dispersed into bodiliness and thus into sexuality" (1984, 137).

Derrida provides an answer which revolves around the negative connotations of conventional philosophical theories of sexual division and distribution.

According to Derrida, the "metaphysical" neutrality of *Dasein* "is not an empty abstraction operating from or in the sense of the ontic", a "*neither-nor*", but rather "the 'not yet' of factual dissemination, of dissociation, of being dis-sociated or of factual dis-society" (1983, 75). This means that whatever division or dispersion comes about, occurs not as some negative encounter which destroys *Dasein's* initial integrity (Derrida uses the word "*décheance*", which means "decline", "degeneration" or "deposition") – as it would in a dialectical structure – but as the *concrete* aspect of *Dasein's* intrinsic possibility:

> It is an originary structure affecting *dasein* with the body, and *hence* with sexual difference, of multiplicity and lack-of-binding [*déliaison*] … (75).

(Sexual) dispersion can thus be read as an affirmative occurrence, or, as Heidegger calls it, a "positivity" or "power" (71).

However, the register of ontology within which Heidegger writes (and which, at least in terms of temporal structure, he seems to challenge) does not allow such a "positive" interpretation. Derrida makes it clear that as soon as one tries to conceive of the particular "body" or "determinate sex" which *Dasein* anticipates, there is no choice but to slide into a conceptual language which carries a negative resonance:

> *Dasein* is separated in its facticity, subjected to dispersion and parcelling out (*zersplittert*), and thereby (*ineins damit*) always disjunct, in disaccord, split up, divided (*zwiespältig*) by sexuality toward a determinate sex (*in eine bestimmte Geschlechtlichkeit*) (76).

The naming of sexuality – the passing to the "thing itself" – seems to cut off the sexual possibility of *Dasein,* because its language is still caught in an order which constrains sexual determination to an act of division; to "being" one of two sexes. It conforms to the binarist logic which Heidegger's ontico-ontological difference complicates.

This considered, Heidegger's insistence on the neutrality of *Dasein* may be very far from being restrictive, or being a denial of sexuality. It may instead be interpreted as an attempt to mark sexual difference in a way which does not limit sexual possibility in the way that it has historically been limited; and continues to be limited. The neutralization may serve as a radical complication of the temporal "ordering" of Being's sexuality which exchanges the possibility of revealing a sexually-essential being, secondary to Being, for the possibility of revealing the manifold sexual *markings* of and within Being. Derrida says that Heidegger's resistance to the conventional ontological order,

> … suggests that the a-sexual neutrality does not desexualize, on the contrary; its *ontological* negativity is not unfolded with respect to *sexuality itself* (which it would instead liberate), but on its differential marks, or more strictly on *sexual duality*. There would be no *Geschlechtslosigkeit* except with respect to "two"; asexuality could be determined as such only to the degree that sexuality would mean immediately binarity or sexual division (71).

Derrida's reading of Heidegger prompts him to suggest (tentatively) a definition of sexuality and sexual difference which "belongs to neither of the two sexes" (72). Like Heidegger's *Dasein* it is a "pre-dual sexuality" which is not necessarily "unitary, homogeneous or undifferentiated". It is something like a primordial sexuality – the sexual possibility *before* sexual determination – which bears a neutral and neutralizing relation to "male" and "female" sexed identities; even while it is what enables a concrete sexual specificity or decision. This may sound altogether too "pure" and originary for a deconstructive ordering, but Derrida is not seeking to divorce his sexual difference from specific categories of being and invest it with transcendent powers. Indeed, it is because he is manifestly resisting such a metaphysical gesture that "Geschlecht" focuses on Heidegger's neutralization of *Dasein* as a *response* to, and reiteration of, pre-existent "categories" of sex. Derrida explains it thus:

> … it is sexual division itself which leads to negativity, so neutralization is *at once* the effect of this negativity and the effacement to which thought must subject it to allow an original positivity to become manifest. Far from constituting a positivity that the asexual neutrality of *Dasein* would annul, sexual binarity itself would be responsible for this negativization (72).

In other words, sexual difference (conceived as sexual binarity) neutralizes sexual difference (conceived as possibility and multiplicity) by determining it as divided beings, and in order that sexual difference be realizable as a possibility "other" than "the one and the two", it must withold from and remain neutral in relation to sexual binarity.

Put like this, the Heideggerian sexual order begins to sound like Derrida's "undecidable" decision: the ironic reiteration of established orders and categories through their own alterity. This is true to an extent, but Derrida is clearly not attempting to claim Heidegger as a proto-feminist. "Geschlecht" is a deconstruction of Heidegger's retreat into metaphysical "purity" as much as an analysis of *Dasein's* potentially different sexuality. The specific details of this are not wholly relevant to my discussion of the sexual theme in "Geschlecht", so I will only attempt a brief sketch of its salient points. Derrida notes that in spite of his careful elaboration of *Dasein's* dispersed "unity" and doubly determined "neutrality", Heidegger remains strangely attached to the idea of an "authentic" articulation of *Dasein*. At times the dispersion, which is considered essential to the concrete potential of *Dasein,* is treated as a sign of (undesirable) inauthenticity, and even decline (81-83). Derrida reads this as an unwillingness in Heidegger to admit that his philosophical project will never be completed. The marking of an originary dissemination brings with it the realization of the necessary endlessness of questioning and negotiation. In spite of figuring an alternative order of being and time *by reiterating* prior structurations of "being and time", Heidegger still wants his philosophy to step beyond these structurations and become independent and autonomous. In "Geschlecht II", Derrida analyses a more reactionary Heidegger, who seeks to "gather" the thought of Being to the site of a more "authentic" language, beyond the "negative" resonances of Christian / Platonic influence.[44] Not only is this impossible, but it is irresponsible, as it fails to acknowledge the negativity and violence of its own heritage. As Derrida points out, the word "Geschlecht" is related to "Schlag", which means "blow" or "strike": the marking of difference, the dissemination of terms, always implies some kind of violence.[45]

Derrida resists the desire for "authenticity", remembering through his risky, double writing the violence and dissymmetry which is part of its "essential heritage"; and which must be continually reiterated and renegotiated if difference-as-alterity is to be properly acknowledged. In its acceptance of this endless contamination, the sexual order is, ironically, less negative, less violent than Heidegger's. While interrogating its own "self-positing", Derrida's writing enables the force of undecidability to strike through the opposed categories of

---

[44] Derrida is careful to point out that there is still a subtle interplay in Heidegger's reading of Trakl between a non-binary idea of "Geschlecht" which can be interpreted as "a certain duplicity, a certain fold of sexual difference" [*das Zwiefache*] and "the duality of the sexes as dissension" [*die Zweitracht der Geschlechter*]. However, Heidegger is now insistent that the "'primordial' non-binary difference is pre-Platonic, pre-metaphysical, or pre-Christian" (1987e, 185-195).

[45] Derrida says that "Geschlecht" "has an essential affinity with the blow, the strike, the imprint" (1989, 106).

"the structure of ipseity" ("... me and you, conscious or unconscious subject, man or woman"), re-marking sexuality as *difference* and sexual determination as a highly specific, contingent decision which does not "belong" to any overarching law (1983, 74). Derrida can then imagine another way of thinking which liberates "the field of sexuality for a very different sexuality, a more multiple one":

> At that point there would be no more sexes [...] there would be one sex for each time. One sex for each gift. A sexual difference for each gift. [...] By definition, one cannot calculate the gift. We are in the order of the incalculable, of undecidability which is a strategic undecidability where one says 'it is undecidable because it is not this term of the opposition or the other'. This is sexual difference. It is absolutely heterogeneous (1987f, 199).

By calling it a "strategic undecidability", Derrida leaves room for specific sexual decisions – which must and will inevitably be made – but reinforces the radical contingency and impurity of such decisions, as they occur within the uncanny, "always-already" temporal order of their writing.

Consequently, the crucial issues to any "feminist" reading of philosophy or narrative are both exaggerated and redefined. The mark of sexual difference is inscribed even before the possibility of Being or being; of having a sexed body or identity and a specific gender. Yet this mark of difference cannot possibly conform to the onto-theological order where a difference "before" implies an origin or essence – a more "authentic" realm of Being than the present. The mark is a possibility of (more than) division and a promise of heterogeneity and multiplicity which allows and partakes in specific sexual "decisions" – biological, behavioural, figural, experiential, orientational – but disallows the appropriation of any of these as the "truth" of being or gender, just as it disallows itself such a status. As a result, the responsibility to the "feminine" other is paramount and endless, but cannot be contained in the "present" revelatory or revolutionary moment of a "knowable" ethics or politics. Responsibility is taken in a "here and now" which performs itself as an anxious-ironic "speculation": it constantly demands an account of the specificity of the "feminine" in the particular context of the analysis, while acknowledging the impossibility of pinning "her" function down to a "proper" position.[46] In keeping her determination

---

[46] Hélène Cixous summarizes this approach in a more phenomenological feminist style when she says "It *is* a question of sexual difference, only sexual difference isn't what we think it is. It is both tortuous and complicated. There is sexual difference, and

open to other possibilities or configurations, we may not be able to constitute a new law of the feminine, but there is a far greater likelihood of being able to make a "just" decision in contexts which demand that we speak of "woman", "women", "gender" or "sex".

Spurs

However, Derrida's "new" style is not without its problems with regard to the feminist project. While it is difficult to lend credence to those who accuse him of "appropriating" feminine metaphors while dispensing with her possible "identity", there are moments when Derrida's sexual undecidability seems to cover rather than probe the anxiety surrounding sexual decisions.[47]

One such moment is in *Spurs / Éperons*, where Derrida uses his analysis of the many, apparently contradictory, "styles" of Nietzsche's philosophical writings to trace the undecidability of the authorial and sexual "subject". In many ways *Spurs* treads over the same ground as *Glas,* as it serves to disband the truth values around which dialectical modes of thought operate. Once again, Derrida focusses on the "fetishistic" functioning of dialectical logic, which treats anything that is "other" to essential, "revealed" presence (accidents, materiality, representation, sexual difference) as both the opposite of and substitute for the "thing itself". "Woman" is the archetype of these "essentializing fetishes" (1979, 54-55), and her truth, "femininity", is one of the "foundations or anchorings of Western rationality": that which shores up the "truth" of masculine subjectivity (1985, 170-71). Derrida traces the relation between Nietzsche's different "styles" and his wildly varying declarations about "woman" and "femininity", in order to explore the difficulty of countering this fetishistic logic, and to suggest implicitly a model of "strategic undecidability" which might successfully resist it.

Like Derrida, Nietzsche seems to acknowledge the risk of any challenge to the prevailing order becoming just another negatively

---

there is what it becomes in its appearances and distributions in each one of us" (1993, 50). I will return to Cixous' version of deconstructive feminism in my final chapter.

[47] I partly have Spivak in mind here, but Irigaray makes the most uncompromising accusations about Derrida's "disposal" of the feminine identity. She acknowledges the necessity of "*screens*, *instruments*, *tools*, *supports*, even *resistance*, for every reinscription of traces", but believes that Derrida disposes "of *eyes*, of *hands*, of *mouths*, of *sex*, and those of *others*" as if they were "tools, instruments, supports" (1985, 164). This accusation presupposes an autonomous physical realm apart from the effects of culture or textuality, and somehow implies that it has claims to be more authentic.

capable opposition that continues truth's logic. His constant enemy is the "dogmatic" philosopher who fails to recognize that the truth he so desperately wants to gaze upon and penetrate is no more transcendent or permanent than a metaphor.[48] This means that the only way for Nietzsche to vanquish his enemy and bypass his dogmatism is to refuse to overcome his "truth" with another – even a "negative" one – and to refuse the "authenticity" of his own, self-present thought and authorship. According to Derrida's reading, philosophy for Nietzsche becomes something close to an art, and the positing of philosophical consciousness a performance: not as a fully-intended subversion of dogmatic logic (mimetic art versus pure reason) but as a way of acknowledging the infinitely different forces, tropes, images and words which constitute even the most "fundamental" truth. Unlike "truthful" philosophy, this philosophy admits to its own ambiguous and contingent constitution, and does not claim to pin down multiple possibilities into a single, "unveiled" truth:

> style […] uses its spur (éperon) as a means of protection against the terrifying, blinding, mortal threat (of that) which *presents* itself, which obstinately thrusts itself into view. And style thereby protects the presence, the content, the thing itself, meaning, truth – on the condition at least that it should not *already* (*déjà*) be that gaping chasm which has been deflowered in the unveiling of the difference (1979, 38-39).

The "style" interposes with a double gesture, holding back from positing itself as certain, truthful presence because the trace of its own alterity has already been posited ("spur" in German means "trace"). "Truth" as "presence, the content, the thing itself, meaning" is therefore impossible. Nevertheless, there is still a residual (trace) return of "presence, the content, the thing itself, meaning" in the necessary structure of (self-)positing (the violent "spurring" of decision). This repeats the simultaneous desire for and fear of final, truthful revelation (the fetishistic "mortal threat" of the "gaping chasm"), but, marked with its other traces, the style no longer believes

---

[48] I am thinking here of Nietzsche's famous definition of truth in his essay "On Truth and Lies in an Extra-Moral Sense": "a mobile army of metaphors, metonyms, and anthropomorphisms – in short, a sum of human relations which have been enhanced, transposed, and embellished poetically and rhetorically, and which after long use seem firm, canonical, and obligatory to a people: truths are illusions about which one has forgotten that this is what they are …" (1979, 82). Derrida's text quotes from many of Nietzsche's works, but the references to "dogmatic" truth and the "feminine" are mainly from *The Gay Science*. I will conduct a more extensive analysis of the links between Nietzschean and deconstructive ideas in my final chapter.

in the authority of this revelation. Differences are and have already been marked, but *the* difference has always yet to be revealed.[49]

While this "strategy" is not the same as Derrida's *différantial* logic – Nietzsche is less wary than Derrida of violently inflicting his "own" style upon his enemies – it has a comparable effect in complicating any notion of a singular origin or presence. "Essence" crumbles in the face of the "other" traces which form and contaminate it; and the determination of categories – including sexual, ontological, and authorial categories – is a matter of "propriation" rather than natural destiny; the force of a whole history of decisions rather than a pre-ordained and revealable "truth":[50]

> The history (of) truth (is) a process of propriation. So property (*le propre*) is not the concern (*ne relève pas*) of an onto-phenomenological or semantico-hermeneutic interrogation (110-11, translation modified).

The fact that Nietzsche's opinions and styles of writing vary so wildly is thus taken by Derrida to mean that Nietzsche is practising a "vertiginous non-mastery" (100-101), which is the only way *not* to write an "onto-phenomenological or semantico-hermeneutic interrogation". He is making himself a master of inauthenticity, parodying the "history of truth" without *properly* calculating his "own" self-positing, so that he does not inscribe another "confession or law table". As Derrida remarks, echoing *Glas*, and underscoring the importance of undecidability within any textual intervention,

> … to use parody […] as a weapon in the service of truth or castration would be in fact to reconstitute religion, as a Nietzsche cult for example, in the interest of a priesthood of parody interpreters (98-99).

Even parody is not immune from the processes of propriation, so Nietzsche's "style" takes care not to become determinedly, monumentally parodic.[51]

---

49 The time of this double style is similar to Heidegger's ontico-ontological difference: "*Already* (*déja*), such is the name for what has been effaced or subtracted beforehand, but which has nevertheless left behind a mark, a signature which is retracted in that very thing from which it is withdrawn" (38-9).

50 Once again, I defer proper examination of Nietzsche's genealogical method until my final chapter. However, for an introductory analysis of this method and its relation to Nietzsche's style of writing, see Allison 1977, xxi - xxvi.

51 Derrida's joke about the "priesthood of parody interpreters" should perhaps be taken to heart in the current context of gender studies, where swathes of earnest interpretations of "parodic" and "performative" formations of gender are being published. I hope my own contribution does not fall into this priestly trap.

Of even greater significance to Derrida is that Nietzsche links this dissimulative art to the figure of "woman":

> The enchantment and the most powerful effect of woman (*der Zaber und die mächtigste Wirkung der Frauen*), is, to use the language of philosophers, as effect at a distance (*eine Wirkung in die Ferne*), an *actio in distans*; but for this it is necessary that there be, primarily and above all – *distance!* (*dazu gehort aber, und vor allem – Distanz!*) (46-47, quoting Nietzsche 1974, translation modified).

While at first glance this might simply be read as another idealized figuration of the "truth" of the woman's alterity, Derrida detects a doubleness in Nietzsche's writing (specifically, in the hyphenated injunction about the necessity of "*Distanz*") which warns the reader off approaching, interpreting and determining this distant woman too quickly. "A distance from distance must be maintained": a double distance which interrupts the dogmatic philosopher's use of the other for the purposes of subscribing (his) "truth" (48-49). Derrida comments:

> If it is necessary to keep one's distance from the feminine operation, from the *actio in distans,* […] it is perhaps because "woman" is not a determinable identity. Perhaps woman is not some thing which announces itself from a distance, at a distance from some other thing.

In other words, in this context the logic of fetishistic "truth" is suspended. The "distant" woman parodies the language of philosophy because, historically, she is "other" to its "truth". Yet if her "otherness" is not to become a simple inversion of "truth", and thus a repetition of its binary logic, it must not be determined as her defining position; her "essential" identity. Some other "otherness" must remain if the differences of and within "truth" – in particular, the sexual differences – are to be marked. The philosopher must therefore follow the "woman's" example of distance and not try to define her as the (possessed, appropriated) "other" *of* his "proper truth": the "thing itself".

Nietzsche, according to Derrida, is rewriting the "allegorical" figure of feminine "truth" (woman as "lack of truth" or "truth-substitute") in a way that opens it up to a play of differences beyond the binary choices of fetishism (truth / untruth; the thing / nothing; whole / castrated). She is still idealized to some degree, as Nietzsche claims that truth is "like a woman" in witholding its beauty.[52] However, this ideality is a returning "trace" (*spur*) which is no longer sustained as the "truth of woman" because, being defined according to its capacity to "withold", its final definition is deferred. Woman as *distant* "truth" makes *present* truth impossible:

> she is woman precisely because she herself does not believe in truth itself, because she does not believe in what she is, in what she is believed to be, in what she thus is not.
>
> In its maneuvers distance strips the lady of her identity and unseats the philosopher-knight (52-53).

Like Heidegger, Nietzsche enables a pattern of sexual decision and sexual difference which maintains a crucial "undecidability". Unlike Heidegger, Nietzsche does not seek to figure this pattern within a philosophy of "authentic" Being.

Derrida uses Nietzsche's version of "strategic undecidability" to warn off the common assumption that if there is to be such a thing as a specifically "feminist" agency, it must take a subjective form and seek a "proper", independent identity for "woman". He reasserts his belief that to follow this assumption is to repeat the blind philosophical faith in essential "truth" and thus to preclude alterity. Alternatively, Nietzsche's "distant" woman, like the "maverick" feminist Derrida refers to in "Choreographies", ridicules this faith through her ironic reiteration of her own (ironic) alterity, and posits her difference as one of many possible propriations. Rather than opposing the logic of the fetish, she ceases to give credence to the whole dialectic of fetishism. As Derrida says,

> 'Woman' – her name made epoch – no more believes in castration's exact opposite, anti-castration, than she does in castration itself. Much too clever for that […] she knows that such a reversal would only deprive her of her powers of simulation, that in truth a reversal of that kind would, in the end, only amount to the same thing and force her just as surely into the same old apparatus (60-61).

Sexual difference thus becomes a matter of infinite potentiality and possibility, which is not tied to "present" being. Sexual decision, like authorial propriation, is a contingent performance interrupted by the "other" time of its writing.

---

[52] Describing the true nature of life, Nietzsche says that it "puts a golden-embroidered veil of lovely potentialities over itself, promising, resisting, modest, mocking, sympathetic, seductive. Yes, life is a woman!" (quoted in Derrida 1979, 50-53).

However, Derrida is so concerned with the way in which Nietzsche's "inauthentic" propriation resists the ontological order, and refuses "this term of [sexual] opposition or the other", that he does not sufficiently attend to the degree to which Nietzsche's styles reinscribe the phallocentric hierarchy.

The pretext of Derrida's analysis is that some "trace" return of binarist logic is always likely as part of the written intervention: Nietzsche's realization of his own violence in "self-positing" lies at the (displaced) centre of Derrida's reiteration. He quotes Nietzsche's musings in the *Untimely Meditations* on the fact that every philosopher is always considering a "predetermined decision and answer to predetermined selected questions" because of the unchangeable "'das bin ich' ("this is I")" which speaks with every thought (104-5). Significantly, Nietzsche's comment is a strategic disclaimer which precedes his positing of "a few truths about 'woman as such'", and Derrida reads it as further evidence of Nietzsche's interruption of essential "truth": the "truths" about "woman" are largely symptomatic of the inevitable propriations of the writing "I", and are not to be construed as authoritative. The disclaimer extends to his "subject" – "woman as such" (or the "eternal feminine") – which has no more permanence or authenticity than his own posited truths. In fact, Derrida doubles back on this, by suggesting that Nietzsche's inauthentic "self-positing" is prompted by the figure of "woman".

> The question of the woman suspends the decidable opposition of true and non-true and inaugurates the epochal regime of quotation marks which is to be enforced for every concept belonging to the system of philosophical decidability (106-7).

This makes sense with regard to the logic of undecidability, and shares the already-divided temporality of Derrida's other texts on sexual difference. As in *Glas*, the "double" status of the woman – as man's "castrated" other and as the suspended other of this other who does not believe in castration – suspends the dialectical exchange.

Nevertheless – and this is where I would argue a degree of evasiveness enters – it seems odd that in a context which is concerned specifically with the "propriative" interrelation of sexual and stylistic decisions, Derrida does not much question the extent to which Nietzsche's strategic "I" still participates in (and propriates through) a binary sexuality. Much more is made of the effect of "woman's" alterity on her own and Nietzsche's own "proper" truth than of the effect of Nietzsche's "I" on the remains of the category of "woman". As both "subjects" are remaining "traces", each will presumably have an impact on the other; but Derrida does not attend to them equally. Consequently, Nietzsche's famously misogynistic remarks about emancipated women (the "abortions … who lack the wherewithal to have children") and even the perfect woman (whose love would "tear him to pieces") are read as oscillations of Nietzsche's undecidable style, and not as a reiteration of the "eternal" sex war and a garnering of self-conscious authority. While Derrida *does* briefly turn his attention to the trace return of the "old" philosophical tactics,

> The stylate spur [*l'éperon stylé*] […] dismantles […] the truth in its guise of production, the unveiling/dissimulation of the present product. The veil is no more raised than it is lowered; its suspension is delimited – the epoch. To de-limit, to undo, to come undone, when it is a matter of the veil, is that not once again tantamount to unveiling? indeed, to the destruction of a fetish? This question – insofar as a question (between logos and theoria, the spoken and the seen) remains – remains interminably (106-9, translation modified).

he does not linger on this "question" in any specific way. He maintains instead that this "process of propriation" "escapes" ontological decidability and the possibility of an onto-hermeneutic interrogation; and that being "more powerful than the question *ti esti*," one cannot examine it directly (108-117). This effectively blurs the "question" about unveiling – which concerns the propriative decision of written intervention and its effect on the other – by considering it as a question which concerns being. Asking whether "propriation" repeats or simulates the movement of fetishistic revelation is not the same as trying to pin down "*what it is*", especially if the propriative economy takes analysis beyond the possibility of such strictly ontological questions. But this is what Derrida's logic in this passage seems to suggest. Moreover, if we are "beyond" in the sense that no sexual or "authorial" positions are purely present, stable or final, surely the relation of these different simulated "positions" is at least as worthy of consideration as the instability of the "positions"? Yet Derrida privileges the latter by passing onto an analysis of the interrupted nature of Heidegger's ontological investigations (108-9).[53] While he refers to the complications of the new sexual signs, where "man and woman change places, exchange masks *ad infinitum*"(110-11), and the opposition between them can be perceived as "nothing more than a transcendental snare which is produced by the hymen's graphic", he does not attend to the workings of this transcendental

---

[53] As in "Geschlecht", Derrida remarks on the way the "sexual question" is "subsumed" by Heidegger "in the general question of the truth of being." This is ironic considering that Derrida also glides over the sexual question here.

snare other than to note that in many of Nietzsche's analyses of sexual difference, "woman is woman" […] "according to an already formalized law" (108-9).[54]

All of this must be read in context, of course. Derrida is *distancing* himself, in doubly ironic fashion, from subjective and intentional definitions of writing and authorship; and from those areas of the feminist movement which can only imagine a new sexual order based on a self-determining female "subject".[55] To object to *Spurs* on the grounds of Derrida's displacement of feminine "subjectivity" is to miss the *irony* of the text: a very serious irony which is concerned above all with marking and problematizing the idealized figuration of the feminine; whether as metaphors of phallocentric or anti-phallocentric "truth".[56] Derrida's refusal to read Nietzsche's violent declarations conventionally, or take them completely seriously, is thus part of his own not-quite-conscious strategy. *Spurs* attempts to enact a "strategic undecidability" which, through its suspension of oppositional decision-making and dialectical time, reiterates and transforms Nietzsche's "truths" so that even his blatant misogynies are interrupted by alterity. Yet even given these ironic complications, through much of the text it is too difficult to distinguish Derrida's "style" from Nietzsche's for this strategy to be clear. It is almost as if his suspicion of "onto-phenomenological or semantico-hermeneutic" positions is so great that he cannot posit his "own" style: anxiety

---

[54] Of course, in such a contingent and contextualized "structure" as Derrida's, it is, as he says, impossible to elaborate on such numerous appearances of "woman" (108-9). However, in the examples he cites from Nietzsche's texts, the "formalized law" dictates that either "woman" "gives herself" (according to Nietzsche's *Gay Science,* in "complete surrender") or she "*gives herself*" (simulates giving, thus assuring "possessive mastery" for herself in an ironic manner). This means that "man" would either possess woman completely, or (mistakenly) believe he possessed her: he would never "give" himself (108-9, footnote 14). There is a dissymmetry here, which, while not necessarily incompatible with the "infinite exchange of masks," still needs to be considered in relation to the "old" oppositional hierarchy.

[55] In her essay, "'Women' in *Spurs* and Nineties Feminism", Jane Gallop maintains that it is important to view Derrida's "woman-centred" texts as being "of their time": as reactions to the simplistic essentialisms of the political feminist movement of the 'seventies (1997, 7-19).

[56] For an example of blindness to *Spurs*' levels of irony, see Feder and Zakin (1997, 21-51). The authors are justifiably concerned that Derrida's textual performance does not take sufficient account of the different status of masculine and feminine "subjects", as inherited from conventional philosophy. However, they interpret the undecidability of Derrida's own authorial "propriation" as a fully intended parodic "strategy" which leaves "his authorial position […] stable, consistent with that structurally accorded to men" (41). I would argue that the whole point of *Spurs* is to problematize such decidable notions of subjective, authorial "ironic" intention.

about his "proper" intervention and a desire to be thoroughly – perhaps authentically – inauthentic takes over, and swamps his engagement with the binarist legacy. And while I would not go as far as Spivak, who says that in *Spurs* "woman" and "différance" are interchangeable "as two names on a chain of nominal displacements" (1989, 215), or as far as Braidotti, who says that "woman" merely functions as "emblem of the non-truth of truth" (1991, 103), I would argue that the specific sexual decisions taken as a part of authorial propriation are under-theorized in comparison with the propriative aspects of sexual "truth". Considering the text is less confined to ontological questions than "Geschlecht", and far more concerned with the violence and responsibilities of writing, one would expect it to tackle more openly the specific relation of the "new" *différantial* definitions of sexuality to the remains or returns of the "old" definitions. What of the philosopher's "own" gender? Would the philosopher's relation to their own "proper" truth be different if they were already classified as a "woman"? Even if the intervention of Derrida's style – the "event" of the text – is merely a "structurally posthumous necessity" (1979, 136-7), a scriptural and sexual decision has occurred which begs further analysis.

While tracing this moment of obfuscation, I am anxious that it should not be interpreted as a diagnosis (*pace* Spivak and Braidotti) of a kind of generalized resistance in Derrida to defining sexuality beyond the idealized sexual positions of the dialectic. His reiteration of the structure of time liberates the ironic feminine from the shackles of negative capability, and heralds a truly differential, rather than binary, notion of sexual difference. Nevertheless, the obfuscation within *Spurs* does suggest a continued anxiety surrounding the question of femininity, which exceeds the anxiety of other textual decisions. It is interesting to consider that while Derrida's work has returned again and again to questions of patrilineal inheritance, of veiled and revealed "truth", to philosophy's "proper" style, the specifically sexual aspects of propriation are usually approached obliquely; *more* obliquely than these other propriative questions. Whether it is through the scuttling ants of "Fourmis" (1994b), or the mesh of masculine and feminine pronouns and textiles in "A Silkworm of One's Own" (2001a), the style in which Derrida weaves questions of sexual decision is tentative almost to the point of being chivalrous.[57] One might even suggest that it is because sexual difference is such an embedded thread in any deliberation over written decisions and propriations that Derrida finds it difficult to approach directly. The fact that he still employs terms such as "madness", "unconsciousness" and "indecipherability" in relation to these decisions – even though we are no longer speaking of a "present" moment of decision and it has thus lost its redemptive or revelatory import – indicates that they are still proximate to the limit, the irreducible, that which philosophy cannot theorize; just as they were with Kierkegaard.[58] And while it is important to re-emphasize that the "risk" of returning the other to a hierarchy where she is negative and secondary is inherent to the deconstructive approach to ironic agency, one can still say that Derrida's writings about sexual difference are more subject to this risk than the writings which do not have the feminine "as [their] subject". The ground of these texts – at its heights in *Spurs* – is deconstruction at its most dangerous. As such, it is writing at its most (potentially) fertile and yet, paradoxically, least "readable"; even for Derrida, within his own radical context.

All of this suggests the profound intractability of the questions posed by the interrelation of irony, femininity and sexual difference. After Derrida, we cannot look for a single answer, because to accept the deconstructive "strategy" is to accept that "there has never been *the* style, *the* simulacrum, *the* woman [...] nor *the* sexual difference" (1979, 138-9). Nevertheless, it should be possible within specific deconstructive and feminist contexts to analyse in detail the relation of the different "styles" between which the "simulacrum" of feminine sexuality is drawn. This remains to be written in a way which takes account of the different impact the sexually "undecidable" decision

---

[57] Of course, in "A Silkworm of One's Own", the faltering progress of the text represents the constant weaving and dismantlement of what Derrida calls the "great and inexhaustible penelopean scene of sexual difference" (58): once again, it signifies a resistance to pluralizing or indefinite definitions of sexuality. Derrida's assumption of the "loom" is an ironic marker of Freud's and philosophy's designation of weaving as women's only technical invention; and it is thus also a suspension of the castrated status of the Freudian woman. Nevertheless, the flip side of Derrida's writing seems to be that while Derrida insists that one must "disentangle, disencumber, extricate" the threads of specific sexual decisions (61), the text's dispersal of sexual signifiers into a dense fabric of tropes, puns and homonyms wards of the attempt to do precisely that.

[58] "Indecipherability" is a word that recurs throughout *Spurs*. It is interesting to note the frequency with which Derrida quotes Kierkegaard's declaration about the "moment of decision" being "madness" in contexts where the "just" treatment of the other is most at stake. It is arguably the central quotation of "Force of Law" as well as *The Gift of Death*; and provides the epigraph for Derrida's analysis of Foucault, "Cogito and the History of Madness" (1978c).

will have on one who writes "like" a woman – whatever their named gender may be – and on one who writes "as" a woman; who is already named as "woman" whether "she" writes "like" her or not.[59] The two established categories of sex can no longer be taken as God-given, anatomically-irreducible "beings" which pre-exist the writing structure, but as *Spurs* makes clear, the legacy of sexual division lives on and intrudes upon the propriative decisions of authorship. This legacy, and the ways in which it may continue to be rewritten, will be the subject of my final chapter.

---

[59] Elizabeth Grosz says something similar when she distinguishes between an understanding of sexuality as "pleasurable drive" and as "sexed subjectivity". While she is careful to point out that "sexed subjectivity" is not a matter of immutable anatomy, and that neither definition is entirely separable from the other – "how one lives in the first sense depends on how one is sexed in the second sense" – she believes that Derrida's sexual "undecidability" makes more sense in relation to the first definition than the second: "In short, one lives one's sexual indeterminacy, one's possibilities for being sexed otherwise differently depending on whether one is male or female. This is not […] to predetermine how one 'is' male or female, but simply to suggest that there is an ineradicable rift between the two, in whatever forms they are lived" (1997, 94).

Chapter 5

Miming History: Sarah Kofman

"The hymen interposes itself between mimicry and mimesis or rather between mimesis and mimesis." Jacques Derrida (1991a, 219).

"Freud and Nietzsche, [the] two rival 'geniuses' I have always needed to hold together so that neither of them could ultimately win out over the other, or over 'me'. Endlessly playing the one and the other, and playing the one off against the other, in 'me', I prevent both from gaining mastery. […] This is perhaps what constitutes the specificity of my reading." Sarah Kofman (1993a, 371-2).

The point we have reached with Derrida, then, is one where we are no longer seeking a "new" identity, name, or figure of "woman" or "femininity", not because it is impossible without losing access to positionality and signification altogether (Kristeva, Lacan), nor because the feminine is strictly "other" as an infinitely negative mark (Kierkegaard) or ethical obligation (Irigaray, Levinas) in the philosophical system. No identity is sought because the very notion of a closed, self-present, generalized category of gender-as-subjectivity, which will oppose and overturn "old" categories of presence, is self-defeating. It follows the same positivist logic that (re)creates the structure of opposition and exclusion which privileges the masculine term, appropriates the feminine term and forecloses difference. While this has been partially realized by several of the writers analysed in the previous chapters, the various strategies they adopt limit the possibility of alterity by thinking of it as an external force to be imposed upon the prevailing hierarchy of terms. Derrida's logic of *différance* as contamination marks the impossibility of any such strategy being "true" to the language it employs: a language which inevitably works as a relation of possibilities, differences, and "undecidability". This logic creates a temporal structure in keeping with the uncanny, anxious movement of reading and writing; and in so doing delineates a style other to ontological and epistemological modes which determines itself *through* acknowledging the impossibility of final appropriation. This is not a strategy of opposition, a counter-dialectic, but is an internal, affirmative gesture which before any subscription or decision insists on the possibility of otherness. The style is, then, ironic, but not in the strictly negative or parodic sense which relies on a "subjective" experience and a crisis of the unknowable "instant" in relation to mediated "history". What we might call the "agency" for change in Derrida's structure preserves the performative complications of existential irony while losing its reliance on a resolution in a completely "other" time or incarnation. Consequently, the feminine other ceases to function as a facilitator of the dialectical drive towards (masculine) self-consciousness. Sexual difference is no longer figured as the relation of two generalized categories ("man" and "woman"), but as the possibility of any number of contingent, highly contextualized, sexual decisions.

In spite of Derrida's transformation of the whole temporal and sexual order, the imperative to keep questioning this order, and his style, remains. As my last chapter revealed, there are limits to Derrida's style when read in a specifically feminist context because his concern to mark the undecidability of sexual decisions sometimes precludes an analysis of exactly what *is* decided sexually in these undecidable decisions, and the extent to which they repeat the "old" sexual hierarchy. I believe more needs to be said about these possible repetitions, and the impact they might have on a written intervention by a feminist, before we can embrace the deconstructive mode of irony as a "style" for feminism.

Of course, to deviate from the path that Derrida takes in relation to questions of sexual decisions is also, in an ironic sense, to remain loyal to his legacy, because it maintains the deconstructive sense of responsibility for other contexts and other styles. The double-bound dilemma of the deconstructive style is always on "what footing" to make a "fresh start",[1] and having encountered this anxiety, any further considerations of sexual difference, "femininity", and writing "as" or "like" a woman will be more strenuous, more caught up in questions

---

[1] Derrida asks "on what footing" he should make a "fresh start" after admitting to fatigue in the face of the "inexhaustibility" of his "penelopean" weavings around the "veil" and the "effect of the veil […] of nudity, of modesty, of shame, of reticence […] of the law, of everything that hides and shows the sex, of the origin of culture and so-called humanity in general" (2001a, 99, footnote 18).

of "propriation" and inheritance than they would have been previously.

With this ironic anxiety in mind, I intend to return to a more explicit feminist context with a different pair of feet, specifically through an analysis of the writing of Sarah Kofman. In a sense this chapter will repeat the concerns of the chapter on Kristeva: it will stage an encounter between a female writer with feminist sympathies and a series of philosophical and psychoanalytic theories written by men; and attempt to trace the feminine other within these texts in the hope of exposing an alternative form of writing that would not violate or appropriate this other. Once again, I will be focussing on the more "feminine"-centred texts in a large corpus of work, which covers many other subjects than "woman". However, in Sarah Kofman's post-Nietzschean, post-Derridean structure, the "subject" of "woman" is already contaminated with the ontological and epistemological ironies that deconstruction engenders. It constantly considers, and manipulates the risk of returning "her" to an idealized category.

Kofman conducts a genealogical analysis of "propriation" as a "sexual operation", in order to explore the mutual influence of authorial and sexual decisions. Kofman traces the way in which textual and logical authority is habitually gained through a protective, divisive gesture which, in the (patriarchal) history of philosophy has always worked to exclude and fetishize the feminine and curtail sexual difference. Her deconstructive readings explore the difficulty of negotiating with this legacy and rewriting the sexual hierarchy without repeating the same sexual "propriations".

Until recently, Kofman has usually been considered in the English-speaking world as an acolyte of Derrida's, and in writing about her "after" Derrida, I risk making the same gesture[2]. However, this risk mirrors the risk that Kofman embraces in her preoccupation with "propriation", and, as I hope to show, is constantly reflected in her writing style. In fact, the dominant theme of this chapter will be Kofman's complex negotiation with not only the "phallocentric" history of philosophy, but with the theorists who have most influenced her approach to wrestling with this history.[3] Kofman's concern with

[2] Volumes such as Deutscher and Oliver (1999) have begun to explore Kofman's writing in its own terms, but the (English) reception of her work has been slow.

[3] Kofman has written a large corpus of work on the phallocentric tendencies within the history of philosophy. Books such as *Aberrations* (1978) and *Le respect des femmes* (1982) trace the paranoid sexual propriations of different authors as part of their claim to autonomy and authority. While there is still much scope for commentary on these works, I am deliberately focussing on Kofman's relation to

the sexual aspects of "propriation" forces her to confront the sexual dissymmetry which persists in even the least "metaphysical" texts, and the impact this has on her status as a "woman" writer. This results in her taking a significantly different approach to claiming her "own" style and also leads her into ironic battle with the masculinist legacies of Derrida, Nietzsche and Freud.

By tracing the intricate manoeuvres of this battle I hope to show that Kofman tackles the questions that were left at the end of chapter 4. Kofman's combining of the comic anxiety of deconstructive analysis with a more sustained exploration of the relation of sexual and authorial decisions, forms a specifically *feminist* style of writing without lapsing into binarist prescriptions of gender or an idealized notion of sexual alterity.

I. Inheritance and Influence

On Writing

Before anything, the work of Sarah Kofman is deconstructive. Following Nietzsche, Freud and Derrida, her main concern is with what has been forgotten persistently by metaphysical philosophy, whether that is the body, the irrational or the written trace. Like her three main influences, Kofman engages in a symptomatic reading of conceptual and rhetorical structures which reveal these "other" traces; not as permanent exiles from the prevailing hierarchy of terms, nor as negative moments (re-)appropriated by a "necessary", positive movement of revelation, but as a constant interference in logocentric categories which is both *internal to* and *constitutive of* those categories. The other is always already there and throws any certainty of presence – including the past and future present – into doubt. This defiance of linearity is figured primarily as an affirmative rather than negative force, because the originary supplementarity is that which makes any textual decisions possible. As Kofman says, paraphrasing Derrida,

> The operations of deduction and citational grafting [*greffes*] are possible only because [writing] belongs to the structure of the sign, of the mark, of being re-marked, doubled, transported, cited in a place other than its own … (1984, 20).

---

authors with whom she has a closer, less critical relationship, in order to reveal the complexities of her feminist positioning in relation to her direct philosophical predecessors.

Thus while decisions are made in a context of radical instability, they do not arise from an empty chasm. Writing may be "incredible, [...] it is not, however, ineffable" (37). Being rooted in possibility and multiplicity, the textual structure insists on a constant reaffirmation of itself as a set of contingent decisions made as part of the "experience" of their impossibility as "proper" events.[4]

For Kofman, this idea of the already-divided origin of writing is a direct descendent of Nietzsche's assertion that "truth" is simply another of the "army" of metaphors which cannot be traced back to an originary source (Nietzsche 1979, 82). Every "proper" thing and text "constitutes a specific, provisional meaning symptomatic of a certain type of life's mastery over the world and over other types of life" (Kofman 1972, 121-2; 1993, 82).

The main thrust of Kofman's work follows on from Nietzsche's typological reading of the history of philosophy; in particular of hierarchies within this history which perpetuate the belief in an absolute Truth beyond the material world. Nietzsche's reading is provoked by his belief that this "ascetic ideal" distorts and represses any true experience of "life" by negating all its (real) mutable characteristics and anticipating the moment when (abstract) Truth will be revealed.[5] According to Nietzsche, this "evolutionary" history is typified by Socrates' purposeful "forgetting" of metaphorical and artistic expression (1972, 32-37; 1993, 19-22). Nietzsche claims that Socrates wishes to banish "mimetic" language not because it takes understanding further from the "essence" of things but because it reveals that there *is* no knowable essence of things. In negating mimetic language and privileging dialectical rationalism, Socrates is fighting a battle of the weak, because he would rather turn away from the rich multiplicity of life's forces than face their complexity. He hides behind an impersonal, "objective" voice – the "proper" voice –

---

[4] The individual occasions on which Kofman employs the different nuances of meaning within the word "propre" – which refers either to propriety, ownership, or the "proper" name – as the hinge to her argument, are too many to mention. However, for an interesting explanation of her particular usage of the term in relation to Derrida's notion of the proper and Nietzsche's meditations on asceticism and "cleanliness", see Kofman 1993, Section V, part 1 & 149-150, note 2.

[5] The battle between worldly and ascetic values in *The Birth of Tragedy* is usually figured in terms of a battle between the more "instinctual" and material art of Dionysus and the cerebral, formalized art of Apollo. In *Nietzsche and Metaphor*, Kofman traces the way in which this battle is initially dialectical in *The Birth of Tragedy* but shifts into a more "metaphorical" interaction of differences rather than opposites where "the same must partake in the other, must be the other" (1972, 26; 1993, 14).

which claims to garner authority from Truth (or God). In fact, all this voice does is engulf and separate itself from "the full panoply of [life's] drives", reducing them to "one alone" – knowledge, which can never be reached – and dividing everything up into a strict hierarchy of terms in relation to this unattainable knowledge (1972, 34; 1993, 20). The aim of Nietzsche's "genealogy" is to expose these "objective" manoeuvres as symptoms of a specific (diseased) "will to mastery", and transmute their values into more "metaphorical", differentiated terms.[6]

Kofman's "return" to Nietzsche as a direct source for her own writing is significant, because it shifts the emphasis of her deconstructive approach. It turns her attention to the history and process of particular "propriative" decisions. While such matters are obviously an important part of Derrida's deconstructive analyses, his prevailing concern with the "remains" of history and process means that the active logistics of "propriation" remain for the most part in the background of his discussions.[7]

Kofman's tendency towards a more "genealogical" method has led to accusations of her work being too "genetic", too obsessed with the root "causes" of logical and textual contradictions, and not with what these contradictions enable.[8] Yet her reading of Nietzsche's genealogical method demonstrates that the deconstructive temporal structure she uses is far from a simple matter of "cause and effect". In *Nietzsche and Metaphor*, Kofman is careful to affirm Nietzsche's central concept, the "will to mastery" or "will to power", but is equally careful to steer away from any interpretations of it as the primary "cause" of everything or the key to overturning the Socratic order and retrieving the "true" life of the instincts. She follows Nietzsche in expressing the idea that "all style reiterates a primary writing, that of the instincts", and also figures particular stylistic and value judgments (including the Socratic one) as being a reflection of the drives of a particular "personality" (1972, 10 & 149-57; 1993, 2-3 & 102-8). However, she insists that this theory is neither biologistic

[6] Nietzsche's, *On the Genealogy of Morals* is the obvious example of this genealogical method.

[7] The exception to this is in Derrida's own writings on Nietzsche, in particular *Spurs / Éperons* (1979) and "Otobiographies" in *The Ear of the Other* (1985).

[8] Paul de Man accuses Kofman of failing to recognize the "logocentric valorization" in Nietzsche's *Birth of Tragedy*. He says Kofman replicates this logocentrism by describing the relation between competing figures of Dionysus and Apollo "in the genetic language of a father / son relationship" (1979, 88-9). Penelope Deutscher (1997, 69-75) makes similar criticisms from a feminist perspective.

nor ontological because it always admits to being infected by an originary "metaphorical activity" (1972, 121; 1993, 82).[9] It is effectively rootless, but because it is still caught in the "grammar" of language and logic it necessarily forms a particular perspective. Kofman explains the "will to power" as,

> … not an ontological truth grasped by an intuition, nor even the result of a deduction or an induction. It is an unhypothetical hypothesis, posited in the name of the method's demand for economy (1972, 135-6; 1993, 93-4).

In other words, Nietzsche's central theory is not to be considered as a central "truth" which refutes and separates itself from the prevailing logic. Its status as "principle" is a function of the economy of the philosophical tradition, and yet it also functions as a parasite within the economy because, unlike the economy, it acknowledges its own contingency. Like a rational concept, it expresses a "proper", but one which is "provisional and multiple", an "appropriation of the world by a specific will" which is itself one of many forces (1972, 149 & 121; 1993, 102 & 82). In this way it unravels, and (provisionally) transmutes the generalized propriation of "objective" dialectical logic. It acts as a "parodic repetition" of conventional logic,

> … a logical principle […] used in order to arrive as a hypothesis which deletes the opposition between the logical and the illogical – the ultimate mockery (1972, 136; 1993, 94).

The terminology here differs from Derrida's: "personality", "will" and "perspective" give a greater sense of a residual "subjectivity" operating than Derrida would allow. But Kofman claims Nietzsche's language is a "parody of the [philosophical] obsession with purity which protects against the common and vulgarizing appropriation of one's 'own' ['*propre*'] thought (1972, 165; 1993, 113-4). Moreover, the temporal and logical movement is very similar to Derrida's. Kofman's figuration of Nietzsche's genealogy is not as a conventional historical method, but as a "style" of interpretation which seeks to establish the "systematic interrelation of various perspectives" and their laws, without believing in their generalized "presence" or absolute truth (1972, 151; 1993, 103-4). She adopts this interpretation as a way of interrogating the "propriations" of whole analytical traditions, and the individual proponents of these traditions. The

---

[9] Kofman describes this in deconstructive terms, saying "any thought of essence is not appropriate to the 'root' of metaphor" and that it does not operate as an "originary music of the world".

resulting theory of writing is a strange hybrid of Derrida's and Nietzsche's ideas which focuses on the contingency and "undecidability" of specific decisions within a genealogy of philosophical "style".

The Genealogical Order

Something of Kofman's combinatory style can be discerned in her consideration of philosophical aporia in *Comment s'en sortir?* In the first, extended section, "Aporie", she traces the overwhelming desire of speculative philosophy to escape from uncertainty into final enlightenment.

Kofman traces the links in philosophy, inescapable and always present, between "poros" (the way or path), "aporia" (paralysis, its apparent opposite) and "Metis" (the Greek figure of wisdom, associated by Plato with rhetoric and sophistry). She begins by noting Plato's denunciation of Metis as a form of intelligence without the singular, rigorous method of science. To him, its mimetic "process" is "oblique, approximate and uncertain," so will always be caught up in contortions and aporia, and can never lead to the truth (1983, 14). It must therefore be banished in favour of the pure and clarifying dialectic. Kofman's interest lies in the process by which this method determines itself and becomes established as the only way to "truth", in spite of the fact that the determination relies so heavily on what is apparently excluded from the method, and final enlightenment never quite arrives. She turns to the Socratic / Platonic myth of the birth of Love in *The Symposium* for her primary example (Plato 1951, 203b-204d). In many Socratic discussions, love is a figure allied to both truth and beauty. Yet even assuming that there can be a single definition of Love, the definition given in the *The Symposium* comes through a pattern of fabrication which says more about the dialectic's desire for neat hierarchies and certain answers than it does about the nature of Love. Love is figured as the son of Poros and Penia. His mother, Penia, is an orphan and represents poverty or lack; while his father, Poros – the "path" of philosophy – is the "son" of Metis. Like Poros' mother, Penia is wily and deceitful, the opposite of Poros and in need of his positivity and determination. So Penia tricks Poros into becoming a father by getting him drunk and seducing him. The resulting baby, Love, inherits a mixture of his parents' characteristics. According to Kofman, Socrates creates a "fantastical genealogy" to show how Love is the philosopher and "intermediary between the learned and the ignorant" (1983, 16, quoting Plato).

Kofman's juxtaposition of Plato's hierarchy of philosophical "method" and his genealogy of "Love" reveals how easily the supposed supremacy of the "rational" dialectic can be undermined. Not only is the "logos" of this scientific "method" only perceptible as "mythos", but the "banished" Metis is the mother and source of the philosophical process and the grandmother of dialectical mediation. As Kofman comments,

> … this genealogical dissymmetry […] suggests that wily, resourceful intelligence that lies at the origin of all *technes* is also one of the ancestors of philosophy, of the love of *sophia* (1983, 15; 1988a, 8-9).

This is, of course, the classic dialectical manoeuvre; what Kofman calls the "philosophical gesture *par excellance*: the gesture of betrayal" (1983, 17; 1988a, 9). The Philosopher seeks a single, final meaning or definition, but is faced with baffling complexity. Rather than tease out this complexity he creates a mythical teleology, which will project him into a process that leads to perceived enlightenment. The resulting structure propels itself forward by dividing everything into opposites ("metis" and science, progression and meandering, "poros" and "aporia", positive and negative, light and dark, enlightenment and obscurity) and swallowing or expelling the "negative" term.[10] These divisions converge most obviously in the sexual resonance of this ironic capability: the "negative", feminine term (Metis or Penia) is figured as the reproductive "source" of the given structure, but is determinedly cast off by rational philosophy and associated with darkness, deviousness and the sensible.

Kofman carefully traces the genealogy of the dialectic, revealing the driving force of the speculative method not as an objectively ordained truth, but as a specific desire or will whose progression is weighed down by the many possibilities of the language it seeks to purify. As the false divisions and oppositions of the teleology proliferate, the confusion and irony they spawn are compounded. Kofman repeats the Platonic metaphor for the philosopher's aporia – the swimmer in the sea of argument, who waits for the chance encounter with a rescuing dolphin – to show how the "rigorous" structure of negative versus

---

[10] Kofman draws an analogy between the philosopher's "swallowing" of the *metis* of the sophists, "in order to use it against them […] so as not to be dispossessed of his mastery" and the story of Zeus, who swallowed Metis, integrating her "into his own sovereignty to prevent her giving birth to wily children who might dispossess him of his power" (1983, 36; 1988a, 16).

positive constantly battles with its own impurity.[11] The irony of the "way out" of the aporia is immediately obvious:

> The way out of discourse, the exit, is a way to safety, a *poros* which appears unexpectedly, which none can be sure of finding, and which is itself always aporetic: a true miracle, an encounter with a dolphin in mid-ocean (1983, 25; 1988a, 12).

In spite of the hierarchy of the Socratic dialectic, rationality cannot forget its "aporetic" other because this other is an integral part of the "rational" determination. The only certain "encounter" is with the hint of anxious, unknown origins and the bastardized compromise that is philosophy; "fathered" and "mothered" not by the single truth of rational science but by the random and multiple differences and deceptions of aporetic language. As Kofman shows, the inevitable "return" of alterity means that Socrates can appear unsullied and rational only through further divisions and separations. Thus, he dictates, there are "good" aporia and "bad" aporia: some sophistical tricks of language bring their victim to the light and their senses; some tricks are simply aporetic and keep the thinker in the perpetual darkness of ignorance. Socrates' own sophistical tendencies are, of course, placed in the former category, so even though he is described as a "stingray" and a "midwife", he is neither flaccid, "slippery" nor effeminate.[12] The divisions continue, the hierarchy of opposites becoming ever more complicated, and ever more reliant on the rhetorical deviations and mimetic inaccuracies which were dismissed initially as the enemy of "proper" logical progress. As Kofman says, the Socratic method attempts to "safeguard" its "purity" and "authenticity" (and protect itself from "madness") by mastering "a mimesis that cannot, ultimately, be mastered" (1983, 39; 1988a, 17).

---

[11] This metaphor was, of course, important to Kierkegaard's mimetic / ironic structure, as analysed in Chapter 2.

[12] In *Meno*, Socrates is compared to a stingray, which is flaccid in appearance, but can deal a sharp and painful blow (quoted by Kofman 1983, 45; 1988a, 19). Throughout this passage of analysis, Kofman draws comparisons between the (hidden) mimetic tendencies of Socrates and the associations in Greek philosophy and mythology between the "dark pit" of the aporia, the "slippery" nature of mimetic language, and feminine sexuality. As she points out, Pandora, the first woman, was compared by Hesiod to "a steep-sided pit from which there is no exit", and "the same word applies to [a woman's] genitals and to the cuttlefish, a particularly slippery, devious, polymorphous and ambiguous creature" (1983, 46-7; 1988a, 20).

The Mimetic Legacy

It is strange that Kofman should say this, as her own style is heavily mimetic; replicating and proliferating the mythical illustrations and allegories of logic, and forging metaphorical links between different instances of dialectical "separation". At times it seems as if she has dropped into a completely fabulous domain, where there is no clear analysis, but simply a chain of contingent, figurative connections. It might be tempting to interpret this as the repetition of the separations of dialectical law from the "other" side of the fence: an Irigarayan irony, which occupies a negative, irrational voice in order to denature habitual philosophical divisions. Yet Kofman's stress on the intrinsic and constitutive nature of alterity is more emphatic than Irigaray's, and her repetition of the mimetic structure seems far closer to the original, and less strategically oppositional.[13] Indeed, towards the end of Kofman's doubling genealogy of doubles, she declares "dialectics provide a good road" even if it is "full of pitfalls". She continues,

> It is too good a way, too divine a way for human thought, which must not seek to go beyond its limitations, which must strive only to remember itself, and which can repeat itself only by reinventing itself, by being always new and always the same (1983, 83-4; 1988a, 38).

Her respect for the "good" road here may seem disingenuous, given that her narrative has just exposed the road's paranoid blind-spots. What would be the "alternative" path of thought within the dialectic – where an aporia is not necessarily considered a profound and dangerous absence – would promise to be far less limiting than the "divine" way. Yet the latter part of this sentence suggests that Kofman's irony partly affirms the dialectical striving; for with the recognition that the "pure" structure was always already mimetic, and without the drive towards absolute enlightenment, the road becomes one which "folds" between repetition and invention. The promise of the "new" road lies in the differences *within* the old one rather than in overcoming, forgetting or swallowing it. Thus Kofman's ironic, "other" path must acknowledge the "double-bind" of deconstructive

---

[13] It is worth remembering that Irigaray maintains a sense of women remaining "elsewhere", so that the deliberate, subversive assumption of the mimetic, "feminine" role that she advocates in *This Sex Which Is Not One,* involves some kind of external agency. Kofman's description of mimetic alterity is far closer to Derrida's notion of the supplement.

analysis, reiterating the (dialectical) striving for "progress" which will never be, as it never was, "properly" the same.[14]

Kofman's style slowly "reinvents" the mimetic form of dialectical irony by being "always new and always the same". She repeats the mythical genealogy of knowledge and oblivion – in particular the negative, feminized figuration of aporia – but rewrites this figuration to show how it need not be construed as absence or lack in relation to presence, purpose and plenitude. Kofman remarks that "if Penia were in fact the paralysing Aporia she would never have tried to escape her distressing situation" (1983, 62; 1988a, 26), and in her wily plot to reproduce through alcohol-aided seduction, it is Poros, not Penia, who plays "the 'passive', 'female' role in the primal scene" (1983, 63; 1988a, 27).[15] In spoiling the division of terms necessitated by an exclusively progressive determination, Kofman enables the figuration of difference without automatic opposition, and reveals apparently "pure" positions to be infinitely divisible:

> Penia is no more the opposite of Poros than is the aporia: the true philosophical aporia, or Penia, is always fertile; in her all opposites are placed under erasure; she is neither masculine nor feminine, rich nor poor, transition nor absence of transition, resourceful nor without resources. [...] Penia is always already pregnant with Love.

And Penia also comes to stand as a metaphor for originary mimesis.

Kofman's re-enactment of the dialectic shifts the privileging of the technologies of presence into a mode of writing and philosophizing which acknowledges that its own determination and intervention are radically contextualized; and whose delineation of "positions" – whether this means sexual identities, conceptual definitions or claims

---

[14] See Derrida 1998, 35-36, where he writes of the "double-bind" of deconstruction in the context of what he considers to be the condition of all analysis: the "stricture" of being a rationalist mode of thought, which cannot "renounce" its "analytic desire" for "the order of reason, of meaning, of the question of the origin, of the social bond"; while following the injunction to "analyze tirelessly the resistance that still clings to the thematic of the simple and the indivisible origin [...]". Derrida argues that the double-bind is neither "merely a classifiable and circumscribable pathology" nor does it reveal "only a transcendental illness of the analytic". In other words, the desire for a secure, known path does not recede – indeed, it is a condition of any analysis – but it is no longer (necessarily) pathological, and is understood to be "multiple, disseminated, in infinitely divisible knots".

[15] Kofman thus also incidentally challenges the Aristotelian model of sexual difference, which figures woman as the "passive receptacle, a matter which has to receive form from the masculine".

to truth – are provisional and performative.[16] Kofman's mimetic style might be said to be miming the mimetic "other" of the dialectical structure to show up its originary status and undermine its "essential" otherness; and, at the same time, miming the "return" of mimesis in the historical legacy of philosophy, which the "new" performative time cannot wholly disown. Thus Kofman can maintain the alterity of the aporia while declaring that "aporetic situations are no longer bad roads [*mauvais passages*] on the main route [*voie de passage*]" (1983, 98).

The way in which Kofman's writing doubles back on itself and compromises its own authority is reminiscent of what Derrida says about parody presupposing a "vertiginous non-mastery" if it is not to become a "confession or law table" (1979, 100). Her mimetic genealogy is also indebted to the irony of Nietzsche's texts. His denunciations of past and present "values" are invariably contextualized by a recognition that these denunciations descend from such values. In *Thus Spoke Zarathustra*, Zarathustra's visions and declarations about the future are framed with repeated disappointments; and Nietzsche admits, in relation to his denunciation of ascetic ideals, that

> … we men of knowledge of today, we godless men and anti-metaphysicians, we too still derive our flame from the fire ignited by a faith millennia old, the Christian faith, which was also Plato's, that God is truth, that truth is *divine* (1967, 152).[17]

The constant intermingling of the "new" and the "same" in Kofman's writing thus fits with her Nietzschean conception of "provisional" truths and personalities: without a historical moment of redemption there is no more likelihood of "overcoming", of forming a clean slate, than there is of replicating some original source. The agency emerging

---

[16] I am using Derrida's definition of "performativity" here, where writing occurs within a promissory structure whose acute awareness of alterity means that decisions, even if made, are never "present." See chapter 4 for my extended explanation.

[17] This confession is reiterated in the section entitled "*How we too are still pious", in The Gay Science* (1974, 280). For analyses of Nietzsche's work as texts which treat ironically their own attempts to "overcome", see Conway 1992 and Pippin 1988. Conway portrays Nietzsche's exploration of the "performative dimension of genealogy" as a direct response to his insight into the impossibility of escaping "his metaphysical yearnings for objectivity, God and Truth" (1992, 75). Pippin reads *Thus Spoke Zarathustra* as a text which uses the repeated failures of Zarathustra's attempts at "self-transformation" as a means of recognizing that there is "no privileged or decisive [ie. redemptive] moment in history" (1988, 55).

from this is a highly contextualized will (not a "proper" subject or a transcendental law) which seeks change by embracing its own mutability and the chance of differentiation that comes with being continually repeated.[18] Kofman's large corpus of work on Nietzsche constantly returns to the simultaneous movement of "appropriation" and "disappropriation" in his writing: his styles are radically different according to context (mimetic; aphoristic; wildly self-determining), but all expressions of the same "will".[19] A similar movement seems to be at work in Kofman's *Comment s'en sortir?* Her mimetic style embodies the anxieties of rewriting the "proper" structure of philosophy through a performative notion of time and determination. In other contexts, the style will be different again.

---

[18] See Kofman 1986b (289-318), where she emphasizes the complicated relation of "unified" and "playful" styles in Nietzsche's *Untimely Meditations* and in *Ecce Homo*. Kofman identifies "two" Nietzsches: the Nietzsche of the earlier work, who borrowed the "decadent" language of his "teachers", Schopenhauer and Wagner, in order to move beyond them and "become" himself; and the Nietzsche of the later, "autobiographical" work, who has "conquered" his style and his "ego" and speaks with "lightning" rather than words (or so he says). As Kofman points out, this change of style could very well indicate a metaphysical movement towards the proper; much like Kierkegaard's ironic communication, which is curtailed in order to "choose" himself. However, the "unity" achieved in "Ecce Homo" is considered by Nietzsche to belong to the plethora of styles across the whole body of his work: as a function of the proliferation of "masks" and personas, rather than as the final finding of his own voice or body and the culmination of his efforts. Thus Nietzsche's apparent (self)mastery could just as easily indicate another *provisional* centre of perspective. Rather than the expression of a centre of "individuality", it might be the expression of the singular will of "styled" language to disrupt the proper; and such a "unity" cannot be possessed (or existentially chosen). Thus the "overcoming" of Nietzsche's autobiography is not an overcoming of the past, as in the appropriation of nature by culture, or the overthrowing of a father by his son, but an overcoming of the illusion of final mastery and predetermined hierarchy; and thus an acknowledgement of the trace of decadence which remains in his own style. As Kofman says: "If the diversity of Nietzschean styles mimes the decadent style, each aphorism is a fibre animated by a single desire. It is not an atomistic fragment, it is energy, intensity, density" (310). This "energy" would then be comparable to Derrida's "force" of writing, and the doubleness it instigates could not be limited to an internalizing, dialectical irony.

[19] The way in which Kofman traces the style of Nietzsche highlights the doubleness of style across the body of Nietzsche's work as a whole, as well as at a local level. *Explosion* (1992 & 1993b) Kofman's two-volumed work on Nietzsche's *Ecce Homo*, reviews the gradual proliferation of Nietzsche's styles and strategies in the context of his own autobiographical review.

Paternity and Authority

However, even if Kofman's mimetic inheritance is taken into account, her style in *Comment s'en sortir?* is significantly more mimetic, and less conceptually determined, than the vast majority of Nietzsche's genealogies or Derrida's deconstructions. In fact, Kofman completes her analysis of philosophical aporia with "Cauchemar", a fabulous account of her own dreams about her "aporetic childhood", which resists any rationally logical conclusions in favour of a free association of images, metaphors and memories (1983, 103-12). Clearly, some other strategy of writing is at work in Kofman's text, which makes it difficult to rest with any "rational" decision or conclusion.

Such a radical shift in style is not wholly typical of Kofman's work in general, for although she has written other autobiographical texts, she usually maintains a distinction between "rational, clear, philosophical" writing and that of a "freer" style (1991, 106). Nevertheless, Kofman has identified an exaggerated mimeticism in her own writing, and has commented on the risk of it leading to a state of "permanent disappropriation" (Kofman quoted in Deutscher 2000a, 155). Moreover, even in those texts which do maintain the "philosophical" style, Kofman's analysis invariably proceeds, as it does in "Aporie", through the textual and logical inconsistencies that surround instances of sexual propriation and exclusion. The question of sexual difference – in particular its relation to the divisions of the dialectic and the *différance* of deconstruction – is obviously going to be a central one in a post-Nietzschean and Derridean "style" of writing, but for Kofman it is evidently crucial. In *Lectures de Derrida*, Kofman insists that "sexual violence, the difference between the sexes", operates as "the best paradigm of différance" (1984, 69). Given the links I made in Chapter 4 between an increased mimesis in Derrida's "style" – in particular, in *Spurs* – and an exaggerated anxiety over the question of sexual difference, this might suggest that Kofman's increased mimesis is the consequence of a more explicit negotiation of this question.

The difference in Kofman's writing appears to lie in her treatment of the legacy of dialectical philosophy; or to be more precise, the question of the "return" of sexual difference as sexual *division*, within the "returning" philosophical legacy. If the "history (of) truth (is) a process of propriation" (Derrida 1979, 110-11), and this propriation occurs primarily as the claiming of an essential, individual "voice" whose presence coincides with objective "truth", then the "proper" is always inscribed to some extent with the "biography" of that individual voice. Derrida hints at the sexual implications of this inscription in *Spurs*, when he writes,

> Although there is no truth in itself of the sexual difference in itself, of either man or woman in itself, all of ontology nonetheless, with its inspection, appropriation, identification and verification of identity, has resulted in concealing, even as it presupposes it, this undecidability.
>
> Somewhere here, beyond the mythology of the signature, beyond the authorial theology, the biographical desire has been inscribed in the text (1979, 102-105).

Kofman's primary concern is with the sexual character of this "biographical desire". In the history of philosophy, this desire has invariably been masculine, and philosophy's "proper" voice has relied upon the separation of itself from different sexuality/ies, thus proclaiming the "female" as its opposite. As Kofman says,

> The metaphysical tradition, essentially masculine, as if moved (set in motion) by a paranoid fear, has always deeply feared the confusion of the sexes [...] and therefore it attempts to separate them categorically. (1991, 105.)

This means that no text, however neutral or "asexual" it seems, is without traces of its sexual propriation:

> Even in a philosophical text, a so-called rational and systematic text, independent of all empirical and pathological subjectivity, and therefore of sexuality, it isn't possible to separate the text from the sexual positioning of its author (105).

The chronology and genealogy of this sexual propriation is, of course, extremely complex, and Kofman is careful to qualify this statement with the assertion that authorial sexual positioning "is not necessarily to be identified with the anatomical sex" (106). The large number of Kofman's works that focus on the "paranoid fear" of the "metaphysical tradition" trace specific propriative movements in particular canonical philosophers: the sexual propriations she highlights are not always oppositional, and the sexual positionings of her subjects are not claimed to be consistent across their whole oeuvre, or even within single texts. Nevertheless, the sexual, biographical traces of the philosophical legacy are still vital enough, biased enough, and hidden enough, to warrant Kofman's singular analysis.

The implications of this analysis for Kofman's own written intervention are profound. For if the deconstructive style exposes "truth" as "propriation", and does this through a writing which resists "propriation" to the extent that it cannot claim to overcome the old structure, then the "new" style will maintain a trace of the old (sexually dividing) "biographical desire", even if it is now considered to be "irreducibly plural" (Derrida 1979, 104-5). While this "return" is problematic and frustrating to a writer like Nietzsche or Derrida, it does not affect the authority of the deconstructive intervention: his style is both "irreducibly plural" and properly masculine in the old sense. But what if, like Kofman, one's biography is already marked out as "feminine"; what if one's "anatomical and social" category is already inscribed as "other"? Surely the return of the proper in the deconstructive style will then to be far more problematic, far more disruptive to one's intervention? No matter how contingent textual authority has become, its return is still inevitable in, and even necessary to, any new writing; and the return still seems to be, at least in part, phallocentric.

How, then, can this sexually divisive return be marked and deconstructed? How can a "woman" – or this particular woman – intervene and claim the deconstructive style as her own? How, in turn, can her own "proper" will be deconstructed? These questions are put into play by Kofman's genealogies, but simmer with particular strength when she writes on, and through, her intellectual allies and forerunners.

II. Intervention

Castration and the Proper

The first of these questions might be approached usefully by turning to Kofman's other great influence – Freud – and analysing the extent to which she inherits and debunks his chronology of sexual division.

More explicitly than Derrida, and from an earlier stage in her writing, Kofman has explored the relation between textual possibility, sexual identity, and "propriety", which the "double gesture" of deconstruction delineates.[20] Just as she adopts a Nietzschean, typological reading of the history of philosophy to mark the

[20] Kofman's writing was a direct influence upon both *The Post Card* and *Spurs / Éperons*, where Derrida tackles "feminist" questions most explicitly. He acknowledges this debt in these texts (1987b, 420, note 4 and 1979, 146-147, note 2).

pathological division and appropriation of the metaphysical tradition (which fears "unknowable", metaphorical language), so Kofman uses the sexualized language of Freud to mark the differentiating violence which is implicit in this constant striving for rhetorical and conceptual purity. This is by no means a straightforward, undivided adoption of terms, however, because such a gesture inevitably treads over the ground around and between Freud's "literal" and "metaphorical" description of sexual division, as well as the question of authorial originality and indebtedness (her own, Derrida's, Freud's and Nietzsche's) which I have just highlighted.

The most prominent of the Freudian concepts adopted by Kofman is that of the castration complex. Preoccupied as she is with the constant origination and repetition of writing, Freud's myth of primary anxiety – the primal "cause" of all culture as well as every individual subject or "personality" – resounds with the possibility and violence of originary difference. What is radical in Freud's theories about the formation of consciousness is strangely similar to what was radical in Nietzsche's genealogical approach to "truth": the notion of other "forces" of life which are repressed (forgotten) in the name of "proper" (habitual) morality, "proper" (objective or universal) expression and a "proper" (pure, self-reflexive) conception of identity.[21] That this repression should be enacted primarily through the Oedipal drama, a cutting of the masculine "self" from instinctual desires to prevent the cutting of his potency, provides Kofman with a startling metaphor for her typological reading of patriarchal "logic":

> "Castration" speaks of the bloody violence of a writing which violates, breaks, tears, rips, cuts and divides itself. Originary castration leading to a fall without return – to the father. […] Performing affirmatively the murder of the father, "castration" cuts into every presence. Without this cut, the present would not present itself, the book would not put itself into play … (1984, 74).

If, as Kofman claims, the history of speculation is marked by a will to mastery which gains control and direction through opposing or assimilating differences, then the shock of the male child "recognizing" its mother's "castration" can be interpreted as a reflection of the genealogy of this history, and the almost-inevitability of its repetition. Kofman repeatedly highlights the way in which Freud's "originary" myth of (sexual) individuation parallels the doublings and divisions of speculative determination. Freud's child

---

[21] A parallel which has been noted by many. Derrida traces the idea of Freud's (denied) indebtedness to Nietzsche in the "Notices (Warnings)" section of *The Post Card* (1987b, 259-291).

gains its independence and (adult) authority by rejecting the breast and fighting off rivals who have been before him. Similarly, philosophy ascribes its "maturity" – its sense of time and absolute insight – to a relinquishing of the "archaic" pleasures of life (155-84). In both cases, the imaginary, feminized origin is both fetishized and repulsed, and becomes the recurring negative term (the aporia) on the path towards "full" consciousness or (self-)knowledge. Moreover, the history of both teleologies is then inscribed as a series of discrete positions, each of which has been established by the overturning of the old (patriarchal) order by the new one; by the son. This is why Kofman emphasizes the links between Freud's theories on sexuality and his theories on the foundation of civilization; maintaining that the idea of castration is rooted "in a myth of the origin of culture, the myth of the murder of the primeval father" (75). Her deconstructive insistence on the mutual contamination of biological, sexual, historical, cultural, written and "experiential" hierarchies means that each determination or "separation" is considered according to its specific determinations while also being (uncannily) representative of the recurring "will to power".

However, as can be seen from the quotation above, Kofman's sexualized metaphor for the workings of "propriation" is not a simple one. "Castration" speaks of the sexually dividing violence of the written structure; but it seems to refer equally to the performative intervention which "cuts into" the oppositionary structure. It is applicable to both the speculative structure which perpetuates the "truth" of these myths, and to the deconstructive analysis which breaks with this truth and ironizes the myth-making. The "metaphor" does not serve to circumscribe the whole history of philosophy into a generalized law of sexual division, but describes the perpetual disruptions and "returns" in the writing of this history in a form which acknowledges the centrality of sexual difference:

> "castration" conveys the problem of the double, of originary mimesis, of the idea of an unending chain of substitutes, without originary signification (70).

In fact, according to Kofman, castration does not operate in a simply referential manner in Freud's own texts. More often than not it is impossible to ascertain whether Freud is engaging in something like Nietzsche's genealogical interrogation of perceived essences in relation to sexual and libidinal differences; or whether he is simply speculating on sexual difference in the metaphysical sense, in order to create his "own" developmental structure. Castration anxiety can function in Freud's texts simply as a symbol of the fear of a particular difference – one of the many instances of the narcissistic drive towards self-completion – and thus no more definitive of the "true" difference between the sexes than any other socially-ordained "truth" of being. Yet the theory can also be read as *the* inevitable and defining cause of the separation of the sexes and that which assures male dominance and female passivity.[22]

It is the ambiguity of Freud's theory which most fascinates Kofman, because it lies with her view of the "double-edged" nature of written intervention. Kofman admits that, unlike Derrida, Freud employs a "mythical language which indicates that [he] is not really considering something like an originary castration" (75-6). The risk of sublation and the final determination of terms is always present. However, this risk, according to Kofman, does not mean that Freud inevitably reinscribes the uncanny and différantial relation of drives and words into a teleological one: far from it, in fact. She believes that unlike speculative dialecticians, Freud does not seek a "strict propriety of terms" that will foreclose the troubling ambiguities provoked by the doubles and substitutions of psychoanalytic interpretation. Thus while Freud refers to Abel's ideas on the "archaic" nature of the language of dreams, the archaisms that Freud traces within dreams are not treated as a simple, singular origin of expression and identity (78). Where Abel sees primitive words as an indication of the evolution of language into clarity (adulthood), and the playful nonsense of dream language as a puzzle whose sense may be resolved through dialectical mediation, Freud emphasizes the infantile pleasure of playing with words, and notes how dream-words are significant as much for their configuration and their sound as for their sense. Dreams, according to Freud's analysis, treat written words as (concrete) "things":

> If the elements of a dream can "signify" themselves or their opposites, it is really because they don't want to say anything: they *mettent en scène*, present the conflict of forces … (81).

While Abel, like Hegel, considers infancy to belong to philosophy, and that it "is intended to be sublated by philosophy", infancy, and the primitive language which is the focus of psychoanalysis is, for Freud,

---

[22] This dual reading is most blatant in Freud's third essay on sexuality, "The Transformations of Puberty", where he interrogates the terms "masculine" and "feminine" in a footnote, concluding that "in human beings pure masculinity or femininity is not to be found either in a psychological or biological sense"; then goes on to distinguish the sexual development of men and women along psychological and biological lines, using the penis (or the woman's lack of one) as the determining factor in mens "activity" and women's "passivity" (1991f, 141-44).

> … meant to underline the permanence of an unsublatable *remainder*: that of the child in the adult, that of archaic traces in the dream, specific to its writing and something which no dialectic can sublimate (80).

Indeed, far from viewing double meaning as "the germ of a dialectical movement", Freud

> … regards the ambivalent duplicity of terms as a means by which the unconscious can express a double determination, an ambivalence, an impassable conflict (81).

According to Kofman, this is not a matter of Freud treasuring the obscurity of a lost "origin" in order to preserve its significance as the inviolable truth of his speculative structure. The import of the archaic terms lies in their capacity to repeat in, remain in and disturb all that Abel would regard as clarity and maturity; presumably even "mediated" language and identity. This means that they also disrupt their capacity to symbolize any one thing. The logic of the Freudian archive is far from linear because its remainder is ever present and always has been. And, according to Kofman, "if everything begins with repetition, delay [*le retard*] is originary"; the "remainder" is there before the beginning of whatever historical or mythical structure speculates upon it (58-60). This "*différance*" is, of course, what is traced and radicalized in Derrida's analysis of the Freudian economy; and Kofman stresses that it is only the language of deconstruction which has done justice to this "fundamental discovery of psychoanalysis" (60). However, for Kofman the "remainder" is still Freud's discovery, which always already implies "a new conception of time, unthinkable according to the criteria of the logic of identity". Freud's ambivalence marks a drive or will more fundamental than the "proper", which exceeds its divisionary ordering of "one" and "two".

Castration and Sexual Difference

This emphasis on the Freudian corruption of origins and archives is important both to the way Kofman's treatment of the psychoanalytic notion of drives and instincts differs from the Kristevan and Lacanian one; and to her staging of the "return" of sexual division in the "return" of the proper. Her analysis is already more open to an uncanny anxiety than the dialectical versions of psychoanalysis which "reinscribe" the notions of castration and the phallus into "the field of the symbolic, of the law, of spoken truth" (76). Even while Kristeva seeks to introduce more mobility and complicate the (symbolic) circularity of her Lacanian structure by focussing on liminal positions – the abject; the "want" of the "object of want"; the metaphorical within the metonymical; the "hainadoration" of primary identification – the doubles and contradictions inscribed by her structure are still necessarily oppositions which arise from and operate within predetermined categories. The "letter" of the law, the castrating signifier, is still primary cause and final truth; and everything which is "other" to it comes to belong to it as its negative means to mediation. The only possible game to be played, therefore, is one which follows the legal operations, which is precisely what Kristeva's system does. Kofman, on the other hand, inhabits symbolic terms only to reveal the uncertainties of "cause" and direction within the psychoanalytic laws. She upholds the centrality of castration anxiety as the "originary" myth of the Freudian structure, but undermines its status as final law or determinant. The "new conception of time" dispels any such possibility and renders castration a double-edged agent. Rather like one of Nietzsche's "transmuted" metaphors, it marks and contaminates the proper truths and values of the prevailing structure, while recognizing that the desire for the "proper" is in some way inevitable; although not indivisible.

However, this does not mean that Freud deconstructs his own "proper" desires; and Kofman believes it is his failure to do so which makes his analyses of sexuality so difficult to interpret. In *L'Énigme de la femme*, Kofman analyses this difficulty, and in so doing throws further light on her own figuration of the sexual markings of the proper.

Kofman shows how Freud's "double-edged" theory of castration translates into an analysis of sexuality which tackles the "problem of the double" and places it at the root of speculation; and yet simultaneously falls back into being a tool through which Freud shores up his own speculative authority and defends the "proper" boundaries of his "masculinity". On the one hand, Freud's theories of sexuality dispense with an essentializing, "metaphysical" view of sexual difference. Biological sexual function and the sexuality of the individual are not conflated; and the basic state of human sexuality is said to be bisexual. According to Kofman, in his "Three Essays on Sexuality", Freud

> … establishes an authentic symmetry between man and woman: bisexuality is claimed to be equally valid for both sexes, the difference between individuals is asserted to be quantitative, the proportion of masculinity and femininity in each individual is said to be eminently variable (1980, 131; 1985, 110).

If sexual difference is considered to be fundamentally "quantitative", then the division of the sexes into opposing, "idealized" positions is not a "natural" or inevitable occurrence (see Freud 1991f, 52-55 & 141-148). The theory

> ... makes it possible to displace the metaphysical categories that it renders problematic, since it proclaims the purely speculative character of the masculine / feminine opposition (1980, 15; 1985, 15).

It is therefore possible to read Freud's theory as a narrative which parallels the deconstructive interrogation of the speculative desire for absolute presence: it traces the attempts of the male "subject" to rid his "proper" self of ambivalence. Thus read, his theories cannot be – as many feminists read them – simply "phallogocentric", or a reflection of homosocial culture, as Freud's own authorial voice does not represent one sex.[23] As Kofman says,

> The thesis of bisexuality [...] implies that Sigmund Freud himself could not have been *purely* and *simply* a man (*vir*), that he could not have had (*purely*) masculine prejudices. That charge only reveals the metaphysical prejudices of those who press it.

On the other hand, there is at least a trace of irony in this comment, because Kofman also points out that Freud uses his own "bisexuality" as a "defense against accusations of anti-feminism", which allows him to return to "the most tenacious, the most traditional, the most metaphysical phallocratic discourse" (1980, 15; 1985, 14). By the time of his later essays on sexuality – most notably his essay on "Female Sexuality" – he has given into his own (historically sanctioned) desire for "proper" masculinity, "discovering" penis envy, and mapping female sexuality as more bisexual than male sexuality; in other words, defined in accordance with and closer to the "masculine" position than the male is to the "feminine" position (Freud 1991g).[24] The "masculine" thus becomes the "norm" of sexuality, and the castration complex now seems both a natural and inevitable part of a developmental process. According to Kofman, it is

---

[23] The target of Kofman's feminist criticism is Luce Irigaray, in particular her *Speculum of the Other Woman*, which accuses Freud of being fundamentally "phallocentric".

[24] Kofman points in particular to the way Freud uses this idea as self-defence, in anticipation of complaints from female psychoanalysts about his theories, as he claims that their analytical intelligence indicates that they are more "masculine" than "feminine". Kofman asserts that the "thesis of bisexuality [...] is in the last analysis used only as a strategic weapon in connection with women" (1980, 15; 1985, 15).

as if Freud cannot stand his own theory of bisexuality, and the ambivalent status of sexual identity that follows from it.[25] Having established its shiftable nature, he shifts its definition into line with his own "proper" fears. In order that he may have authority over his own identity and his own writing, Freud has to return to the "speculative" divisions that his initial theory undermines, and reinstigate a structure which functions through the setting down of "pure" positions.

As such, Freud's theory of castration is both a recognition of the recurrence of differentiating forces within the sexual "economy" – and thus, potentially, a means of displacing the "purely speculative" opposition of "masculine and feminine" – and a "rational" defence of Freud's own (apparently spontaneous) fear of difference, and his own "will to mastery", which manifest themselves as a need to subscribe the perceived chaos of bisexuality:

> Because with 'woman' men never know for sure *with whom* they are dealing, they try to overcome her lack of 'proper nature' and propriety by making her their property, by deciding, given her undecidability, in favor of masculinity; in short, by endowing her with "penis envy" as a definitive mark (1980, 249; 1985, 207).

In treating "castration" as a "transmuted" metaphor, Kofman can read it as a (provisional) truth about creative and mastering "forces", which does not refer to an empirical or essential "knowledge". For Kofman, the theory's analysis of doubleness, and its own double function, reveal the recurrent force within analytical writing to be a force of propriation which necessarily acts through the spatial and temporal markings of sexual "difference" and "division". Significantly, Kofman's genealogy of the return of Freud's "proper" voice also reveals that these markings are not necessarily permanent, and need not always occur in the same order. That they ultimately do in Freud is an indication of his blindness to his own desire to master his speculative inheritance.

Evading Sexual Difference

It is such acts of blindness which Kofman is concerned to mark, both in order to distinguish herself from the "father" figures in her own texts; and to draw out the complexity of the relations between the

---

[25] Kofman uses Freud's own theory against him by describing his fear of ambivalence as the desire "to keep the boy's love for his mother intact and pure" (1980, 203; 1985, 170).

historically sanctioned legacy of philosophy and the styles of writing which attempt to challenge the hierarchies of this legacy. For Kofman, these two purposes are inseparable because they highlight the degree to which philosophical determination is founded on a sexualized economy. Even the most contingent, "perspectival", performative modes of writing rely, at the point of intervention (what Derrida calls "decision") on a proprietorial force which, while being suffused with alterity, still operates by claiming a self-authorizing voice. According to Kofman, this action is sexually differentiating. Freud, Nietzsche and Derrida are cited and analysed as theorists who enable a new order of writing and yet are not immune from the return of "proper" desires. This includes the desire to hide the sexual bias of these "proper" desires behind an impersonal, "objective" voice. Kofman's writing constantly draws attention to this double movement by juxtaposing the different styles and "orders" of her three influences, and tracing the way in which all three figure their ideas on causality through sexualized metaphors. In the process, Kofman's own movement of writing – partly mimetic, partly ironic – explores the nature of deconstructive agency in a way which begins to suggest how it may be applicable in a more explicitly feminist context.

Kofman illuminates the double bind of Freud's theories through her genealogical investigation which, ironically, highlights his reliance on a structure of "forces" that resembles Nietzsche's. Equally, many of Nietzsche's works are shown to share Freud's concern with a sexual paranoia and fetishism lying at the base of apparently rational structures. In *Nietzsche et la scène philosophique*, and throughout *Explosion I* and *Explosion II*, Kofman stresses the recurring images of rejected, "decadent" fathers and dangerous, desirable mothers which Nietzsche uses to represent the determining forces of the philosophical legacy.[26] As with Freud, this would seem to suggest the centrality of sexual difference to philosophical determination; and as with Freud, these markings are no longer "essential", or necessarily constrained to a particular hierarchy.

However, like Freud, Nietzsche has moments of exaggerated misogyny and anti-feminism, which seem to coincide with his desire to claim his "own" textual authority and originality. In *Ecce Homo*, for example, Nietzsche complicates his relation to his "own" (familial) legacy and his "own" name. He resists the idea of a

[26] The most sustained analysis of this is in "Baubô – Perversion théologique et fétichisme" (1986c; 1988b), which I will analyze in the final section of this chapter.

"present" self and a progressive development of self-knowledge, by showing how he lives simultaneously (and provisionally) through both his mother's and father's legacies; neither of which cohere or coincide (Kofman 1992, 167-200). Yet Kofman notes that there is a "dissymmetry" in this "double gesture" because the mother appears only briefly, and is villified and rejected (169). Similarly, in the chapter entitled "Why I am so wise", Nietzsche denies the matriarchal line – saying it is the "most base" – in favour of the "grandeur" of the patrilineal legacy; and this is in spite of what he considers elsewhere to be his father's "decadence" (192-94). Kofman considers this return to the primacy of the father as "a trace, a remainder of the paternal system of evaluations, which, after having pushed them as far as they will go, [Nietzsche] turns into their opposite" (194). In other words, Nietzsche insists on a "pure" legacy of thought so that complete inversion and subversion is possible. He "elevates his father the better to kill him"; which signals the persistence of his desire for "proper" mastery. Parricide, the attempted relegation of the maternal legacy, the "fear" of castration, are all different aspects of the will to mastery which, even in the least metaphysical contexts, cannot be overcome.

Even Derrida is not immune, and it is significant that Kofman should trace his own parricidal tendencies in a context where Freudian castration is under discussion.

Lectures de Derrida is one of Kofman's most explicitly "deconstructive" texts, and one of her most mimetic in style. However, the chapter which focuses on Derrida's radicalization of Freudian ambivalence, "Un philosophe unheimlich", is also where Kofman signals her belief that Derrida parallels Freud in his desire to shore up his own "authority" and "mastery", as well as in his undermining of singular, speculative determination. In "The Double Session", for example, one of the first texts where Derrida relates the notion of castration to the double origin (both revolve around an endless substitution of terms without "return" to the "father"), Derrida's analysis of Freud's essay on "The Uncanny" hints that the fear of castration as portrayed by Freud carries the same status as the final or transcendental signified, functioning as the stop to the seminal play of uncanny interpretation. Fear of castration (which also encompasses the loss of limb or eyesight at the hand of the father) seems to be figured as the root "cause" of the "uncanny" fears traced in the dreamlike narrative of Hoffmann's "The Sandman". Thus Derrida comments,

> Freud – here more than ever attentive to undecidable ambivalence, to the play of the double, to the endless exchange between the fantastic and the real, the 'symbolized' and the 'symbolizer', to the process of interminable substitution – can, without contradicting this play, have recourse both to castration anxiety, behind which no deeper secret (*kein tieferes Geheimnis*), no other meaning (*keine andere Bedeutung*) would lie hidden, and to the substitutive relation (*Ersatzbeziehung*) itself, for example between the eye and the male member (1981a, 268, note 67).

Castration is the primary term in the text's hermeneutical sequence, which Derrida calls "that nonsecret of seminal division that breaks into substitution". Kofman, however, points out that Freud himself categorizes such an interpretation as being a rational one only, which does not account for the sheer complexity of the experience of the uncanny (1984, 71-2).[27] The notion of substitution is inherent to the experience and is what distinguishes it from "normal" fear. As Kofman says,

> ... if this fear did not itself refer to something else, the uncanny effect would not be produced: it must be referred from substitute to substitute as part of a repression which never reveals itself as an ultimate secret, a secret of the depths (71).

For Kofman, then, castration anxiety cannot be considered as the final signified of Freud's multi-layered depiction of the uncanny; and this is borne out by the inexhaustibility of the Freudian narrative.[28] Thus even if it is only Derrida's appropriation of the Freudian structure which has radicalized its potential for disrupting speculative

---

[27] Freud posits the "rational" explanation of the experience of the uncanny as the literal fear of castration, then proceeds to complicate this explanation by hinting at the Oedipal resonances of this fear, and by alluding to other fundamental drives and complexes. He points in particular to the "compulsion to repeat" in the unconscious mind, which manifests itself simultaneously as the "doubling, dividing and interchanging of the self" and as "the constant recurrence of the same thing" in uncanny incidents (Freud 1990, 352-65).

[28] I am paraphrasing Kofman here. See in particular her footnote describing the series of substitutions and divisions which operate in Hoffmann's tale (72-3), and her assertion of the final indecision of Freud's text (87-88). Unlike Derrida, Kofman does not problematize the distinction Freud makes towards the end of his essay between "real" and "fictional" experiences of the uncanny. If, like Kofman, one accepts that Freud is rehearsing the doubling and repetition of the "experience" of the uncanny as much as seeking empirical definitions of it, then one can interpret this division simply as another substitution in the open-ended chain of "experiential" interpretation, and not as a bracketing or "setting aside" of the literary. That Freud clearly points to the fact that he has "not exhausted the possibilities of poetic license and the privileges enjoyed by story-writers in evoking or in excluding an uncanny feeling" would then indicate a more ironic "conclusion" than Derrida allows the essay to have.

teleologies, and for recognizing the true impact of the force of the "double" and the "undecidable", this appropriation also represses the degree of playfulness permitted by the Freudian text:

> Derrida […] solicits the text, putting at once more and less into play than Freud himself, thanks to a certain cutting …(71).

Derrida cuts – castrates – the chain of substitutions in the Freudian text in exactly the same way as he accuses Freud of doing in analysing his "father" text. The irony of this is emphasized in Kofman's knowing use of the double meaning of "coupure", which encompasses both to cut off / curtail and divide. Derrida frequently plays on the same double meaning – particularly in relation to his philosophical adoption of "castration" as a signifier of hermeneutical anxiety – and so to use this pun against him is both a way of paying homage to his project and a reminder that he remains partially within the curtailing, dividing legacy. Like Freud, he unifies his own analysis by reducing the possibilities of the other text.

Kofman's remarking of Derrida's parricidal gesture is not a *general* denunciation of his practice, or an accusation of a simple return to the "proper" paranoia of dialectical speculation. Derrida repeatedly acknowledges some degree of return to be inevitable; indeed, as we saw in Chapter 4, he highlights its central function in maintaining and sustaining the "transcendental seriousness" or urge to question in philosophy. Rather, Kofman marks the return to the "proper", objective voice *in this particular context*, because, in this particular context, Derrida does not admit it, and hides behind the general, philosophical "truth". On this occasion, when it comes to defining his "own" style and claiming his "own" authority within and in relation to the speculative legacy, the will to mastery (the "transcendental sickness of the analytic") is not marked and is solidly in place rather than "infinitely divisible".[29]

Although Kofman is usually far from critical in her engagement with Derrida, such moments as the one in *Lectures de Derrida* are significant, not simply because they prove her capacity to deconstruct her main influence, but because they carry wider implications for Kofman's different definition of writing, and for the delineation of her "own" style.[30] They demonstrate the centrality of the "propriating"

[29] I refer back to footnote 14 and Derrida's comments in *Resistances*.

[30] Kofman's implied critique of Derrida in some ways resembles Derrida's critique of Levinasian ethics. Both are barely distinguishable from the theorist they analyse in

trope in any speculation or genealogy, and, more importantly, its phallocentric, parricidal tendency. By implication, this suggests a specific element within the affirmative intervention of the deconstructive project which is neglected, and which, I would argue, Kofman's mimetic / ironic style addresses.

This specific element is the way the return of the "proper" might bring with it a return to sexual paranoia and fetishism. To some extent, on occasion, Derrida sidesteps the problem of the returning "proper" voice (the "biographical desire") at the level of his own style. There are particular contexts – usually when the question of sexual difference arises – where specific consideration of this problem seems to be evaded for the sake of preserving the independence of the deconstructive project; because such a consideration would not be "affirmative" enough, or would risk sounding too "existentialist" or "ontological".

Derrida's reading of sexual difference in *Spurs* could, perhaps, be thought of as one such context. Derrida's avoidance of the specifically sexual and sexualizing aspects of the "propriative" movement of "style", and his dismissal of the returning oppositionary sexual hierarchy in Nietzsche's work as "nothing more than a transcendental snare", indicate a fear of compromising the novelty and authority of deconstruction's "affirmative" structure. And in "Choreographies", a discussion which centres on a similar reinvention of sexuality and "style", Derrida makes the same protective / evasive move explicitly:

> The question proceeds, so to speak, from the end; it proceeds from the point where the thought of the gift and that of "propriation" disturbs without simply reversing the order of the ontology, the authority of the question "what is it", the subordination of regional ontologies to one fundamental ontology. From this point, which is not a point, one wonders whether this … idea of the gift can still maintain an essential relationship to sexual difference. One wonders whether sexual difference […] does not remain derived from and subordinated to either the question of destination or the thought of the gift (1985, 172).

The final sentence of this extract is particularly strange, as it seems to imply a neutral or even authentic "thought" outside the realm of manifested "being", in much the same way as Heidegger's ontological questioning did.[31] In so doing he defines his "own" deconstructive

---

terms of their overall projects, but both take the theorist to task for not sufficiently admitting the violence of their own structure in certain contexts.

[31] Both the quotation from "Choreographies" and the evasive movement in *Spurs* come in (perhaps through) the context of a discussion about Heidegger. It is therefore interesting to note that Kofman has most clearly distinguished herself from Derrida through her attempts to distance "deconstruction" from Heideggerian influence. As

boundaries and "subject" more easily, but as in "The Double Session", does not acknowledge the curtailing and (sexually) objectifying action of this self-defining movement.[32]

This is what I would consider to be the cutting point between Kofman's work and Derrida's; and what explains Kofman's obsession with the return of the "proper", and the heightened mimeticism of her own style. Given her (more Nietzschean) reading of philosophy in terms of specific types of "mastery", Kofman's greatest concern is to pursue and decipher as many specific incidents of mastery in as many provisional contexts as possible. Thus questions about the ways in which particular figurations of sexual difference might be symptomatic of a certain historical or structural will to mastery, are more urgent than "the question of destination or the thought of the gift". Indeed, the latter question and thought could only ever be approached through the analysis of their particular manifestation in a specific context – such as one where a "new" style of writing refigures "old" hierarchies of masculinity and femininity. Considered in any other way the risk of falling into a generalized conceptual mode of expression would be too great. This is the risk that Derrida runs rather than risking what he considers to be too "subjective" or (self-)present an approach. Kofman, on the other hand, is far less anxious to distinguish her style from the language of subjectivity because according to her, a typological analysis of subjective propriation is not

---

she says, "For my part, I'm not borrowing [the] word [deconstruction] from Derrida, who borrowed it from Heidegger, but from Nietzsche" (1991, 112).

[32] In the introduction to his translation of *Nietzsche and Metaphor*, Duncan Large remarks on "the scant and somewhat cryptic 'global' acknowledgement Derrida delivers at the outset of [*Spurs*] to those (including Kofman, as a footnote makes clear) whose recent readings of Nietzsche provided the backdrop to his 'sally'" (Kofman 1993b, xx). Derrida says he "owes these readings a great debt", but does not refer to them individually "because they have opened up that problematic field to the very margin in which […] [he] shall remain [and therefore] that debt should not be fragmented here, but at each moment presupposed in its totality" (Derrida 1979, 36-37). Large comments, "The convenience of this strategy – which capitalizes on "the death of the author" so as to dispatch the authors – contrasts markedly with Kofman's candid recognition of her indebtedness the other way round" (Kofman 1993b, xxviii-xxxix). Derrida's "propriative" glossing over of the sexual aspects of the question of his "own" style in *Spurs* could perhaps be compared with his "dispatching" of the "French Nietzscheans" at the beginning of the text. That Derrida's and Kofman's intellectual relationship was difficult is acknowledged in Derrida's elegiac piece on Kofman in *The Work of Mourning* (2001b, 168-88). For an intriguing analysis of this piece, and the ethics and sexual politics of Derrida's and Kofman's mutual indebtedness, see Deutscher 2000b.

at odds with the (post-)Nietzschean "stripping away of individuality" and essence (1993b, 122, note 27). It simply reveals a particular perspective or "personality" which is one of many "provisional and multiple" propriations (102).[33]

Conscious as she is of her indebtedness to Derrida – indeed of the general debt of writing which suspends "progression" and "conclusion" – Kofman returns to a more personal vocabulary. This is both because "after" Derrida there can be no return to self-possession; and because it is at the point of claiming one's own style, one's written "specificity", that the risk of violating alterity is greatest; even, as we have seen, for Derrida. Kofman's interweaving of Derridean performativity with Freud's theories of castration and parricide, and with Nietzsche's "will to power", shows that she regards this point of intervention as perhaps *the* inevitable decision. Even if the deconstructive "style" eschews the possessiveness of "proper" writing and challenges the "ontological truth", the "undecidable" decision of writing, when reduced to its specificity, can only operate through a residual self determination.[34] It is racked with the deferrals and differences of performative time, but self-determined nevertheless, and thus necessarily "propriative". If it were not, it would still be ethical, metaphysical, and reliant on an originary Other. Derrida freely admits this, of course, but it is not usually his primary concern or explicit context.[35] The impossibility of overcoming the "legacy" of

[33] As she says of the metaphorical style: "To express oneself metaphorically one must simultaneously be outside oneself and express oneself, whereas the concept is the deliberate concealment of the personality in the interest of speaking "properly" and objectively" (1993b, 122, note 27).

[34] In fact, Ernesto Laclau rechristens the undecidable decision the "subject" because its inevitably failing structural determination demands a supplementary decision "in order to explain actuality". This has to be "in some way self-determined, because it cannot appeal as its ground to anything different from its own singularity" (1996, 55). While quick to reject any comparisons between this model of decision and ideas of existential "choice", Laclau is ready to accept the language of subjectivity because he sees the supplementary decision as an act of *simulation*.

[35] Just as Derrida's analyses of Freud have increasingly explored questions of legacy and indebtedness, so too has he entered into more explicit considerations of the "subject" and propriation. See in particular "Eating Well: Or the Calculation of the Subject", where Derrida follows a Kofmanian sequence of movements between "propriation" and "disappropriation" in discussing the "self's" non-identicality to itself (1991, 115); and *The Politics of Friendship* (1997), which offers an extended meditation on the ironies of "fraternity" and its (social, historical and philosophical) exclusion of female relations. This is not to suggest that Derrida is returning to a classical model of subjectivity, but that, having established the profound difference between deconstructive "presence" and that of the grand metaphysicians – having affirmed his "own" style – he can afford to return to such topics without risking a

mastery, which is also the problem of the specificity of "style", with all its connotations of creativity and violence, is fundamental to Kofman's analysis, and could be described as its driving force. It is her recurring context, and is always tied to the divisions of sexual authority and "subjection". Implicit in this is Kofman's concern for her "own" propriating will. If she is to write from her "own" perspective, as a female writer, she must challenge the historical legacy which may figure its determination as both a will to mastery and a will to renunciate (the question of destination and the question of the gift) but, in order to define itself, invariably assigns to "woman" the renunciating will alone.[36]

Kofman's challenge is thus to rework the uncanny irony of Derrida's depiction of "experience" – the undecidable "here and now" between and beyond history, memory and determination – in a register which, before anything, addresses the aspect of this experience which will always seek to authorize and master itself. This is the case even if – especially if – the experience knows it will only ever be provisional, a simulation in a highly specific context. By subjecting each of the "fathers" of her writing to the analytical "styles" of the others, Kofman highlights the inevitability of the "proper" return; marks its historical manifestation as a patriarchal, phallocentric, and sexually divisive trope; and shows that none of the perspectives given is

---

"real" return. That Kofman, with the luxury of coming "after" Derrida, should have picked up on Derrida's parricidal tendencies in his early texts, and have treated *explicitly* the possibility of "subjective" simulation before Derrida, is particularly interesting in the current context of considering genealogical ironies.

[36] "Mastery" and "renunciation" are, of course, tied closely to Nietzsche's "concept" of "eternal recurrence." See "*Of the Bestowing Virtue*", "*Of Old and New Law Tables*" and "*The Convalescent*" in *Thus Spoke Zarathustra*. The attribution of sexual characteristics to these two "wills" is by no means straightforward, or consistent, in Nietzsche's texts, as Kofman's analyses make clear. Nietzsche's "new" hierarchy of terms does not consider them as opposites: the "man of renunciation" referred to in *The Gay Science* is strong and *masterful* in his renunciation of "endless trust" in absolutes, and this strength is the same as the strength required to act "at a distance" and resist the unveiling of truth; which are acts associated with women and femininity. (See 1974, 38; section 60, 123-124; section 285, 229-230). However, Kofman's point is that when Nietzsche (like Freud or Derrida) claims his "own" style and perspective – an act of propriation which is necessary to creation and thus an affirmatory aspect of the will to power – he "returns" to the more oppositionary sexual hierarchy. See for example his description of men's and women's rights in love, where the woman's love is defined by "its unconditional renunciation of rights" (she "wants to be taken and accepted as a possession") and the man's love consists of his "wanting to have and not of renunciation and giving away" (section 363, 319-320). This alignment of the "woman" with the act of renunciation intersects with Derrida's playful reiteration in *Spurs*.

permanent or finally authoritative.[37] Each is a specific, provisional and highly contingent style which will be complicated or undone when placed in relation to another. It is this contingency which enables Kofman to stage her own anxious relation to their legacies. Significantly, not only does Kofman's "force" of writing not quite resemble Derrida's, but it is neither quite existential enough to be like Nietzsche's conception of instinct, nor quite biological enough to be like Freud's archaic drive. Instead it is suggestive of yet another "other" context where some provisional "decision" or "personality" may, at times, affirm itself alongside and as part of the "experience" of the impossible. That it writes itself somewhere between graphical, historical and biological determination and between, or beyond, three "(post-)patriarchal" styles brings to the fore the violence and doubleness of Kofman claiming her "own" authority and her "own" difference. And since the question of sexual difference and "propriation" is paradigmatic of the movement of authority and difference in writing, this context may also suggest what may be, for a writer who is, historically, the "other" of her (topical) subject and her (own) subject, "her" only proper style.

The Return of the Feminine

If we consider again the shifts of perspective that were taking place in "Aporie", we can perhaps detect the doubleness of approach deemed necessary by Kofman in the creation of her alternative genealogy. There is an element of "returning" violence throughout Kofman's family saga of the aporia, not simply in the constant repetition of the dialectical hierarchy, but in the deconstructive genealogy which interrupts this repetition. Primarily this is played through the "battle of the sexes". The figure of Metis (sophistry, rhetoric) and the Thracian maidservant who laughs at the trapped philosopher are reactive forces in line with the mimetic structure of speculation. One is the original "risk" of darkness and irrationality

[37] See in particular the "Rhapsodic Supplement" of *Explosion II*, quoted in the epigraph of this chapter, where Kofman situates herself as a "child" of Nietzsche, but also marks her propriation and exposure of Nietzsche and Freud to each other's "ears" "so that neither of them could ultimately win out over the other or over 'me'" (1993a, 372). It is perhaps not too far-fetched (though beyond the scope of this chapter) to make an oblique connection between Kofman's "philosophical" positioning and her "autobiographical" writings, which return repeatedly to the loss of her father, and her painful upbringing divided between two "mothers". For more extended considerations of this connection, see Duroux (1997), and Deutscher (1999).

which, paradoxically, is also the source of the ultimate means to escape. The other is the copy of this risk, the aporia of the ironic method, whose ridicule will bring the philosopher to (temporary) enlightenment. Both are "properly" ironic, and "properly" feminine: dangerous, possibly castrating, in league with negativity and abandoned to irrational laughter. However Penia, as read through Kofman's doubling and splitting of dialectical logic, reacts differently. She too is seemingly excluded and deceitful (a poverty-striken seducer), but fails to repeat the oppositional structure that is the basis of the speculative lineage. She cannot be hived off and separated: she is not a separate, definable "she" and part of the poros / aporia division. She is *already* pregnant with love because she is the instigator of the plot, and other to paralysis, not the embodiment of it and the opposite of Poros. She "breaks with the logic of identity" (1983, 63). Hence she can be the producer of possibility, even plenitude, without relying on the authority of ultimate enlightenment or certain direction. Yet in not being a separate copy of original "truth", she is a repetition: the ironic feminine *does* return at the very point of Penia's divergence from the path, in her resemblance to the vengeful maidservant and the untrustworthy Metis, and most of all, in her strange similarity to the effeminate "midwife" Socrates, who is a dialectical intermediary. Penia's "own" difference and authority come, ironically, with the return of the same, which, infused as it is with "originary" alterity, is now also the violation of all sameness. Her doubly repeated (sexual) otherness is an appropriation which makes propriation insufficient and invalid.

This return can, in turn, be brought back to the writer of the genealogy herself, for while the "path" of writing is now too dissymmetrical for any allegories to be drawn, the figuring of this appropriation through the "first" separation of sexual difference is surely not accidental. In fact, the diversion in allegorical direction, and the way in which it highlights the possible "biographical" element in the narrative, may well be the point behind Kofman's discussion of aporias. The "newness" of Kofman's genealogy, the marking of her "own" authorial difference and authority not only engages with the secondariness of coming after and writing over the speculative history of division, but with this secondariness being the attributed "nature" of the "fundamental ontology" of the feminine which is her own starting point.

Kofman is performing the double dissymmetry between the return of the proper (the simulated "personality", the biographical trace) that is a necessary and inevitable part of the disturbance of speculative order, and the sexual division (hierarchical secondariness of the historical legacy) which seems to return even as one moves into the dream of a more-than-binary structure. She thus shows that it is quite possible to be true to the logic of the hymen while inscribing one's "own" sexualized style, for there could not even be Derrida's question of "destination" (even if it is not a "straight" question) without this dissymmetrical return of "originary" sexual division and self-possession.

These complicated manoeuvrings illuminate Kofman's mimeticism and suggest a way in which a woman writer can intervene in both speculative and deconstructive structures. However, a question remains concerning the relation of this mimeticism to the negative figuration of feminine sexuality in the history of philosophy. Kofman's dissymmetrical repetitions may mark and treat ironically the returning hierarchy of sexual difference in the propriative structure of writing, but do they actually transmute the representations of masculinity and femininity? Even if the marking of the "subjective" propriation does not return to the belief in essentialist notions of gender, does it not seem to suggest that there is something irreducible about the historical determination of these categories, and the writer's relation to them? I intend to tackle these questions in the final section of this chapter by comparing Kofman's ironic / mimetic intervention with those of two other "feminist" theorists.

III. Irony, Mimesis and the History of Propriation

Cixous and Irigaray

Like Kofman, Hélène Cixous and Luce Irigaray repeat and ironize apparently "natural" gender positions as a way of revealing their historical and cultural instigation.

Hélène Cixous is probably the closest to Kofman in her analysis of binarism and separatism in the patriarchal economy of thought. She follows Derrida's deconstruction of the "metaphysics of presence", and plays up the différantial "time" of writing; claiming it as a realm where the propriating hierarchies of phallocentric logic are most exposed. The register of writing is always, "not the one not the other, neither one nor two – it is always more: a *plus*, one plus, one more", which leads Cixous to write of it as being "entredeux", bisexual, the "neuter"(1997, 50-52). The "bisexuality" of her writing ["*écriture*"] works as the "non-exclusion either of the difference or of one sex"

(1975, 46; 1980, 254). Rather than seeking to eliminate differences for the sake of a universal norm, it "stirs them up, pursues them, increases their number". This definition distinguishes itself from the Freudian definition in not perceiving bisexuality as the first stage of a sexual development that leads to a sexual identification based on two mirrored halves. Rather, Cixous stresses that these male / female sexual identifications only occur *belatedly* in the psyche of the individual, and that a complex relationship between different "libidinal economies" is and should be maintained (1984, 131). This means that sexual difference

> … is not a block between two blocks, it is exchange itself. […] It cannot be seen. What we see is only appearance, not difference. The visible does not make the difference (1997, 53).

What does "make the difference" is a constantly shifting set of psychic identifications and investments, which may be "masculine", "feminine", death-driven, life-driven, active, and / or passive beyond the binary associations of one sex with one set of attributes. Cixous' writings on sexuality seek to follow the movement of these identifications and economies, "exchanging, spending and retaining" rather than forging one theoretical position (1984, 131). Her "poetic" register resists singular, speculative decisions and, following Derrida's example, keeps an ear open to alterity. Indeed, Cixous' and Derrida's sequence of texts on each other's work builds a dialogue which exchanges their common figurations and tropes without treading exactly the same ground.[38]

However, there are some peculiar inconsistencies in the way Cixous balances her "new" configuration of sexual difference with the "old" configurations. She acknowledges the impossibility of simply leaving behind conceptual binarisms and says that we must "resign ourselves to keeping words like 'feminine' and 'masculine'", not because "anatomical sex […] determines anything" but because "one never escapes" history and "cultural schema" (1988, 18). Yet the way in which this translates into her written evocations of "masculine" and "feminine" libidinal economies seems at once too sexually prescriptive, and too eager to leave the complications of the historical legacy behind.

Her descriptions of propriation are a case in point. Like Kofman, Cixous associates the determination of speculative structures with a sexual propriation: propriation is a self-determining act, and a

[38] See Derrida 1994b and 2001a; Cixous 1994, 2001a and 2001b.

response to the "fear of expropriation, of separation", typically manifested as a fear of sexual otherness (1985, 80).[39] Yet where Kofman analyses its occurrence in specific writing contexts, Cixous forms a broad diagnosis of it as a symptom of the "masculine" libidinal economy:

> The Realm of the Proper, culture, functions by the appropriation articulated, set into play, by man's classic fear whose response is all of History. Everything must return to the masculine. 'Return': the economy is founded on a system of returns. If a man spends and is spent, it's on condition that his power returns (1976a, 7; 1981, 50).

Propriation is irreducibly masculine, always a response to castration anxiety and is the foundation for the whole of History – in capital letters. What Kofman analyses as a contingent web of relations (the propriative will is inevitable, but performative rather than essential, so does not always "propriating" in the same direction, for the same sex) Cixous seems to draw as a general rule. This quotation is from one of Cixous' polemical texts, which may account for a certain deliberate rhetorical exuberance, but even in more recent, more "dialogic" writings she tends to equate propriation with masculinity. Her musings on Derrida's "Circonfession" take up his anxious play with his "own" sexual markings – the circumcision that marks him as "man" and as "Jew", that confirms his proper name, and proper style – and translates it into a very literal "female" equivalent:

> The female-difference [difference-femme] is often localized, placed, hidden with[in] ourselves, in the body, and I believe that it isn't inscribed, not with a knife, not with a style, not to the bone [lit. aux dents]. It is a fleshly mystery without tragedy. And if there is a trace, and if there is a scene, it isn't before, it is later, it's tomorrow, it's 'when I grow up', it is to imagine. […] We invest in the promised rite of the proper body. It will come about (also) with the loss of blood, but tomorrow, and the loss of blood is received as a gift (1994, 42).

What in Derrida's writing signals a tension between the impossibility and the "event" of the defining sexual mark, becomes in Cixous' feminized reiteration an idealized picture of possibility and futurity, with all violent and negative traces forgotten; presumably because they are assigned to the masculine realm of the Proper.

---

[39] Cixous cites Hegel as a typical proponent of the "history of propriation", the "drama of the Selfsame (*propre*)" (79).

This figuration is not a simple biologism because Cixous is clearly writing in economic terms.[40] However, it *is* a case of structural determinism which – most strangely for a deconstructionist – leaves little room for hierarchical changes in the legacy of philosophical history. An opposition seems to be resurrected between a "proper" rational masculine History and an instinctual women's writing which "depropriate[s] unselfishly, endless body, without 'end', without principal 'parts' (1980, 259-60). Cixous even goes so far as to deny the possibility of writing analytically about "her":

> In the domain of woman nothing can be theorized. […] The only thing is that writing can not tell or theorize it, but play with it or sing it. […] Being a woman cannot be demonstrated, it must be felt, […] it is the experience of a pleasure (1989, 11).

Even if the "truth" about men and women can never finally be "known", this does not mean that nothing can be said about the many different "positions" or performances that identify themselves as womanly or feminine; or that any feminine experience should necessarily remain non-verbal and bodily. And although Cixous' notion of *l'écriture feminine*, or *l'écriture dite feminine*[41] is bisexual insofar as it is a challenge to "phallic monosexuality" (1986, 85), the register in which she writes of it suggests that rather than exemplifying the logic of supplementarity, it is completely "other":

> Her scene of wild writings forever escapes vigilance, armed reason, force, jealousy, death wish, Schadenfreude, the traps and bites of life's enemies.
>
> … Her art of living her abysses, of loving them, of making them sing, change, resounding their air with the rhythms of her earth tongues, regardless of the littoral and acoustic delimitations of their syllabysses (1976b, 205-6).

Quite apart from the question of how this writing can "forever escape" propriation when it is never without the other, such a rhapsodic and triumphant register cancels out the anxiety (for the other) and the irony (of never completing one "position") which should surely be ingrained in any alterity-conscious, non-prescriptive writing. Cixous seems to have embraced the affirmatory element of deconstruction to

[40] I am thinking here of Toril Moi's critique of Cixous (1985, 108-113) which accused her of "biologism". Cixous is always careful to stress that she is talking about a sexual *economy*: "I think that […] a feminine libidinal economy is an economy which has more supple relation to property, which can stand separation and detachment, which signifies that it can also stand freedom – for instance, the other's freedom" (1984, 137).

[41] See 1984, 129-134, for Cixous' explanation of why she uses these terms.

such an extent that, ironically, her writing evades the specific decisions of sexual differentiation completely.

Cixous' problem here is clearly a recurrence (in different clothing) of the old problem of "post-dialectical" agency: how can one change historically constituted gender categories which are founded on and determined through the propriative desire for (absolute) self-presence, without repeating the propriative gesture, and in a context where there is no historical record of the feminine other being figured as anything but the negative of the masculine positive? The influence of Derrida's deconstructive intervention has clearly changed the parameters of this problem, by interrupting the propriative "will" with its own internal and (self-)constituting alterity. While this also interrupts the belief in the possibility of overcoming the old order, and so demands a highly contextualized, anxious / ironic intervention, this intervention is still *acutely* anxious when the sexual hierarchy is under analysis; because, as Kofman's ironic doublings of masculine / feminine hierarchies point out, it is more difficult to intervene in a way which decentres "neutral" "phallogocentric" presence if, historically, as a "woman" writer, one is already "properly" marked as excentric. This is not to say that historical categories and positions of gender are inescapable or irreducible; but it *is* to say that they should be more *specifically* addressed in the context of the question of sexual difference and women's writing. Cixous does comment on this problem on occasions when she writes about historical and political "identities", but when she writes about writing, she avoids the complications of the "new" order's relation to "old" hierarchies altogether.[42] Her too-rigid division between philosophical and "poetic" writing banishes the problem of "propriation" along with masculinist History and steps into an idealized space of perfect multiplicity and difference.

Given Cixous' evasion of historical and sexual propriation, the doubling mimesis of Kofman's writing seems a more promising way

---

[42] For example, Cixous writes of the problems of possessing a particular "History" for one who is Jewish and a woman (a "Jewoman"), and having commented that "in the domain of women nothing can be theorized" and that "being a woman […] must be felt […] is the experience of a pleasure", she leaps into a description of the theatre as a place where "from one sentiment to another one can reach an understanding even in a foreign language" (1989, 11-12). Later, she describes the theatre as a place where "the human heart has no sex", but says that she writes "with the body […] [as] a woman" (15). This logical sequence demonstrates the way Cixous tends to fly from questions and problems associated with her "own" propriative desires, and those of history, into a "pure" space of fiction where temporal and historical problems seem to have dissolved inexplicably, and blatant sexual contradictions (gender as multiple and neutral; gender as essential) co-exist without provoking anxiety.

of figuring sexual difference differently in relation to the historical legacy. However, as Kofman (like Cixous and Derrida) is well aware, the risk of a mimetic / ironic register crumbling into "pure" negativity and a desire for existential "revelation" is great.

This is the trap into which Luce Irigaray falls in her analysis of Nietzsche's "affirmative" structure (1991). Like Kofman and Cixous, she stresses the prevalence of sexual propriation in philosophical writing, and the problematic legacy it leaves for the woman writer, but she mistakenly believes that a levelling up of gendered presences could achieve a new space and time of equality. Far from regarding Nietzsche's performative structure as a potential liberation from divisive figurations of sexual difference, she views it as a shoring-up of masculine independence from femininity which is founded in a fear of difference:

> I was your resonance.
> Drum. I was merely the drum in your own ear sending back to itself its own truth (1991, 3).

Writing from the other side of the "film" that keeps her and Nietzsche apart (she writes "you [tu] and me" as a signal of the intimate relation between the sexes to which she aspires in her writing), Irigaray portrays Nietzsche's "hammering philosophy" as another means by which the male philosopher gains self-possession and authority at the expense of the "other" woman (5).[43]

The implication of *Amante marine* is that the Nietzschean refiguration of philosophy as a history of propriation does not pass into a realm beyond ethics where alterity is an integral part of any signification or signature; but that it ignores the other or uses her as a sounding board or mirror in the manner of speculative philosophy:

> … it is left to her to reflect your destiny as superman … when finally you allow her to speak, it is only to bring about – your perspective, your art, your time,

---

[43] Irigaray's point is that while the "performative" structure serves to emasculate Nietzsche's philosophical predecessors, it still does not allow any figuration of feminine "experience". For an elaboration of this point of view, see Oliver 1995. Oliver argues that to regard the emasculation of philosophical "propriation" as a feminist act, as Nietzschean and Derridean "feminists" do, is to "presume that the feminine is merely the lack of the masculine" (xii). She makes an Irigarayan call for the retrieval of "feminine" experience by using "the maternal body and its relation to the fetus […] [as] a model for an intersubjective theory of subjectivity as a process of exchanges" (xvii). I will return to this idea later in the chapter.

> your will. The last pattern of your being that she must still reproduce or mimic (36).[44]

Sexual difference is a matter of sexual division, and Nietzsche's "gay science" of surface, beauty, masks and "action at a distance" is simply a defensive strategy for preventing real contact with the other. The defence is deemed necessary because her "absence" in relation to masculine "presence" resembles the very limit of his existence; and is proximate to (his) death.

> To share the life of the other without stealing the other's goods is a threshold you refuse to cross. A circle you will not break. A skin you will not shed.
> And when you claim to digest the whole in your stomach, is it not here that your sickness lies?
> […] Within you, something of the other becomes nothing – resists absorption. And something becomes death – the difference of the bodies that you claim in this way to overcome (15).

According to this passage, the banishment of the ethical concern as ascetic "weakness" is simply an enactment of Nietzsche's desire to consume the whole history of philosophy. Far from deconstructing the metaphysical hierarchy, where the body is subordinated to the mind, and far from digesting and expelling the old pleasure-denying order in preparation for a new, healthier diet, Nietzsche's physiological analysis effaces difference under the force of his own solipsistic appetite for self-determination. The distinctions between corporeality and incorporeity are erased rather than transmuted and multiplied, and alterity is lost – becoming abyssal and deathly.

This claim may seem strange given Nietzsche's assertion that "the body is […] a multiplicity with one sense, […] which does not say 'I' but performs 'I'" (1969, 61-62), but it is prompted by the same "misogynist" incidents as the ones which provoke Kofman's more occasional remarks about Nietzsche's "proper" desire for authority and autonomy. The difference is that whereas Kofman does not regard the philosophical desire for mastery as inherently phallocratic – but historically constituted as such – Irigaray regards the whole conception of history in Nietzsche's structure as indivisibly phallocratic; and whereas Kofman considers the return of the "proper", regardless of its sexual bias, as inevitable, indeed necessary to any philosophical order and style, Irigaray regards it as inevitable only insofar as Nietzsche's order repeats the patriarchal fear of the

[44] Hence the water and mirror imagery which runs throughout the book. The water also serves as a metaphor for Irigaray's writing which acts as a (womanly) undercurrent to Nietzsche's philosophy.

feminized origin. She believes that in seeking to "overcome" philosophical history through genealogical analysis, Nietzsche attempts to erase the memory of its birth and becoming, by (metaphorically) giving birth to himself:

> And, going back to the source of all your children, you want to bring yourself back into the world. […] But in fact isn't it your will, in the here and now, to pull everything back inside you and to be and to have only one sun? And suspend the ascending and descending movement of genealogy? And to join up in one perfect place, one perfect circle, the origin and end of all things? (34).

This means that the eternal recurrence is not a figuration of the complex interaction of "sameness" and "difference", but a figuration of the same: and it translates into a profound resentment of maternal creativity. Nietzsche mimics "the gestation of nature" in his apparent affirmation of the body, while in reality "annihilating it" as a creative act that belongs to another who is very different from himself (60). Not content with possessing verbal power, he seeks to take over the only function or identity that the other has been permitted.

Irigaray's concern for the ethical relation between philosophy and its other(s) has lead her to place a Kierkegaardian-like emphasis on the *division* between what is posited in the "present" structure and what this excludes. Her depiction of Nietzsche's misogyny reads like a gendered replay of the ironic dialectic between mediated history and the unknown "instant." The singular logic of masculinity comes to terms with the unfathomability of the other by ignoring it and indulging in a kind of parthenogenetic fantasy. Meanwhile, there is a whole other logic at work outside and beyond this obsessive (self-) mastery, which, if it were allowed to make its presence felt, could perhaps unite with the masculine side in a marriage of mutual respect. Irigaray's figuration of these divided realms is, of course, an ironic repetition and reflection of the "divided" structure that she sees as the creation of masculine sexual paranoia. She is "play[ing] with mimesis": throwing back (in the sense of ventriloquizing, as well as returning and discarding) the harassed and silenced "feminine" position that Nietzsche and history has assigned her (1985b, 76). The writing space she inhabits is thus not simply contradictory, because her assumed feminine role "is not closed up or around one single truth or essence" (1991, 86). She is "already […] double in her self: both one and the other. Not: one plus an other, more than one". This means that the divisions are not accepted as being natural, and, like Cixous, she cannot accurately be accused of "biologism".

Nevertheless, the implication of this ironic reduplication is that only if the other is revealed and made "present" will a truly differential structure be attainable. Irigaray seems to assume that because she is "double", any manifestation of the (feminine) other would automatically take account of *its* other in a way which masculine presence never does: as she insists, "the possessive mark of belonging does not belong to her" (87). Yet how even a non-self-identical presence can eschew possessiveness and be non-propriative is far from certain, especially judging by the revelatory structures that I analysed in the first part of this book.[45] Moreover, in relying on a teleological ("theological") determination, Irigaray's anticipated "identity" resides in a semi-mystical futurity which leaves the "woman" silent in the here-and-now. Hence she anticipates a figure like Christ (this is a counter movement to Nietzsche's demolition of the "idol") because of his message of love and the fact that his incarnation can be interpreted as a mutually accepting marriage between the masculine "word" and the feminine "body":

> He is made flesh. Continues on in the flesh. Closes with and is close to himself, from within a living body. That can be affected by *pathos* – his own and that of others (182).

He defies the logic of mastery and law because his conception "was not marked by the language of a father husband" (180). He "does not act to defer the possibility that the presence will occur" (181)· Irigaray adopts this incarnation as a model for a future age where full presence will be possible through an act of consummation between "spirit" and "flesh", where the flesh is represented by the natural, maternal figure of the Virgin Mary, who remains "in excess to the existing world". How this excessive, affirmatory union will make its presence felt is, however, uncertain, because she is a "Grace that speaks silently through and beyond the word" (190).[46] Irigaray's ironic intervention marks and inverts Nietzsche's sexual propriations, but her attempts to reconstruct a differential economy evades awkward questions about her own possible violence through the utopian anticipation of perfect

---

[45] David Farrell Krell voices similar suspicions of Irigaray's claims to be without ressentiment (1994, 197-8).

[46] Irigaray is returning to the category of the "natural" and asserting sexual differences as "natural" phenomena, in contradiction to what she considers Western philosophy's anthropocentric notion of nature as an "immediate" substance that needs to be overcome by human subjectivity. This "return" is implicit in *Marine Lover*, but is outlined more explicitly in more recent works such as *I Love to You* (1996). For a sympathetic commentary on this "return", see Cheah and Grosz (1998).

synthetic plenitude.[47] Indeed, quite apart from the structural, temporal similarities between her maternal incarnation and Kierkegaard's "personality", Irigaray's silently signifying fleshly mother strongly resembles Kristeva's "herethical" mother – which is strange, considering the vehemence of her rejection of Freudian and Lacanian models of femininity, and Hegel's incorporation of alterity.

Cixous' and Irigaray's battles with the philosophical legacy prove that the margin within which the specificity of the feminine can be addressed in the "post-dialectical" structure is minute. The risks of being either too affirmative or too negative are peculiarly heightened given the apparent centrality of sexual decisions to written / philosophical interventions, and the excentric positioning of feminine sexuality within the history of philosophy.

I would argue that Kofman manages to maintain the difficult balancing act needed to write "improperly" as a woman without falling into sexually evasive affirmation or theological negativity. By threading Derrida's différantial structure back through Nietzsche's and Freud's historical / "instinctive" readings of "propriation", she writes a complex narrative which admits to the "self-determining" nature of structural decisions, and relates this to the complications and anxieties surrounding historical figurations of sexual difference and feminist interventions in this history. Propriation is figured as *the* primary determinant of thought and writing. Sexual propriation – the division of "experience" according to gendered marks in order to claim and possess a distinct perspective – is perhaps the primary form of this determinant. However, propriation is still performative rather than essential, so is "infinitely divisible" in terms of the actions and directions it may take. The perpetual desire of writing for a "proper" (objective) voice is thus constantly undermined by the otherness of its own deferred constitution.

This relation of terms retrieves some notion of "subjective" agency but rids it of ontological and epistemological authority. It thus enables Kofman to highlight her different relation to the history of propriation – as one whose "subject" is already marked as secondary and other – while affirming the deconstructive resistance to essential categories of gender. Kofman's ironic intervention marks and decenters the sexual propriations of dialectical philosophy and those of her non-dialectical

---

[47] Penelope Deutscher draws crucial distinctions between Irigaray and Kofman on the basis of Irigaray resisting "disappropriation" in her engagement with Nietzsche and Freud (2000a, 155-178).

"fathers", without dismissing propriation as inherently, irreducibly phallocentric, or claiming a reductive and historically-sanctioned account of female bodily "experience" as the authentic voice of alterity. Instead, her double style also mimes her "own" propriation, thus affirming its specific perspective and "other" sexual history while debunking any claims it might make for generalized authority or authenticity.

Baubô

This complex web of irony and deferral is most clearly played out in an oblique and whimsical essay by Kofman, on Nietzsche, called "Baubô: Theological Perversion and Fetishism" (1986c; 1988b). Like much of Kofman's other work, "Baubô" traces the way in which Nietzsche's interrogation of the fundamental assumptions of philosophy transmutes apparently fixed values and truths. The essay also serves as a deconstructive analysis of Nietzsche's own values and methods, and, most importantly, a feminist interrogation of the sexual and sexualizing aspects of these methods.

"Baubô" focuses on Nietzsche's typological analyses of "causality" and what he perceives as its fetishistic roots. In *Twilight of the Idols*, Nietzsche traces what he calls a "primitive psychology" at the origins of language, reason and metaphysics, whereby humans "think of the self as a substance and as the cause of their actions" (1986c, 225-6; 1988b, 175, quoting Nietzsche). This belief – and it can only be a belief because it is not grounded in an objective "truth" – extends to a belief "in will as cause in general" and eventually, the attribution of everything to a "being" which "*produces an effect*". Nietzsche calls it fetishistic because he maintains that it derives from a "feeling of fear" and a concomitant wish "*not* to see something that one does see; wishing not to see something *as* one does see it" (1986c, 227; 1988b, 176). In other words, man has created the fiction of God and of his own proximity to God and power as a response to his anxious ignorance and feeling of insignificance.[48] This notion of causality becomes fixed, becomes the "truth of things", when in fact it is merely a "*moral-optical* illusion" (Nietzsche 1990, 49).

[48] Nietzsche's "psychological" explanation is that "to trace something unknown back to something known is alleviating, soothing, gratifying and gives moreover a feeling of power. Danger, disquiet, anxiety attend the unknown – the first instinct is to *eliminate* these distressing states" (1990, 62).

This decentering of the "onto-theological grammar" of metaphysics is familiar ground for Kofman. However, she wonders if the term "fetishistic" carries more significance than might at first be apparent: if, rather than simply expressing Nietzsche's belief in the general perversity of the "system of theological judgments", the term refers to a more precise definition of fetishism, which is strangely close to that of Freud's. After all, as Kofman points out, Freud's definition of fetishism also revolves around a fear of seeing:

> For Freud, abnegation is the particular process of fetishism whereby castration is at once recognized and denied, and where the absence of a penis in women, more particularly in the mother, is both grasped and disregarded (1986c 227; 1988b, 176).

Moreover, "woman, a woman, an old woman, accomplice to the belief in the existence of God, continuously haunts Nietzsche's text".[49] If this were the case, then not only would it imply that sexual fear and propriation are central to Nietzsche's explanations of the derivation of causality, but it would significantly alter any reading we might make of Nietzsche's own attitudes towards women. On the one hand, it might suggest that Nietzsche is himself acknowledging the fear that is inspired by the unknowable, "castrated" woman; on the other hand, it might suggest that he is attributing this fear and the very notion of castration to the perversity of the theological perspective which tries to dominate "to the point of excluding anything that is not itself". Kofman poses a double question in response to these ambiguities:

> Does Nietzsche not himself repeat the ancient theological misogyny that woman is the locus and source of all evil? ... Or should this famous misogyny not itself be rethought and reevaluated from a standpoint that would differentiate it into types? (1986c, 228; 1988b, 177)

She proposes to "knit a cloth" out of the relation of the two possible sexual attitudes to the concept of causality.

The premise of Kofman's text might sound overly biographical or genetic: Kofman psychoanalysing Nietzsche in order to discover the cause of his placing of fear at the root of all structures. However, it is clear from the start that Kofman's analysis resists the belief in single, substantial "causes" as much as Nietzsche. Her text hinges on the uncanny nature of written decisions and determinations, and this

---

[49] The most obvious example of this haunting is in Nietzsche's quip: "'Reason' in language: oh what a deceitful old woman! I fear we are not getting rid of God because we still believe in grammar" (1990, 48).

brings to light the complex interaction of "proper" desires with their transmutation in Nietzsche's intervention. His ambiguous sexual attitudes are not simply read as symptoms of a problem he had with his mother, but as symptoms of the fight he has with his desire to create and possess his "own" authoritative voice.

This fight revolves around the "perverse" and "fetishistic" "theological" perspective, which fails to affirm "life" and constantly projects itself towards future perfection: in other words, the "theological" perspective which lives out the obsessions of the "proper". For Nietzsche, perhaps the worst aspect of this perspective is its claims to be objective, its denial of "the perspective that is part of the vital condition of all that lives" (1986c, 244; 1988b, 190). Nietzsche calls its world of objectivity and abstraction "antinatural" and "degenerated," terms which might sound somewhat anti-cultural and oppositional for one who is aiming to emphasize difference. However, as Kofman points out,

> Like most of the other 'old words', 'nature' (as well as denaturation and thus also perversion) needs to be revalued, read as if crossed-out. This is because the abstract, 'denatured', 'antinatural' world is still a 'natural' world: it too is the expression of a certain form of life. In this sense, all 'culture' is natural (1986c, 230; 1988b, 178).

In other words, the whole dialectic of natural versus unnatural is itself a symptom of the perverse moralistic view which imposes its rejection of worldliness on everything:

> That which is perverse and against nature is the will to impose one's own nature on another, [...] is to designate as "supernatural" the fictitious world and not to will to recognize its natural, too natural character.

This is the familiar problem of deconstructive agency: how to pass beyond the theological perspective without repeating its oppositionary structure and divisive definitions; how to conceive of a truly perspectival "causality"? For Kofman, this immediately translates into a feminist deliberation, because the failure of the "theologians" to admit any other perspective is portrayed by Nietzsche as a weakness much like the "weakness" of women: "they try to seduce, they charm, by misrepresenting and disguising nihilistic values under gilded trim" (1986c, 231; 1988b, 179). Nietzsche seems to be using a figuration of otherness in a propriative way – creating a sexual opposition – in order to authorize his own perspective. As Kofman says,

> It would seem that, on the one hand, he 'deconstructs' metaphysics and theology and denounces the ascetic ideal, but, on the other, remains caught in the net of the theologians (1986c, 232; 1988b, 180).

However, it is possible that this apparent misogyny needs to be "crossed-out" in the same way as his use of terms such as "anti-natural", because the "weak" women he speaks of may also be symptoms of the theological legacy, with its fiction of fixed categories and immutable hierarchies: woman as other, as weakness and nothingness. Kofman asks whether it is woman that Nietzsche denounces or simply a "*certain* woman"? After all, he also seems to scorn the art of seduction here, and in other contexts this is portrayed as "the special art of Dionysus". Such misogynistic moments might, then be interpreted as Derrida interprets them: as the decentering of the "history of truth", where the (initially Platonic, subsequently divided) idea "is a form of truth's self-presentation" and the "becoming-female of the idea is the presence or presentation [*mise en scène*] of the truth" (Derrida 1979, 86-87).[50] The "certain" woman that Nietzsche denounces is the philosopher's woman who represents "truth" in her elusiveness and otherness (1986c, 231-2; 1988b, 179-80). She is longed for and hated in equal measure, and the philosophers are sure her naked being will be revealed to their gaze at the end of their self-determining, divinely inspired reasoning. Nietzsche would thus be denouncing her in the same way as he denounced Socrates – as a "decadent" – for both use artistry perversely, with the aim of pinning things down to one fixed truth. Countering this is Nietzsche's notion of "true art", which repeats the world,

> … not in order to devalue it but to enhance the creative capacity [*pouvoir*] of life. Thus art wills for life yet again its eternal return in difference, a Dionysian mimetic power at one with creation and affirmation (1986c, 233; 1988b, 181).

According to this reading, once this affirmatory art is admitted to the thinking structure, neither this "proper" conception of woman, nor the "proper" causality are feasible. Sexual characteristics, "authors", truths, are performative; struck through with the "eternal return in difference". Thus even if the historical / theological terms and metaphors return – in Nietzsche's "weak" women, in his analyses of "health" and "sickness", "high" values and "baseness" – they are

---

[50] Of course, we should remember that Derrida wrote this after Kofman wrote "Baubô", and was directly influenced by her interpretation of Nietzsche's "misogyny".

transmuted by the (differential) admission of perspective. They serve now as "a denunciation of the metaphysicians/ fundamental prejudice for the autonomy and the opposition of values" (1986c, 238; 1988b, 185).

Kofman's genealogy of Nietzsche's genealogies brings us to a point where Nietzsche is retrieved from any (generalized) accusations of misogyny. "Women" and sexual propriation are considered to be central to Nietzsche's writing because femininity is the primary "other" of the perverse philosophers and the object of their fetishistic pursuits of "truth." The *many types* of women in Nietzsche's texts thus serve as a metaphor for his transmutation of values from the abstract and monumental to the specific and contingent. Nietzsche's antipathy towards certain "types" of woman (the sterile woman; the old woman) is based in a rejection of the trope of "truthful" woman who is the other side of the belief in the "castrated" woman (1986c, 247; 1988b, 192). Alongside this woman sits the "feminist", the "self-reliant" woman who makes "clumsy attempts ... at scientific self-exposure" (1986c, 247-8; 1988b,192, quoting Nietzsche 1974). Kofman explains Nietzsche's disgust at these women as an antipathy towards their will to "truth", their desire to reveal themselves like philosophers, and not as an antipathy towards woman-in-herself or her desire to alter existing hierarchies. In fact, a woman who seeks "self-exposure" simply repeats the ascetic negation of life and creativity. As Kofman says, "such a woman differs not at all from the man of *ressentiment* and like him erects her perspective as an absolute" (1986c, 248; 1988b, 193).

The truly affirmative woman or feminist would, according to Nietzsche, rather seek to transmute traditional hierarchies by refusing to accept the philosophical history of truth, which views her fetishistically in terms of the masculine ideal. She would reject the abstract "*moral-optical* illusion" of divinely determined, supernatural "truth". She would "consider it a matter of decency not to wish to see everything naked, or to be present at everything and 'know' everything" (1974, 38). She would affirm her sexuality as *different* rather than as a negated version of fully-present maleness; she would figure her "truth" as a specific type of truth – one of many perspectives – made up of many layers and without the comfort of a certain centre.[51] In other words, she would *perform* herself as an ironic

[51] Presumably it is this lack of certainty that provokes Nietzsche into figuring such a woman as a dangerous being (tiger, criminal) even while her celebrates her. "She" is

work of art: ironic because she holds back from monumental self-presentation, and not because she represents pure negativity (the "other" side of self-presentation), seducing her way towards positive revelation. Such a woman is specified by Nietzsche in *The Gay Science*:

> Perhaps truth is a woman who has reasons for not letting us see her reasons? Perhaps her name is, to speak Greek, *Baubô*? Ah, these Greeks! They knew how to live! What is demanded is to stop courageously at the surface, at the fold, the skin, to adore appearance, to believe in forms, tones, words in the whole Olympus of appearance. These Greeks were superficial – *out of profundity* (1974, 38).

She is named, but fleetingly, and her relevance to the affirmatory structure is not explained. This is where Kofman steps in and over-steps Nietzsche's figurations of affirmatory sexuality.

Baubô, Kofman explains, is a mythical figure who appears in the mysteries of Eleusis. She made the goddess Demeter laugh, when she was mourning the loss of Persephone, by pulling up her skirts and showing her belly. On her belly was drawn a figure of "an obscure deity", "thought to be [...] Iaachos, the child of Demeter, [...] sometimes identified with Dionysus" (1986c, 254; 1988b, 196). Kofman takes this strange and little-recorded event as her cue for an elaborate and fantastical analysis of the significance of Baubô. She interprets Baubô's gesture as an "apotropaic" gesture (1988b, 196, note 23).[52] Kofman suggests that as in many myths "the belly of the woman plays the role of the head of the Medusa", Baubô's lifting of her skirt was "suggesting that she go and frighten Hades, or that which comes to the same, recall fecundity to herself". This sounds like a crudely Freudian reading which, if taken as the reason for Nietzsche's reference to Baubô, would replicate rather than transmute the fetishization of woman. However, Kofman's interpretation continues:

> By displaying the figure of Dionysus on her belly, [Baubô] recalls the eternal return of life: 'Demeter recovers joy in the thought that Dionysus will be reborn. This joy, which announces the birth of the genius, is Greek serenity' (1986c, 255; 1988b, 197, quoting Nietzsche 1974).

Baubô's action now seems to represent a prophecy: not simply of a literal birth, but of a transmutation of values, which is represented by

---

uncanny and provokes anxiety, but Nietzsche does not wish to make her familiar or feel secure.

[52] As the footnote here explains, "apotropaïque" is a "neologism from the Greek 'apotropos': to displace in space".

the return of Dionysus and recovery from loss and darkness. Sure enough, Kofman continues to draw analogies, suggesting that Baubô is not only the predictor of Dionysus' birth, but "the female double of Dionysus". Kofman claims that the word Baubô derives from an "improper" word for female genitalia; that Dionysus was reputed to have used a "*baubôn*" – a figwood phallus – to gratify himself sexually; and in the Eleusian mysteries the female sexual organ is "exalted as the symbol of fertility and eternal return of all things".

It is at this point that Kofman's metaphorical reading becomes clear. Baubô is not an archetypal representation of a castrating woman; nor is she "revealing" her (biological, reproductive) truth by revealing her body. In fact, she is highly uncanny: apparently replicating the gestures of a negative ironic woman, but identifying herself with a figure (Dionysus) who defies "reproductive" sexuality. She heralds a movement towards a sexual hierarchy which is forever shifting ("men" and "women", real and "fake" genitalia, sexual orientations all changing) because it is not determined by the laws of division and "propriety" but by the difference of the eternal return:

> The figure of Baubô indicates that a simple logic could never understand that life is neither depth nor surface, that behind the veil, there is another veil, behind a layer of paint, another layer.

Baubô does this by defying conventional morality, by performing her otherness (while recognizing its "fertility" as part of "all things" (all determinations?)), and by acknowledging her contingent "self". The laughter she provokes is the work of an affirmatory ironist.

And yet, why does Kofman consider it necessary to dwell upon such a marginal figure as Baubô? Why does she patch together Baubô's history out of fragments of myths and etymologies of words? Why does she enthrone Baubô as the "female double of Dionysus" even as she stresses that Dionysus "crosses himself out [*se rature*] of the distinction between veiled and unveiled, masculine and feminine, fetishism and castration" (1986c, 255-6; 1988b, 197-8)? Is it because Kofman cannot concede to the deconstructive attempt to resist self-presentation and propriation? Is she trying to insert a model of "true" female identity into the philosophical structure, like one of Nietzsche's "sterile", "emancipated" women?

The answers to these last two questions are yes and no, because "Baubô" is another example of Kofman's double writing – much like "Aporie" – which upholds deconstructive interventions in speculative history, but also marks the way in which the (necessary) propriations of the "new" order repeat the problematic sexual discriminations of the old.

Kofman's interest in the idea of causality in Nietzsche not only stems from his capacity to transmute values and hierarchies, but *how* he achieves this transmutation. Once again, Kofman quotes the passage from *Ecce Homo*, where Nietzsche attributes his flexibility to the double set of judgments he inherited from his father and mother. "He is always his own double", which enables him to flit between many perspectives, to admit alterity into each of his own perspectives (1986c, 241; 1988b, 187). He calls this the "fatality" of his existence:

> This dual descent, as it were, both from the highest and the lowest rung on the ladder of life, at the same time a *decadent* and a beginning – this, if anything explains that neutrality, that freedom from all partiality in relation to the problem of life, that perhaps distinguishes me (1967, 222).

Kofman's reading of this "fatality" is close and ironic. The shift from (theological) "causality" to (affirmatory) "fatality" in Nietzsche's writing hinges on him regarding the doubleness of his inheritance as "freedom". Kofman shows that this notion of freedom corresponds to an "oneiric experience" which is frequently related in Nietzsche's writings. The experience takes the form of feelings of flight, where the dreamer

> … knows the feeling of a certain divine frivolity, an 'upward' without tension and constraints, a 'downward' without condescension and humiliation – without *gravity*! (1986c, 241; 1988b, 187, quoting Nietzsche).

This experience is not as transcendental as it may sound, because its psychological re-evaluations are "anchored in the body". Indeed, one could say that it closely resembles the "gift-giving" virtue that Zarathustra speaks of, where "mind and spirit" advance and elevate themselves as and through the body without letting aspiration "beat with its wings against the eternal walls" (1969, 102). However, we know from *Thus Spoke Zarathustra* that the "gift-giving" virtue is never fully enacted because Zarathustra cannot finally overcome the old law tables. Similarly, while the "dream" of freedom and "equilibrium" *does* affect the values of the dreamer's perspective in his waking life, the perspective will never be as free as the dream, because in its creative and (self-)defining movement it can never wholly escape the propriations of its history. Sure enough, Nietzsche admits to the "all-too-human" element of every artist's perspective, the "camera obscura" which inscribes "particular errors, illusions, or lies … on the general background or error inside this unsurpassable dream" (1986c, 244; 1988b, 190).

Kofman's reading of the causal shift in Nietzsche's values follows the dream flight and (disappointing) reality of his perspectival art, but highlights the sexual metaphors within this journey. In doing this she shows that while Nietzsche's "flight" "effect[s] an equilibrium between [the] double tendencies" of masculine and feminine histories, his "own" perspective – the artistic creation or propriation of his "existence" as "author" in *Ecce Homo* – repeats the old sexual hierarchy. He demotes the mother and elevates the father. A kind of double causality is at work in the creation of Nietzsche's "fatality", where Nietzsche's admission of "perspective" wounds the "proper" causality of the theological perspective, enables the change in sexual values, but also repeats the (historical) sexual propriations in order to distinguish his perspective from the old one. To only mark the transmutation of sexual values would thus be to fall into a mistaken Zarathustrian hubris; and this is precisely what Kofman avoids in weaving Nietzsche's transmuted causality back through the sexual bias of its own birth and determination.[53]

This ironic weaving can also be seen in Kofman's analytical shifts throughout the main body of her essay: from discussing theological "fetishism" to marking Nietzsche's ambivalent attitude to women; to analysing Nietzsche's dreamlike transmutation of terms through his "double" parental heritage; to discussing the "errors" of the "camera obscura"; and then to Nietzsche's typological analysis of women and her own (fabulous) exploration of the significance of Baubô. This trajectory retrieves Nietzsche from accusations of a generalized misogyny, but also shows that the specificity of the feminine term is not accounted for specifically enough. It shows Nietzsche's "new" conception of "cause" and "being" to be genuinely non-essentialist. It's "perspective" or performative "personality" is constantly interrupted by alterity and thus can only ever be a simulation of "self-presentation".[54] Nevertheless, it is still "self"-determined, insofar as there is no external force with which it reacts and authorizes itself. As such, the "proper" forces return, and with them the temptation to fall

---

[53] I would argue that this is what Hélène Cixous *does not* avoid in her figuration of the space of writing as a realm of sexual freedom. It is also the mistake Derrida makes in *Spurs* when he puts such an emphasis on the fact that "Man and woman change places *ad infinitum*" in Nietzsche's analysis of sexual difference (1979, 110-111).

[54] Thus it treats ironically feminist demands for an "authentic" female "experience", such as Kelly Oliver's call for a body-based "intersubjective theory of subjectivity". See footnote 43.

back into the historical sexual order. Kofman's sexualization of Nietzsche's causality clearly marks this path and completes the reading by tracing her "own" contingent perspective. Her figuration of Baubô as the "female" equivalent of Dionysus redresses the sexual balance in the historical legacy that determines the "new" order, without being an unproblematized insertion of the feminine term. (After all, both Baubô and Dionysus are simulations of "sex" as much as they are of a particular biological "sex".) Baubô deconstructs the fetishistic sexual hierarchy and opens out onto a more dissymmetrical and less phenomenologically-conceived sexuality, *while* playing back and ironically underscoring the sexual secondariness of her position in Nietzsche's "proper" returns, and of her and Kofman's position in the historical legacy. She is thus fetishistic in the theological sense, an interruption of fetishism, and an ironic simulation of fetishism, which maintains its anxious ambivalence without anticipating a final division of terms.[55]

The final passages of "Baubô" tie together this web of ironic repetition, deconstruction, affirmation and performative decision. Framed by the dissymmetrical return of the feminine "Baubô", and a phrase and footnote about Nietzsche's need for a protecting "umbrella" – which echo Derrida in pointing to the final "undecidability" of any text – Kofman's symptomatic reading of Nietzsche's letters, describing his "love" of and "injustice" towards women, can only be interpreted as an ironic commentary on the way "new" styles and structures repeat, while transmuting, their "own" history (1986c, 258-9 & note 43; 1988b, 198-200 & note 29).[56] Nietzsche fears and protects himself against the "abyssal"

---

[55] This is the biggest difference between Kofman's analysis of Nietzsche's women and Irigaray's. While both wish to create a more balanced sexual hierarchy than Nietzsche in their writing, Irigaray's analysis revolves around her desire for a redemptive moment in the future when a perfect marriage of different sexes will be realized. Apart from the fact that this desire is startlingly heterosexist, it also replicates the classic theological manoeuvre of abstraction by generalizing Nietzsche's misogyny. Ironically, this makes Irigaray's analysis in *Marine Lover* less ethical, because she violates the specificity of Nietzsche's style.

[56] Kofman's last comments refer to Derrida's "commentary" in *Spurs* on Nietzsche's marginal aphorism, "I have forgotten my umbrella", which shows that there is "no totality to Nietzsche's text" (and by implication, no one "subject" or signature for Nietzsche or "woman") by making various playful, textual associations between this phrase and Nietzsche's remarks on himself and on women (1979, 134-5). Derrida attributes his reading of this aphorism to Kofman (124, note 14 & 125, note 20) which is interesting considering that Derrida's (more influential) reading is more evasive than Kofman's about the different relations of "men" and "women" to the history of propriation.

undecidability of sexual difference, even as he moves towards a style which embraces it. Kofman makes her own sexual "propriation" by reiterating and laughing at this ambivalence. Propriative and sexual anxieties are never "cured" and always return; even in deconstructive texts. Nevertheless, if the determination of these potentially divisive and oppressive forces is vigilantly differentiated and denatured – as it is in Kofman's text – these forces need not permanently define the sexual hierarchy.[57]

Kofman's ironic, typological reading manages to interpose itself "between mimicry and mimesis" while actively tracing a specific form of feminist agency; and without compromising the promissory possibilities of either.

---

[57] Like Baubô's "apotropaic" gesture, the emphasis put on the need to "laugh" in the final passages and quotations of the essay suggest again the *comic* anxiety which, according to Kofman and Derrida, is the only responsible stylistic response to the uncanny experience of writing. A postscript quoting similar jokes and aphorisms by Freud and Nietzsche was added to the translated edition of Kofman's text (1988b, 200).

Afterword: The Lesson of Irony, The Future of Feminism

I am wary of writing a conclusion to this book, for fear of compromising its subject. I need only refer to Kierkegaard's attempts to end the aesthetic and ethical complications in *The Concept of Irony*, and the "curtailment" of irony, and sacrifice of alterity, which ensued. Perhaps, then, it will be more faithful to the spirit of irony, and its sense of otherness, to record how my initial questions about irony as a form of feminist agency have changed as a result of my analysis.

The first question concerns what we have been seeking: what constitutes feminist emancipation in the written structures I have analysed? Most of the theorists I have looked at are suspicious of anticipating a "new", independent identity for "woman" because this would conform to essentializing principles. However, the feminist "impulse" has still altered, from Kristeva's structure, which sought a more liminal position for certain feminized functions within the symbolic structure, to Derrida and Kofman, who ceaselessly interrogate such positions. Their motivation is a definition of emancipation which is at once broader and more specific. They seek a form of writing which will permit sexual specificity to exist without being drawn into a fixed function or generalized category; for such categories cut off the possibility of other sexual configurations arising. While they continue to analyse the economic function of the "feminine" in particular contexts, they no longer believe in the authority of this function as a determining part of the system's totalizing (sexual) "truth". Sexual difference is thus redefined as the possibility of many "other" sexual decisions and contexts (physical, psychological, behavioural, orientational, etc.) rather than as the dialectical movement between two predetermined terms.

These redefinitions are the consequence of taking seriously the irony of the feminine in the prevailing, binary structure; of treating its alterity as something specific, something "other" than the other *of* some "universal" term. Ironically, the "woman" ceases to "be" the "irony in the life of the community": the fetishized, liminal, negatively capable "other" which persists as an idealized figure even in more ethical structures such as those of Levinas and Irigaray. The never-wholly-present time of deconstruction allows a doubly ironic gesture, which decentres even this negative idealization, making the status of the feminine less certain yet more affirmative.

The second question – how feminism can stop repeating the "old" sexual hierarchy – is both altered and responded to by this temporal shift. In part, the whole point of irony as a trope is to admit that these repetitions cannot be prevented. The idea of a complete "break" or "rupture" with the past is not only impossible (any "currency" we have, whether in the present or future, is dependent upon this past), it is also irresponsible, even violent, because its only "knowable" authority is self-justified. The presumption of such an authority is what the irony of Kierkegaard, Derrida and Irigaray ridiculed most in Hegel.

However, this is not to say that the repetitions cannot and will not be repeated differently. In withdrawing from a self-believing act of "positing", the register of irony embraces the time of its own writing, which is highly susceptible to interruptions and alterations – other meanings and interpretations. Thus, change comes through the acknowledgement of alterity. Derrida exaggerates this register, withdrawing from the (residual) expectation of a revealed and knowable "truth" beyond this time, and heightening the awareness of the violence of this "truth". He defines a radical form of responsibility for the other, "beyond" ethics, which acknowledges alterity and "iterability" in every minute context and decision.

The effort to transform the sexual hierarchy thus comes as an uncanny, radically contingent negotiation; its agency the immanent alterity of its (never-) "present" writing. This makes the possibility of viewing irony as an aimed "strategy", or intended, subversive parody difficult, as we are talking about something unstable and "vertiginous", which some political theorists might not regard as sufficiently independent. However, I hope my book has emphasized the importance of feminism remembering the past – its own violent as well as violated history – and in some ways affirming the phallocentric legacy, because this is the only way in which feminism can be truly responsible to the other, and, indeed, benefit from the other's capacity to alter things through its reiteration.

This brings us to the question of the "point" of textual intervention: the "time" or "space" in which interruption and transmutation of the prevailing structure takes place. This "point" has changed its guise, in line with the alteration of other structural relationships, from being a "known", self-conscious "moment", to being an unknown, anxious, subjective "leap of faith", to being an undecidable decision or "propriation", which cannot be made without responding to the other possibilities which will always constitute, interrupt and alter its particular recitation. This is also another acknowledgement of the violence of any such intervention.

In my final chapter I suggest that it is desirable to "return" to a more "subjective" vocabulary when writing of this "propriation". I still want to qualify this, by saying that the "subject" I speak of bears little resemblance to the transcendent, existential, phenomenological, even, psychoanalytic subject. It is, to paraphrase Derrida and Laclau, an "operation" or "effect" of subjectivity insofar as it repeats a form of self-determination; but this does not mean that it is irreducible, or claims an "authentic", "authoritative" experience (Derrida 1984a, 125; Laclau 1996, 55). Nevertheless, in the context of feminism, where anxieties about the legacy of phallocentrism – its historical authority and "returning" violence – are heightened, it enables a further interrogation of the peculiar relation of femininity (and the feminist) to this legacy. In Kofman's genealogical analysis it provokes a detailed investigation of the sexual and sexualizing operations of "propriation"; a further ironic, reflexive gesture.

The issues of emancipation, repetition, responsibility and intervention are not, of course, separable, and any mode of writing and theorizing which sets out to treat seriously the complications surrounding the question of feminist agency must maintain a difficult balance between them; between the marking of alterity and the return of "propriation". If my final chapter suggests that, out of all the theorists I have analysed, Kofman treads this balance most nimbly, it is not because I want to suggest her method as the general "solution" to the problem of feminist agency. I am not asserting that her particular mimetic genealogy is *the way* in which a feminist may subvert the prevailing sexual order, for her irony only works in her "own" highly specific context. Rather, it is to argue that the querying of categories, relations, hierarchies and times must continue forever; in other contexts. This, perhaps, is the lasting lesson of irony, and what gives feminism its future.

Works Cited

Abraham, Nicolas, and Torok, Maria. 1994. "Mourning *or* Melancholia: Introjection *versus* Incorporation". In *The Shell and the Kernel. Renewals of Psychoanalysis.* Volume 1, edited and translated by Nicholas Rand, 125-138. Chicago: Chicago University Press.

Agacinski, Sylviane. 1988. *Aparté: Conceptions and Deaths of Søren Kierkegaard*, translated by Kevin Newmark. Tallahassee: Florida University Press.

Althusser, Louis. 1979. *For Marx*, translated by Ben Brewster. London: Verso.

Benhabib, Seyla. 1991. "On Hegel, Women, and Irony". In *Feminist Interpretations and Political Theory*, edited by Mary Lyndon Shanley and Carole Pateman, 129-45. Oxford: Polity Press.

Bennington, Geoffrey. 1994. "The Frontier: Between Kant and Hegel". In *Legislations: The Politics of Deconstruction*, 259-73. London and New York: Verso.

Bennington, Geoffrey and Derrida, Jacques. 1993. *Jacques Derrida*, translated by Geoffrey Bennington. Chicago and London: The University of Chicago Press.

Berry, Wanda Warren. 1995. "Kierkegaard and Feminism: Apologetic, Repetition and Dialogue". In *Kierkegaard in Post / Modernity*, edited by Martin Matustík and Merold Westphal, 110-124. Bloomington and Indianapolis: Indiana University Press.

Booth, Wayne. 1974. *A Rhetoric of Irony*. Chicago and London: University of Chicago Press.

Brandt, Joan. 2001. "Revolt or Concensus? Julia Kristeva in the 1990s". Esprit Créateur 41. 1 (Spring): 85-96.

Braidotti, Rosi. 1991. *Patterns of Dissonance: A study of women in contemporary philosophy*, translated by Elizabeth Guild. Cambridge: Polity Press.

Budick, Sanford, and Iser, Wolfgang, eds. 1989. *Languages of the Unsayable: The Play of Negativity in Literature and Literary Theory*. New York: Columbia University Press.

Butler, Judith. 1992. "Contingent Foundations: Feminism and the Question of Postmodernism". In *Feminists Theorize the Political*, edited by Judith Butler and Joan Scott, 3-21. London: Routledge.

—— 1993. *Bodies That Matter: On the Discursive Limits of "Sex"*. London: Routledge.

—— 1999. *Gender Trouble: Feminism and the Subversion of Identity*. 2nd Edition. London and New York: Routledge.

Chanter, Tina. 1990. "The Alterity and Immodesty of Time: Death as Future and Eros as Feminine in Levinas". In *Writing the Future*, edited by David Wood, 137-54. London and New York: Routledge.

—— 1995. *Ethics of Eros: Irigaray's Rewriting of the Philosophers*. London and New York: Routledge.

Cheah, Pheng and Grosz, Elizabeth. 1998. "Of Being – Two. Introduction". *Diacritics* 28. 1: 3-18.

Cixous, Hélène. 1975. "Le Rire de la Méduse". *L'Arc*, 61: 39-54.

—— 1976a. "Le Sexe ou la tête?". *Les Cahiers du GRIF*, 13: 5-15.

—— 1976b. *La*. Paris: Éditions Gallimard.

—— 1980. "The Laugh of the Medusa". In *New French Feminisms*, edited by Elaine Marks and Isabelle de Courtivron, 245-64. Brighton: Harvester.

—— 1981. "Castration or Decapitation?", translated by Annette Kuhn. *Signs*, 7, 1: 41-55.

—— 1984. "An Exchange with Hélène Cixous", with Verena Andermatt Conley. In *Hélène Cixous: Writing the Feminine*, edited by Verena Andermatt Conley, 129-161. Lincoln and London: University of Nabraska Press.

—— 1986. *The Newly Born Woman*, translated by Betsy Wing. Manchester: Manchester University Press.

—— 1988. "Extreme fidelity", translated by Ann Liddle and Susan Sellers. *In Writing Differences: Readings from the Seminar of Hélène Cixous*, 9-36. Milton Keynes: Open University Press, and New York: St. Martin's Press.

—— 1989. "From the Scene of the Unconscious to the Scene of History", translated by Deborah Carpenter. In *The Future of Literary History*, edited by Ralph Cohen, 1-18. New York and London: Routledge.

—— 1993. *Three Steps on the Ladder of Writing*, translated by Sarah Cornell, Deborah Jenson, Ann Liddle and Susan Sellers. Cambridge, Massachusetts: Harvard University Press.

—— 1994. "Contes de la Différence Sexuelle". In *Lectures de la différence sexuelle*, edited by Mara Negrón. 31-68. Paris: des femmes

—— 2001a "Savoir", translated by Geoffrey Bennington. In *Veils*, by Hélène Cixous and Jacques Derrida, 1-16. Stanford, California: Stanford University Press.

—— 2001b *Portrait de Jacques Derrida en jeune saint juif.* Paris: Galilée.

Cixous, Hélène, and Calle-Gruber, Mireille. 1997. *Hélène Cixous, rootprints: memory and life writing*, translated by Eric Prenowitz. London: Routledge.

Clarke, Tim. 1986. "Being in mime: Heidegger and Derrida on the ontology of literary language". *Modern Language Notes* 101. 5:1003-21.

Conway, Daniel W. 1992. "Comedians of the Ascetic Ideal: The Performance of Genealogy" in *The Politics of Irony: Essays in Self-Betrayal*, edited by Daniel W. Conway and John E. Seery, 73-95. New York: St. Martin's Press.

Cornell, Drucilla. 1992. *The Philosophy of the Limit*. New York and London: Routledge.

Cornell, Drucilla, Rosenfeld, Michel, and Carlson, David Gray. eds. 1992. *Deconstruction and the Possibility of Justice*. New York and London: Routledge.

Critchley, Simon. 1992. *The Ethics of Deconstruction*: Derrida and Levinas. Oxford: Blackwell.

—— 1998. "A Commentary Upon Derrida's Reading of Hegel in *Glas*". In *Hegel After Derrida*, edited by Stuart Barnett, 197-226. London and New York: Routledge.

Cross, Andrew. 1998. "Neither either not or: The Perils of reflexive irony". In *The Cambridge Companion to Kierkegaard*, edited by Alistair Hannay and Gordon D. Marino 125-53. Cambridge: Cambridge University Press.

Deleuze, Gilles. 1983. *Nietzsche and Philosophy*, translated by Hugh Tomlinson. London: The Athlone Press.

De Man, Paul. 1979. *Allegories of Reading: Figural Language in Rousseau, Nietzsche, Rilke and Proust*. New Haven and London: Yale University Press.

—— 1996. "The Concept of Irony". In *Aesthetic Ideology*, edited by Andrzej Warminski, 163-84. Minneapolis and London: University of Minnesota Press.
Derrida, Jacques. 1972a. *La dissémination*. Paris: Éditions du Seuil.
—— 1972b. *Positions*. Paris: Les Éditions de Minuit.
—— 1977. "Limited inc abc", *Glyph* 2: 162-254.
—— 1978a. "Violence and Metaphysics". In *Writing and Difference*, translated by Alan Bass, 79-153. London and Henley: Routledge and Kegan Paul.
—— 1978b. "Structure, Sign and Play in the Discourse of the Human Sciences". In *Writing and Difference*, translated by Alan Bass, 278-93. London and Henley: Routledge and Kegan Paul.
—— 1978c. "Cogito and the History of Madness". In *Writing and Difference*, translated by Alan Bass 31-63. London and Henley: Routledge and Kegan Paul.
—— 1979. *Spurs: Nietzsche's Styles / Éperons: Les Styles de Nietzsche*, translated by Barbara Harlow. Chicago: University of Chicago Press.
—— 1980. *La carte postale: de Socrate à Freud et au-delà*. Paris: Aubier-Flammarion.
—— 1981a. *Dissemination*, translated by Barbara Johnson. London: The Athlone Press.
—— 1981b. *Glas*, 2 volumes. Paris: Éditions Denoël / Gonthier.
—— 1982a. "Tympan". In *Margins: of Philosophy*, translated by Alan Bass, ix-xxix. Brighton: Harvester Press.
—— 1982b. "Différance". In *Margins: of Philosophy*, translated by Alan Bass, 1-27. Brighton: Harvester Press.
—— 1982c. "Signature, Event, Context". In *Margins: of Philosophy*, translated by Alan Bass, 307-330. Brighton: Harvester Press.
—— 1983. "Geschlecht: sexual difference, ontological difference", translated by Ruben Berezdivin. *Research in Phenomenology* 13: 65-83.
—— 1984a. "Deconstruction and the Other". In *Dialogues with contemporary continental thinkers: the phenomenological heritage: Paul Ricoeur, Emmanuel Levinas, Herbert Marcuse, Stanislas Breton, Jacques Derrida*, edited by Richard Kearney, 107-126. Manchester: Manchester University Press.
—— 1984b. "Of an apocalyptic tone recently adopted in philosophy", translated by John P. Leavey Jr, *Oxford Literary Review* 6.2: 3-37.
—— 1985. *The Ear of the Other: Otobiography, Transference, Translation*, translated by Peggy Kamuf, edited by Christie McDonald. Lincoln: The University of Nebraska Press.

—— 1986a. *Glas*, translated by John P. Leavey Jr. and Richard Rand. Lincoln: University of Nebraska Press.
—— 1986b. " 'Proverb: 'He that would pun …'' ". In *Glassery*, by John P. Leavey Jr, 17-20. Lincoln and London: University of Nebraska Press.
—— 1986c. *Parages*. Paris: Éditions Galilée.
—— 1987a. *Positions*, translated by Alan Bass. London: The Athlone Press.
—— 1987b *The Post Card: from Socrates to Freud and Beyond*, translated by Alan Bass. Chicago: The University of Chicago Press.
—— 1987c. "En ce moment même dans cet ouvrage me voici". Reprinted in *Psyché: inventions de l'autre*, 159-202. Paris: Galilée.
—— 1987d. "Psyché: invention de l'autre". In *Psyché: inventions de l'autre*, 11-61. Paris: Éditions Galilée.
—— 1987e. "Geschlecht II: Heidegger's Hand", translated by John P. Leavey Jr. In *Deconstruction and Philosophy*, edited by John Sallis, 161-96. Chicago and London: The University of Chicago Press.
—— 1987f. "Women in the Beehive: A Seminar with Jacques Derrida". In *Men in Feminism*, edited by Alice Jardine and Paul Smith, 189-203. New York: Methuen.
—— 1988. "Afterword: Toward an Ethic of Discussion", translated by Samuel Weber. In *Limited Inc*, 111-60. Evanston, Illinois: Northwestern University Press, 1988.
—— 1989a. "How to Avoid Speaking: Denials". In *Languages of the Unsayable: The Play of Negativity in Literature and Literary Theory*, edited by Sanford Budick and Wolfgang Iser, 3-70. New York: Columbia University Press.
—— 1989b. *Of Spirit: Heidegger and the Question*, translated by Geoffrey Bennington and Rachel Bowlby. Chicago: The University of Chicago Press.
—— 1991. "'Eating Well', or the Calculation of the Subject: An Interview with Jacques Derrida". In *Who Comes After the Subject?*, edited by Eduardo Cadava, Peter Connor and Jean-Luc Nancy, 96-111. New York and London: Routledge.
—— 1992a. "Donner le mort". In *L"éthique du don, Jacques Derrida et la pensée du don: Colloque de Royaumont, décembre, 1990*, edited by Jean-Michel Rabaté and Michael Wetzel, 11-108. Paris: Éditions Métailié-Transition.
—— 1992b. *Given Time: 1. Counterfeit Money*, translated by Peggy Kamuf. Chicago and London: The University of Chicago Press.
—— 1992c. "Force of Law: the 'Mystical Foundation of Authority'", translated by Mary Quaintance. In *Deconstruction and the*

Possibility of Justice, edited by Drucilla Cornell, Michel Rosenfeld and David Gray Carlson, 3-67. New York and London: Routledge.
— 1992d. "The Law of Genre". In *Acts of Literature*, edited by Derek Attridge, 221-52. New York and London: Routledge.
— 1992e. From "Psyche: Invention of the Other". In *Acts of Literature*, edited by Derek Attridge, 310-43. New York and London: Routledge.
— 1992f. "Ulysses Gramaphone: Hear Say Yes in Joyce". In *Acts of Literature*, edited by Derek Attridge, 253-309. New York and London: Routledge.
— 1994a. *Force de loi: Le "Fondement mystique de l'autorité"*. Paris: Éditions Galilée.
— 1994b. "Fourmis". In *Lectures de la différence sexuelle*, edited by Mara Negrón. 69-102. Paris: des femmes.
— 1995. *The Gift of Death*, translated by David Wills. Chicago and London: The University of Chicago Press.
— 1996, "Remarks on Deconstruction and Pragmatism". In *Deconstruction and Pragmatism: Simon Critchley, Jacques Derrida, Ernesto Laclau, Richard Rorty*, edited by Chantal Mouffe, 77-88. London and New York: Routledge,
— 1997. *Politics of Friendship*, translated by George Collins. London: Verso.
— 1998. *Resistances: of psychoanalysis*, translated by Peggy Kamuf, Pascale-Anne Brault and Michael Nass. Stanford: Stanford University Press.
— 2001a. "A Silkworm of One's Own", translated by Geoffrey Bennington. In *Veils*, by Hélène Cixous and Jacques Derrida, 17-108. Stanford, California: Stanford University Press.
— 2001b. *The Work of Mourning*, edited by Pascale-Anne Brault and Michael Naas. Chicago: University of Chicago Press.
Deutscher, Penelope. 1997. *Yielding Gender: Feminism, deconstruction and the history of philosophy*. London and New York: Routledge.
— 1999. "Complicated Fidelity: Kofman's Freud (Reading *The Childhood of Art* and *The Enigma of Woman*)". In *Enigmas: Essays on Sarah Kofman*, edited by Penelope Deutscher and Kelly Oliver, 159-73. Ithaca and London: Cornell University Press.
— 2000a. "Disappropriations: Luce Irigaray and Sarah Kofman". In *Resistance, Flight, Creation. Feminist Enactments of French Philosophy*, edited by Dorothea Olkowski, 155-178. Ithaca: Cornell University Press.

—— 2000b. “Pardon: Sarah Kofman and Jacques Derrida (On Mourning, Debt and Seven Friendships)”. *Journal of the British Society for Phenomenology*. 31. 1: 21-35.

Deutscher, Penelope and Oliver, Kelly, eds. 1999. *Enigmas: Essays on Sarah Kofman*. Ithaca and London: Cornell University Press.

Duroux, Françoise. 1997. “Comment philosophe une femme”. *Les Cahiers du GRIF* (nouvelle série) 3 (Printemps): 87-105.

Elam, Diane. 1994. *Feminism and Deconstruction: Ms. en Abyme*. London and New York: Routledge.

Feder, Ellen K. and Zakin, Emily. 1997. “Flirting with the Truth: Derrida’s Discourse with ‘Woman’ and Wenches”. In *Derrida and Feminism: Recasting the Question of Woman*, edited by Ellen Feder, Mary C. Rawlinson and Emily Zakin, 21-51. New York and London: Routledge.

Fichte, J. G. 1970. *Science of Knowledge, with the First and Second Introductions*, edited and translated Peter Heath and John Lachs. New York: Appleton-Century-Crofts.

Fraser, Nancy. 1992. “The Uses and Abuses of French Discourse Theories for Feminist Politics”, in *Revaluing French Feminism: Critical Essays on Difference, Agency and Culture*, edited by Nancy Fraser and Sandra Lee Bartky, 177-194. Bloomington: Indiana University Press.

Freud, Sigmund. 1990. “The Uncanny”. In *Penguin Freud Library, Volume 14: On Art and Literature*, translated by James Strachey, edited by Albert Dickson, 339-376. London: Penguin.

—— 1991a. “Beyond the Pleasure Principle”. In *Penguin Freud Library, Vol. 11: On Metapsychology*, translated by James Strachey, edited by Angela Richards, 269-338. London: Penguin.

—— 1991b. “The Ego and the Id”. In *Penguin Freud Library, Vol. 11: On Metapsychology*, translated by James Strachey, edited by Angela Richards, 339-407. London: Penguin.

—— 1991c. “On Narcissism: An Introduction”. In *Penguin Freud Library, Vol. 11: On Metapsychology*, translated by James Strachey, edited by Angela Richards, 59-97. London: Penguin.

—— 1991d. “Negation”. In *Penguin Freud Library, Vol. 11: On Metapsychology*, translated by James Strachey, edited by Angela Richards, 435-442. London: Penguin.

—— 1991e. “Group Psychology and the Analysis of the Ego”. In *Penguin Freud Library, Vol. 12: Civilization, Society and Religion*, translated by James Strachey, edited by Albert Dickson. London: Penguin.

—— 1991f. "Three Essays on the Theory of Sexuality". In *Penguin Freud Library, Vol. 7: On Sexuality*, translated by James Strachey, edited by Angela Richards, 31-169. London: Penguin.

—— 1991g. "Female Sexuality". In *Penguin Freud Library, Vol. 7: On Sexuality*, translated by James Strachey, edited by Angela Richards, 369-92. London: Penguin.

—— 1993a. "On The Grounds For Detaching A Particular Syndrome From Neurasthenia Under The Description 'Anxiety Neurosis'" In *Penguin Freud Library, Volume 10: On Psychopathology*, translated by James Strachey, edited by Angela Richards, 31-65. London: Penguin.

—— 1993b. "Inhibitions, Symptoms and Anxiety". In *Penguin Freud Library, Volume 10: On Psychopathology*, translated by James Strachey, edited by Angela Richards, 227-333. London: Penguin.

Fuss, Diana. 1989. *Essentially Speaking: Feminism, Nature and Difference*. New York and London: Routledge.

Gallop, Jane. 1982. *Feminism and Psychoanalysis: The Daughter's Seduction*. London: Macmillan Press.

—— 1997. "'Women' in *Spurs* and Nineties Feminism". In *Derrida and Feminism: Recasting the Question of Woman*, edited by Ellen Feder, Mary C. Rawlinson and Emily Zakin, 7-19. New York & London: Routledge.

Gillespie, Michael Allen, and Strong, Tracy B., eds., *Nietzsche's New Seas: Explorations in Philosophy, Aesthetics and Politics*. Chicago and London: University of Chicago Press, 1988.

Grosz, Elizabeth. 1994. "Sexual Difference and the Problem of Essentialism". In *The Essential Difference*, edited by Naomi Schor and Elizabeth Weed, 82-97. Bloomington and Indianapolis: Indiana University Press.

—— 1997. "Ontology and Equivocation: Derrida's Politics of Sexual Difference". In *Feminist Interpretations of Jacques Derrida*, edited by Nancy J. Holland, 73-101. University Park Pennsylvania: The Pennsylvania State University Press.

Hegel, G. W. F. 1942. *Philosophy of Right*, translated by T. M. Knox. Oxford: Clarendon Press.

—— 1970. *The Philosophy of Nature*, edited and translated by M. J. Petry. London: Allen & Unwin.

—— 1974. *Lectures on The History of Philosophy*, edited by Elizabeth Sanderson Haldame and Frances H. Simson. Volume 1. London: Routledge and Kegan Paul.

—— 1975. *Lectures on the Philosophy of World History*, translated by H. B. Nisbet. Cambridge: Cambridge University Press.

—— 1976. *The Science of Logic*, translated by A. V. Miller. New York: Humanities Press.

—— 1977. *The Phenomenology of Spirit*, translated by A. V. Miller. Oxford: Oxford University Press.

—— 1993. *Introductory Lectures on Aesthetics*, translated by Bernard Bosanquet, edited by Michael Inwood. London: Penguin.

Heidegger, Martin. 1962. *Being and Time*, translated by John Macquarrie and Edward Robinson. Oxford: Blackwell.

—— 1984. *The Metaphysical Foundations of Logic*, translated by Michael Heim. Bloomington: Indiana University Press.

Howe, Leslie A. 1994. "Kierkegaard and the Feminine Self". *Hypatia* 9. 4 (Fall): 131-57.

Hutcheon, Linda. 1991. *Splitting Images: Contemporary Canadian Ironies*. Toronto: Oxford University Press.

—— 1994. *Irony's Edge: The theory and politics of irony*. London and New York: Routledge.

Irigaray, Luce. 1974. *Speculum de l'autre femme*. Paris: Les Éditions de Minuit.

1977. *Ce sexe qui n'en est pas un*. Paris: Les Éditions de Minuit.

—— 1980 *Amante marine. de Friedrich Nietzsche*. Paris: Les Éditions de Minuit.

—— 1984. *Éthique de la différence sexuelle.* Paris: Les Éditions de Minuit.

—— 1985a. *Speculum of the Other Woman*, translated by Gillian C. Gill. Ithaca: Cornell University Press.

—— 1985b. *This Sex Which Is Not One*, translated by Catherine Porter and Carolyn Burke. Ithaca: Cornell University Press.

—— 1991a. "Questions to Emmanuel Levinas". In *The Irigaray Reader*, edited. and translated by Margaret Whitford, 178-189. Oxford: Blackwell.

—— 1991b. *Marine Lover of Friedrich Nietzsche*, translated by Gillian C. Gill. New York: Columbia University Press.

—— 1993. *An Ethics of Sexual Difference*, translated by Carolyn Burke and Gillian C. Gill. London: The Athlone Press.

—— 1996. *I Love To You: Sketch of a Possible Felicity in History*, translated by Alison Martin. New York: Routledge.

Jameson, Fredric. 1991. *Postmodernism, or, The Cultural Logic of Late Capitalism*. Durham, N. C: Duke University Press.

Jantzen, Grace M. 1998. *Becoming Divine: Towards a Feminist Philosophy of Religion.* Manchester: Manchester University Press.

—— 2003. "'Death, Then, How Could I Yield To It?' Kristeva's Mortal Visions". In *Religion in French Feminist Thought: Critical*

Perspectives, edited by Morny Joy, Kathleen O'Grady and Judith L. Poxon, 117-130. London and New York: Routledge.

Jardine, Alice, and Menke, Anne M., eds. 1991. *Shifting Scenes: Interviews on Women, Writing, and Politics in Post-68 France*. New York: Columbia University Press.

Joyce, James. 1993. *Ulysses, the 1922 text*, edited by Jeri Johnson. Oxford: Oxford University Press.

Kearney, Richard, ed. 1984. *Dialogues with contemporary continental thinkers: the phenomenological heritage: Paul Ricoeur, Emmanuel Levinas, Herbert Marcuse, Stanislas Breton, Jacques Derrida*. Manchester: Manchester University Press.

Kierkegaard, Søren. 1939. *The point of view etc., including The point of view for my work as an author, Two notes about "the individual" and On my work as an author*, translated by Walter Lowrie. London: Oxford University Press.

—— 1980. *The Concept of Anxiety: A Simple Psychologically Orienting Deliberation on the Dogmatic Issue of Hereditary Sin*, edited and translated by Reidar Thomte and Alber B. Anderson. Princeton: Princeton University Press.

—— 1983. *Fear and Trembling; Repetition*, edited and translated by Howard V. Hong and Edna H. Hong. Princeton: Princeton University Press.

—— 1987. *Either / Or: A Fragment of Life*, 2 volumes, edited and translated by Howard V. Hong and Edna H. Hong. Princeton: Princeton University Press.

—— 1989. *The Concept of Irony; With Continual Reference to Socrates*, edited and translated by Howard V. Hong and Edna H. Hong. Princeton: Princeton University Press.

—— 1992a. *Either / Or: A Fragment of Life*, abridged and translated by Alastair Hannay. London: Penguin.

—— 1992b *Philosophical Fragments, Johannes Climacus*, edited and translated by Howard V. Hong and Edna H. Hong. Princeton: Princeton University Press.

—— 1992c. *Concluding Unscientific Postscript to Philosophical Fragments*, 2 volumes, edited and translated by Howard V. Hong and Edna H. Hong. Princeton: Princeton University Press.

Knox, Dilwyn. 1989. *Ironia: Medieval and Renaissance Ideas on Irony*. Leiden: Brill.

Knox, Norman. 1961. *The Word Irony and Its Context, 1500-1755*. Durham, N. C: Duke University Press.

Kofman, Sarah. 1972. *Nietzsche et la métaphore*. Paris: Payot.

—— 1973. *Camera obscura, de l'idéologie*. Paris: Éditions Galilée.

—— 1974. *Quatres romans analytiques*. Paris: Éditions Galilée.
—— 1978. *Aberrations: Le devenir-femme d'Auguste Comte*. Paris: Aubier Flammarion.
—— 1980. *L'Énigme de la femme, la femme dans les textes de Freud*. Paris: Éditions Galilée.
—— 1982. *Le respect des femmes (Kant et Rousseau)*. Paris: Galilée.
—— 1983. *Comment s'en sortir?*. Paris: Éditions Galilée.
—— 1984. *Lectures de Derrida*. Paris: Éditions Galilée.
—— 1985. *The Enigma of Woman: Woman in Freud's Writings*, translated by Catherine Porter. Ithaca and London: Cornell University Press.
—— 1986a. *Nietzsche et la scène philosophique*. Paris: Galilée.
—— 1986b. "Le / Les 'concepts' de culture dans les *Intempestives* ou la double dissimulation". In *Nietzsche et la scène philosophique*, 289-318. Paris: Galilée
—— 1986c. "Baubô – Perversion théologique et fétichisme". In *Nietzsche et la scène philosophique*, 225-59. Paris: Galilée.
—— 1988a. "Beyond Aporia", translated by David Macey, in *Post-Structuralist Classics*, edited by Andrew Benjamin, 7-44. London: Routledge.
—— 1988b. "Baubô: Theological Perversion and Fetishism". In *Nietzsche's New Seas: Explorations in Philosophy, Aesthetics and Politics*, edited by Michael Allen Gillespie and Tracy B. Strong, 175-202. Chicago and London: University of Chicago Press.
—— 1989 "Ça cloche", trans. Caren Kaplan in Hugh J. Silverman, ed., *Derrida and Deconstruction*, 108-138. London and New York: Routledge.
—— 1991. "Sarah Kofman", with Alice Jardine. In *Shifting Scenes: Interviews on Women, Writing, and Politics in Post-68 France*, edited by Alice Jardine and Anne M. Menke, 104-112. New York: Columbia University Press, 1991
—— 1992. *Explosion I, De l' "Ecce Homo" de Nietzsche*. Paris: Éditions Galilée.
—— 1993a. *Explosion II, Les enfants de Nietzsche*. Paris: Éditions Galilée.
—— 1993b. *Nietzsche and Metaphor*, trans. Duncan Large. London: The Athlone Press.
Krell, David Farrell. 1994. "To the Orange Grove at the Edge of the Sea: Remarks on Luce Irigaray's *Amante Marine*". In *Nietzsche and the Feminine*, edited by Peter J. Burgard, 185-209. Charlottesville and London: University Press of Virginia.

—— 1996. "Lucinde's Shame: Hegel, Sensuous Woman, and the Law". In *Feminist Interpretations of G. W. F. Hegel*, edited by Patricia Jagentowicz Mills, 89-107. University Park, Pennsylvania: Pennsylvania University Press.

Kristeva, Julia. 1974. *La révolution du langage poétique*. Paris: Éditions du Seuil.

—— 1977a. *Polylogue*. Paris: Éditions du Seuil.

—— 1977b. *About Chinese Women*, translated by Anita Barrows. London: Marion Boyars.

—— 1980a. "Julia Kristeva: Oscillation between power and denial", interview with Xavière Guthier. In *New French Feminisms*, edited by Elaine Marks and Isabelled de Courtivron, 165-7. Brighton: The Harvester Press.

—— 1980b. *Desire in Language: A Semiotic Approach to Literature and Art*, translated by Thomas Gora, Alice Jardine and Leon S. Roudiez. New York: Columbia University Press.

—— 1982. *Powers of Horror: An Essay on Abjection*, translated by Leon S. Roudiez. New York: Columbia University Press.

—— 1983. *Histoires d'Amour*. Paris: Éditions Denoël.

—— 1984a. *Revolution in Poetic Language*, translated by Margaret Waller. New York: Columbia University Press.

—— 1984b. "Evénement et révélation". *L'Infini* no. 5 (Winter): 3-14.

—— 1984c. "Julia Kristeva in Conversation with Rosalind Coward". *Desire*, edited by Lisa Appigannesi. New York: ICA Documents.

—— 1986a. "The System and the Speaking Subject". In *The Kristeva Reader*, edited by Toril Moi, 24-33. Oxford: Blackwell.

—— 1986b. "Women's Time". In *The Kristeva Reader*, edited by Toril Moi, 187-213. Oxford: Blackwell.

—— 1986c. "A New Type of Intellectual: The Dissident". In *The Kristeva Reader*, edited by Toril Moi, 292-300. Oxford: Blackwell.

—— 1987a. *Tales of Love*, translated by Leon S. Roudiez. New York: Columbia University Press.

—— 1987b. *Soleil Noir: Dépression et Mélancholie*. Paris: Gallimard.

—— 1987c. *In the Beginning Was Love: Psychoanalysis and Faith*, translated by Arthur Goldhammer. New York: Columbia University Press.

—— 1989. *Black Sun: Depression and Melancholia*, translated by Leon S. Roudiez. New York: Columbia University Press.

—— 1991. *Strangers to Ourselves*, translated by Leon S. Roudiez. New York: Harvester Wheatsheaf.

—— 1993a. *Les nouvelles maladies de l'âme*. Paris: Fayard.

—— 1993b. "Les nouvelles maladies de l'âme". *L'Infini* 42 (Summer): 67-73.

——1994a. "Monstreuse intimité (de la littérature comme expérience)". *L'Infini* 48 (Winter): 55-61.

—— 1995a. "Bulgarie, ma souffrance". *L'Infini* 49 (Spring): 42-52.

—— 1995b. *New Maladies of the Soul,* translated by Ross Guberman. New York: Columbia University Press.

—— 1996a. "L'expérience littéraire est-elle encore possible?". *L'Infini* 53 (Spring): 20-46.

—— 1996b. *Sens et non-sens de la révolte. Pouvoirs et limites de la psychanalyse* vol. 1. Paris: Fayard.

—— 1997. *La Révolte intime. Pouvoirs et limites de la psychanalyse* vol. 2. Paris: Fayard.

—— 1999. "Le sens de la parité". *L'Infini* 67 (Autumn): 47-54.

—— 2000. *The Sense and Non-Sense of Revolt: The Powers and Limits of Psychoanalysis*, vol. 1, translated by Jeanine Herman. New York: Columbia University Press.

Lacan, Jacques, and the École Freudienne, 1982a. "The Meaning of the Phallus". In *Feminine Sexuality,* translated by Jacqueline Rose, edited by Juliet Mitchell and Jacqueline Rose, 74-85. London: Macmillan Press.

—— 1982b. "God and the *Jouissance* of ~~The~~ Woman". In *Feminine Sexuality*, translated by Jacqueline Rose, edited by Juliet Mitchell and Jacqueline Rose, 137-148. London: Macmillan Press.

—— 1972. "Seminar on *the Purloined Letter*", translated by Jeffrey Mehlman, *French Freud, Yale French Studies*, 48:38-72.

Laclau, Ernesto. 1996. "Deconstruction, Pragmatism, Hegemony." In *Deconstruction and Pragmatism: Simon Critchley, Jacques Derrida, Ernesto Laclau, Richard Rorty*, edited by Chantal Mouffe, 47-67. London and New York: Routledge.

Leavey, Jr., John P. 1986. *Glassery*. Lincoln and London: University of Nebraska Press.

Lévinas, Emmanuel. 1969. *Totality and Infinity: An Essay on Exteriority*, translated by Alphonso Lingis. Pittsburgh: Duquesne University Press.

—— 1974. *Autrement qu'être, ou au-delà de l'essence*. The Hague: M. Nijhoff,

—— 1977. *Du sacré au saint*. Paris: Les Éditions de Minuit.

—— 1978. *Existence and Existents*, translated by Alphonso Lingis. The Hague: M. Nijhoff.

—— 1979. *Le Temps et l'autre*. Paris: Fata Morgana.

—— 1981. *Otherwise Than Being; or Beyond Essence*, translated by Alphonso Lingis. The Hague: M. Nijhoff.

—— 1984. "Dialogue with Emmanuel Lévinas". In *Dialogues with Contemporary Continental Thinkers: the Phenomenological Heritage,* edited by Richard Kearney, 49-70. Manchester: Manchester University Press.

—— 1985. *Ethics and Infinity*, translated by Richard A. Cohen. Pittsburgh: Duquesne University Press.

—— 1986. "The Trace of the Other". In *Deconstruction in Context*, edited by Mark Taylor, 345-59. Chicago: The University of Chicago Press.

—— 1989. *The Levinas Reader*, edited by Sean Hand. Oxford: Blackwell.

Lyotard, Jean-François. 1984. *The Postmodern Condition: A Report on Knowledge* translated by Geoff Bennington and Brian Massumi. Minneapolis: University of Minnesota Press.

Melburg, Arne. 1995. *Theories of Mimesis*. Cambridge: Cambridge University Press.

Moi, Toril. 1985. *Sexual / Textual Politics*. London and New York: Routledge.

Muecke, D. C. 1970. *Irony and the Ironic*. London and New York: Methuen.

Nietzsche, Friedrich. 1966. *Beyond Good and Evil: Prelude to a Philosophy of the Future*, translated by Walter Kaufmann. New York: Vintage Books.

—— 1967. *The Birth of Tragedy and The Case of Wagner*, translated by Walter Kaufmann. New York: Vintage Books.

—— 1967 [1989]. *On the Genealogy of Morals and Ecce Homo*, translated by Walter Kaufmann and R. J. Hollingdale. New York: Vintage Books.

—— 1968a. *Twilight of the Idols and The Anti-Christ*, translated by R. J. Hollingdale. London: Penguin.

—— 1968b. *The Will to Power*, translated by Walter Kaufmann and R. J. Hollingdale. New York: Vintage Books.

—— 1969. *Thus Spoke Zarathustra*, translated by R. J. Hollingdale. London: Penguin.

—— 1974. *The Gay Science, with a prelude in rhymes and an appendix of songs*, translated by Walter Kaufmann. New York: Vintage Books.

—— 1979. *Philosophy and Truth*: Selections from Nietzsche's Notebooks or the early 1870's, edited and translated by Daniel Breazele. New Jersey: Humanities Press.

Oliver, Kelly. 1993. *Reading Kristeva: Unravelling the Double-Bind.* Bloomington: Indiana University Press.

—— 1995. *Womanizing Nietzsche: Philosophy's Relation to the "Feminine"*. London and New York: Routledge.

Oxford English Dictionary. 1989. 2nd Edition. Oxford: Oxford University Press.

Pippin, Robert B., 1988. "Irony and Affirmation in Nietzsche's 'Thus Spoke Zarathustra'". In *Nietzsche's New Seas*, edited by Michael Allen Gillespie and Tracy B. Strong, 45-71. Chicago: University of Chicago Press.

Plato. 1951. *The Symposium*, translated by Walter Hamilton. London: Penguin.

—— 1956. *Protagoras and Meno*, translated by W. K. C. Guthrie. London: Penguin.

—— 1973. *Phaedrus and Letters VII and VIII*, translated by Walter Hamilton. London: Penguin.

—— 1987a. *The Republic*, translated by Desmond Lee. London: Penguin.

—— 1987b. *Theaetetus*, translated by Robin A. H. Waterfield. London: Penguin.

—— 1993a. *Euthyphro*. In *The Last Days of Socrates: Euthyphro; Apology; Crito; Phaedo*, translated by Hugh Tredennick and Harold Tennant. London: Penguin.

—— 1993b. *Apology*. In *The Last Days of Socrates: Euthyphro; Apology; Crito; Phaedo*, translated by Hugh Tredennick and Harold Tennant. London: Penguin.

—— 1993c. *Phaedo*. In *The Last Days of Socrates: Euthyphro; Apology; Crito; Phaedo*, translated by Hugh Tredennick and Harold Tennant. London: Penguin.

Poole, Roger. 1993. *Kierkegaard: The Indirect Communication*. Charlottesville and London: University Press of Virginia.

Prosser, Jay. 1998. *Second Skins: The Body Narratives of Transsexuality*. New York: Columbia University Press.

Redfield, Mark. 2000. "Lucinde's Obscenity". In *Rereading Romanticism*, edited by Martha B. Helfer. Amsterdamer Beiträge zur neuren Germanistik. Bd. 47: 103-130.

Rorty, Richard. 1989. *Contingency, Irony, and Solidarity*. Cambridge: Cambridge University Press.

Rose, Jacqueline. 1993. *Why War?* Oxford: Blackwell.

Royle, Nicholas. 1995. *After Derrida*. Manchester: Manchester University Press.

Sallis, John. 1995. *Double Truth*. Albany: State University of New York Press.

Sartre, Jean-Paul. 1972. "L'universal singulier". In *Situations IX*, 152-190. Paris: Gallimard.

Schlegel, Friedrich von, 1971. *Lucinde and the Fragments*, translated by Peter Firchow. Minneapolis: University of Minnesota Press.

Schrift, Alan D. 1997. *The Logic of the Gift: Toward and Ethic of Generosity*. London and New York: Routledge.

Silverman, Hugh J., ed. 1989. *Derrida and Deconstruction*. London and New York: Routledge, 1989.

Smith, Robert. 1995. *Derrida and Autobiography*. Cambridge: Cambridge University Press.

Spivak, Gayatri Chakravorty. 1983. "Displacement and the Discourse of Woman". In *Displacement: Derrida and After*, edited by Mark Krupnick, 169-195. Bloomington: Indiana University Press.

— 1989. "Feminism and Deconstruction, Again: Negotiating with Unacknowledged Masculinism". In *Between Feminism and Psychoanalysis*, edited by Teresa Brennan, 206-223. London: Methuen.

Stanton, Domna C. 1989. "Difference on Trial" A Critique of the Maternal Metaphor in Cixous, Irigaray and Kristeva". In *The Thinking Muse: Feminism and Modern French Philosophy*, edited by Jeffner Allen and Iris Marion Young, 156-179. Bloomington: Indiana University Press.

Stringfellow, Frank Jr. 1994. *The Meaning of Irony: A Psychoanalytic Investigation*. Albany, New York: SUNY Press.

Taylor, Mark, ed. 1986. *Deconstruction in Context*. Chicago: The University of Chicago Press.

Whitford, Margaret. 1991. "Introduction". In *The Irigaray Reader*, edited and translated by Margaret Whitford, 1-15. Oxford: Blackwell.

Wilde, Alan. 1981. *Horizons of Assent: Modernism, Postmodernism, and the Ironic Imagination*. Baltimore and London: Johns Hopkins University Press.